AFTER THE KILLING FIELDS

Lessons from the Cambodian Genocide

Craig Etcheson

PRAEGER

Westport, Connecticut
London

Library of Congress Cataloging-in-Publication Data

Etcheson, Craig, 1955–
    After the killing fields : lessons from the Cambodian genocide / Craig Etcheson.
      p. cm.
    Includes bibliographical references and index.
    ISBN 0–275–98513–X (alk. paper)
  1. Cambodia—History—1953–1975. 2. Cambodia—History—1975–1979. 3.
Cambodia—History—1979– 4. Genocide—Cambodia. 5. Parti communiste du
Kampuchea. I. Title.
DS554.8.E73 2005
959.604—dc22   2004022487

British Library Cataloguing in Publication Data is available.

Library of Congress Catalog Card Number: 2004022487
ISBN: 0–275–98513–X

First published in 2005

Praeger Publishers, 88 Post Road West, Westport, CT 06881
An imprint of Greenwood Publishing Group, Inc.
www.praeger.com

Printed in the United States of America

The paper used in this book complies with the
Permanent Paper Standard issued by the National
Information Standards Organization (Z39.48–1984).

10 9 8 7 6 5 4 3 2 1

This book is dedicated to

the staff of the Documentation Center of Cambodia,

who have been bravely and selflessly

searching for the truth about the Cambodian genocide

for ten years.

CONTENTS

PREFACE

I write these words on the twenty-ninth anniversary of the day that a guerilla movement called the "Khmer Rouge" seized state power in Cambodia. That event ushered in a brief, but catastrophic, period known in Cambodia as the "Killing Fields." It has now been more than a quarter century since the Khmer Rouge were driven from power. After the Killing Fields, Cambodia was forever transformed, and the rest of the world has been slow to learn the lessons of that tragic episode. It has been slower still in attempting to deliver justice for the massive crimes committed in that time. Yet, finally, in 2004, both Cambodia and the world at large appear to be on the verge of rectifying this historic lapse. Justice may soon be coming for the Khmer Rouge.

My 1984 book on the Khmer Rouge, *The Rise and Demise of Democratic Kampuchea*, traced the history of Cambodian communism from its origins in the 1920s up through the fall of the Khmer Rouge regime in 1979. *After the Killing Fields* picks up the narrative in 1979 and brings the Khmer Rouge story forward to 2004, five years after their final defeat on the Cambodian battlefield. Beginning with a brief overview of the three decades of war and genocide that the Khmer Rouge inflicted on the Cambodian people, this book relates the struggles since 1979 to end the war and bring the perpetrators to account for their massive human rights abuses.

Chapter 1, "The Thirty Years War," and Chapter 2, "A Desperate Time," are pieces prepared specifically for this book. Chapter 3, "After the Peace," is a heavily revised version of "Cambodia after the Peace," a briefing paper prepared for the U.S. Institute of Peace in 1994. Chapter 3 also draws on "Cambodia, the UN and the Aftermath," which I presented in 1994 at the School of Oriental and African Studies, University of London, and the Center for Southeast Asian Studies, Free University of Berlin. Chapter 4, "Documenting Mass Murder," is a revised version of an internal working paper prepared for the Documentation Center of Cambodia under the title, "A Brief History of the Cambodian Genocide Program and the Documentation Center of Cambodia." Chapter 5, "Centralized Terror," is a revised version of a paper that I delivered to the Annual Meeting of the Association of Asian Studies in 1997. Chapter 6, "Terror in the East," is a lightly revised version of a paper I originally presented to the Annual Meeting of the Society for Historians of American Foreign Relations in 1997.

Chapters 5 and 6 report on research conducted in part under the auspices of the Cambodian Genocide Program at Yale University. The Cambodian Genocide Program was a large-scale team project involving literally hundreds of individuals in several countries. Thus, the information reported in these chapters is the result of the team efforts of many colleagues; I am grateful for their contributions to this book. I would particularly like to acknowledge the assistance of Youk Chhang, director of the Documentation Center of Cambodia, and the very able staff of the Documentation Center, for their help in selecting and translating some of the documents discussed in these and other chapters, as well as for their intrepid fieldwork and many other forms of research assistance. For chapters 5 and 6, the author also acknowledges the support of the U.S. Department of State. The project that gave rise to these chapters was funded, in part, through Cooperative Agreement Number S-OPRAQ-95-H-0537. The opinions, findings, and conclusions or recommendations expressed herein are those of the author and do not necessarily reflect those of the Department of State. The mass grave mapping project, in particular, was also funded in part by grants from the Department of Foreign Affairs and Trade of the Commonwealth of Australia, the Foreign Ministry of the Netherlands, and the U.S. Agency for International Development. The author gratefully acknowledges this support, while recognizing that the findings herein do not necessarily reflect the views of the granting agencies.

Chapter 7, "Digging in the Killing Fields," draws heavily on an internal report prepared for the Documentation Center of Cambodia in July 2000, titled " 'The Number'—Quantifying Crimes against Humanity in Cambodia," and shares part of the title of an earlier paper I presented to the

International Conference on Khmer Studies in 1996. Chapter 8, "The Persistence of Impunity," is a revised version of a paper originally presented at the International Conference on Reining [*sic*] in Impunity for International Crimes and Serious Violations of Fundamental Human Rights, Siracusa, Italy, in 1997. It appeared as pages 231 to 243 in Christopher C. Joyner, ed., *Reining in Impunity for International Crimes and Serious Violations of Fundamental Human Rights: Proceedings of the Siracusa Conference, 17–21 September 1998* (Érès: Association International de Droit Penal, 1998), and is reprinted here by permission of the International Association of Penal Law. Chapter 9, "The Politics of Genocide Justice," is a revised version of presentations given by the author at Harvard University's Kennedy School of Government and the U.S. Foreign Service Institute. A slightly different version of this chapter has been published in Cesare Romano et al., eds., *International Criminal Courts and Tribunals* (Oxford: Oxford University Press, 2004), and is reprinted here by kind permission of Oxford University Press. Chapter 10, "Challenging the Culture of Impunity," is a heavily revised version of a paper originally presented to the Second International Conference on Khmer Studies, Royal University of Phnom Penh, in 2000.

Over the last decade as I carried out the work that informs this volume, I received assistance from many, many more people than I can even remember, indeed, many more than it would be reasonable to list here—including some whom I cannot name for reasons of security or confidentiality. I thank them all for their many contributions to my work. Even so, there are a few whose help I cannot fail to mention, for I could not have completed this book without them.

My wife, Mychelle Balthazard, has been a perceptive reader of my work and, indeed, in many ways is my most fierce critic. She has encouraged me to persevere in preparing this book, gently insisting that it must be done and must be done well. I also gratefully acknowledge R. John Pritchard; John has been an inspiration to me. I also thank David P. Chandler, who is rightly regarded worldwide as the dean of modern Cambodia studies and who has certainly served as a mentor to me. I thank him for being a valued friend and colleague.

My discussions with, and readings of the work of, other numerous colleagues have been crucial in forming and refining my understanding of the issues discussed here, particularly (though in no particular order) Steve Heder, David Ashley, Sorn Samnang, Judy Ledgerwood, Peter Maguire, Kenton Clymer, Raoul Jennar, Eva Mysliwiec, Dith Pran, Nate Thayer, Fred Brown, Karl Jackson, Naranhkiri Tith, Catharin Dalpino, Michael

Vickery, Sorpong Peou, Patrick Raszelenberg, Elizabeth Becker, Yossi Shain, Ken Quinn, Jacques Bekaert, Chanthou Boua, Stephen Morris, Sara Colm, Greg Stanton, David Hawk, Brad Adams, Chhang Song, Henri Locard, Anette Marcher, Evan Gottesman, Jason Abrams, Steve Ratner, Carl Thayer, Jim Scott, Serge Thion, and William Shawcross. A number of people helped with advice on legal and comparative issues, as well as other forms of input, including Lili Cole, Philip Gourevitch, Pippa Scott, Anne Harringer, Ben Ferencz, Francisco Forrest Martin, Anthony D'Amato, Catherine Fitzpatrick, George Lombard, Ewen Allison, Victor Conde, and M. Cherif Bassiouni. I would be remiss if I did not also thank Fred Brown and the Johns Hopkins University School of Advanced International Studies for providing the intellectual space required to get some serious writing done.

Again, my numerous colleagues at the Cambodian Genocide Program, especially Ben Kiernan, Youk Chhang, Helen Jarvis, Nereida Cross, Kristine Mooseker, and Leslie Timko, along with the staff of the Documentation Center of Cambodia, particularly Phat Kosal, Sim Sorya, Lay Putheara, Ea Meng-try, and Im Sothearith, all know the contributions they have made to this volume and to our other work together, as well. I thank them for their collaboration and for our friendship.

Finally, Peter Maguire, Peter Sainsbury, Steve Etcheson, Mychelle Balthazard, David Chandler, and Jeannette Smyth gave careful readings of various drafts of the manuscript, providing invaluable comments and criticism that tremendously enhanced the quality of the resulting book. Jeannette delivered a particularly robust critique on a late draft of the manuscript. Good critics are a writer's best friend, and I am most grateful for the time and effort they devoted to assisting me in this project. Of course, I am obliged to note that although the colleagues and others acknowledged here made it possible for me to complete this book and have improved the final product in thousands of ways large and small, any errors of fact or interpretation that may remain are solely my own responsibility.

Craig Etcheson
Takoma Park, Maryland
April 17, 2004

1

The Thirty Years War

Something terrible happened in Cambodia, but many people—many Cambodians—do not believe it. It would seem that this terrible thing should have been hard to miss, since it went on for the entire last third of the twentieth century. In trying to explain what happened, pundits, politicians, and publicists have resorted to many different claims, some absurd, many essentially ideological. All this rhetoric has added to the sense of disbelief some feel. But what happened is really quite simple: the Khmer Rouge happened. One can go on and on about all of the factors antecedent to Cambodia's tragic modern history and all the factors incidental to its unfolding—the legacy of Angkor, Norodom Sihanouk, the Vietnam War, the Cold War, regional rivalries, superpower games, and so forth—but the essence of what happened was that the Khmer Rouge launched a war, and they continued that war for thirty long years.

Those born after the Khmer Rouge fell from power in 1979 now constitute a majority of the Cambodian population. Khmer Rouge killing became sporadic once they were driven from the capital, so most of these young people have no personal experience of Khmer Rouge atrocities. They do not learn about it in school, because what happened during the Khmer Rouge regime is not part of the public school curriculum. As a result, some children know only what they have heard from their parents. In many cases, however, parents and grandparents have preferred to say very little about it. The older generation has often been reluctant to speak to their children about life under the Khmer Rouge, finding it too difficult for words or too ugly for tender ears or simply not wanting to recall the suffering that still eats at them from within.

Those who have attempted to explain Cambodia's dispiriting modern history to their children often find that they are simply not believed. Many youth just cannot imagine that as Cambodians, the Khmer Rouge could have done to other Cambodians what is said that they did. An example of this is found in the 11-year-old son of Pen Samitthy, who is the publisher of Cambodia's leading newspaper, *Rasmei Kampuchea*. Of his boy, Samitthy says, "He knows about the Khmer Rouge, about Pol Pot, what they did. But the problem is he doesn't believe it happened."[1] In one sense, this book is for Samitthy's son and others like him who do not yet comprehend the terrible truth about what the Khmer Rouge did to Cambodia.

Why should they believe it? There is virtually nothing about it in Cambodian textbooks. Everyday life in Cambodia today seems perfectly normal, at least to those who grew up in that environment. If such crimes really were committed, would not the perpetrators have been brought before the law and thrown into prison? That has not happened; far from it. Instead, with one or two exceptions, the surviving leadership of the Khmer Rouge has continued to live unmolested, treated with respect by the government, and free to go about their business. That business has included the establishment of a sort of cottage industry devoted to denying that the Khmer Rouge committed any crimes, portraying themselves instead as patriots who saved the nation from extinction. The propaganda emanating from this effort contributes materially to the sense among many Cambodian youth today that the Cambodian genocide never really happened. It is as if Himmler, Goebbels, and Göring had all retired to Munich after World War II, spending the remainder of their lives publishing tracts asserting that no Jews were ever killed by the Nazis and that any troubles the Jews might have had they had deservedly brought upon themselves. It is a morally untenable situation. If this state of affairs endures until the Khmer Rouge leaders have all died peaceful deaths in their beds—as several of them already have—then it is difficult to see how Cambodian society can ever recover its moral compass.

BACK TO THE BEGINNING

It is an extraordinary situation. Cambodia is a country where as much as a third of the population died in one of the worst genocides of modern times, and many Cambodians do not believe it happened. How can it be that so much destruction occurred so recently, yet so few are aware of this history? In order to explain how this peculiar situation came about and perhaps to help to correct it, we must start at the beginning of the Thirty Years War.

That war began in 1968, when the Communist Party of Kampuchea—popularly known as the "Khmer Rouge"—declared armed struggle against the government of Cambodian leader Prince Norodom Sihanouk. Over the course of this war, the conflict took many different forms, went through many phases, and involved a list of participants nearly as long as the roster of the membership of the United Nations. The country changed its name six times during the Thirty Years War, beginning as the Kingdom of Cambodia, changing to the Khmer Republic in 1970, Democratic Kampuchea in 1975, then the People's Republic of Kampuchea in 1979, the State of Cambodia in 1989, and finally back to the Kingdom of Cambodia again in 1993. These contortions reflected the extraordinary violence of the underlying turmoil. Cambodia finally emerged from the Thirty Years War in 1999, with the capture of the last Khmer Rouge military leader still waging armed resistance.

The Thirty Years War wrought upon Cambodia a level of destruction that few nations have endured. At the epicenter of all this violence, from the beginning until the end, there was one constant, churning presence: the Khmer Rouge. Though they have now ceased to exist as a political or military organization, Cambodia continues to be haunted both by the influence of the individuals who constituted the Khmer Rouge and by the legacy of the tragedy they brought down on the country. The social, political, economic, and psychological devastation sown by the Khmer Rouge will take generations to heal, if indeed it ever can be healed. This epic saga of havoc is so complex and confusing that scholars do not even entirely agree on how to name all the ruin.

Many historians describe the conflicts in Southeast Asia during the second half of the twentieth century in terms of three Indochinese wars.[2] The First Indochina War was the war of French decolonization in Vietnam, Laos, and Cambodia, beginning in 1946 and ending with the Geneva Conference of 1954.[3] The Second Indochina War can be said to have run from 1954 to 1975; it is typically known in the United States as the "Vietnam War" and in Vietnam as the "American War," a dichotomy that reveals much about who was centrally involved. In this war of Vietnamese unification, as the United States attempted to prevent the consolidation of communist

rule over all of Vietnam, the war also spread to engulf both Laos and Cambodia.[4] The Third Indochina War began hard on the heels of the second,
when from 1975 to 1991, the issue of who would rule Cambodia and how
it would be ruled drew deadly interest from virtually every country in the
region and from all the world's major powers.[5]

From 1968 onward, it appeared to many Cambodians that these wars
flowed from one into the other, as inexorably as the Mekong River flows
into the sea. The 1991–1993 United Nations peacekeeping mission in
Cambodia marked the end of the Third Indochina War, but the fighting
in Cambodia continued for nearly another decade afterward. The outlines
of the conflict in Cambodia changed with the United Nations intervention, but the basic issue underlying the war—the Khmer Rouge drive for
power—was not resolved by the peace process. Combat continued between
the central government and the Khmer Rouge until the government finally prevailed in 1999. Thus, what historians characterize as distinct wars
with distinct protagonists appeared to many Cambodians to be simply one
long war, with one central protagonist—the Khmer Rouge—driving the
entire conflict.

A CAREER OF EVIL

Some view the Khmer Rouge as simply one political actor among many,
another player in history's sprawling cast, as legitimate as any other. Some
Cambodians even see them as a particularly patriotic and incorruptible
force in Cambodian history or, at a minimum, as nothing to be particularly concerned about. Like Pen Samitthy's son, it is hard for many young
people in Cambodia, and not a few older people as well, to believe that
Cambodians could kill millions of their fellow Cambodians. There must
be another explanation, a mysterious, malevolent external force that was
responsible for the violence. The fact that many external forces were indeed involved in Cambodia's Thirty Years War makes it that much easier
to identify potential villains. The real source of Cambodia's tragedy, however, lies within, and attempting to cast blame outside the borders of the
country only obscures the bitter truth.

The truth about the Khmer Rouge is that they perpetrated a level of
violence upon the people of Cambodia that has rarely been matched in
the history of the world. This violence was fundamentally criminal in nature. Though its partisans prefer to think of the Khmer Rouge as a political movement, it makes more sense to view it as a criminal organization.

For the last five years of its existence, in fact, the Khmer Rouge was formally branded a criminal organization under Cambodian law. Prior to that time, the criminal nature of the Khmer Rouge was all too apparent from its methods. The Khmer Rouge operated outside the law even when they controlled the state apparatus. They rejected the very concept of law, abandoning it as an artifact of the "feudal, reactionary, imperialist" order against which they stood. From the very beginning, the Khmer Rouge relied extensively on extrajudicial murder.

The Khmer Rouge began their long war with a style of revolutionary violence that would become their trademark.[6] After declaring armed struggle in 1968, the top leadership of the Communist Party of Kampuchea retreated to the remote jungles of northeastern Cambodia. There they set about establishing their authority over Ratanakiri, Mondolkiri, and Stung Treng Provinces, using murder to liquidate the existing administration. The nascent revolution moved from village to village, purging local leaders and appointing revolutionary leaders to take their place. "Between four and 10 people were killed in most villages . . . primarily former commune and village chiefs."[7] This technique became a long-standing pattern of Khmer Rouge behavior over the next three decades.

Another "innovation" the Khmer Rouge put in place during their early jungle years in the northeast was the recruitment of children as soldiers, often beginning their indoctrination at ages as young as 6 years old. One man in Ratanakiri Province has described how he was recruited into *Angkar*, or the "Organization," as the Khmer Rouge styled themselves, at the age of 11:

> At that time the teachers made propaganda in the classroom itself for the students to go to the jungle. The Khmer Rouge had infiltrated the teachers, who told us our country needed communism to develop and become prosperous, to overcome the royalists. I went with Angkar because at that time in my village there was no salt, no food to eat. Angkar had food, and taught us how to serve our country. I was too young to understand their political agenda.[8]

Soon the Khmer Rouge would come to see children as the core of the revolution, easily shaped to carry out virtually any task—a particularly useful trait in the security services. As one party publication put it, "the forces of youth . . . became the nucleus, the wick of the struggle."[9] As Prince Norodom Sihanouk described it, the child soldiers were trained to believe that the society against which they fought—and which they came to understand that Sihanouk more than anyone else represented—was "despicable, contemptible, corrupt, unjust and oppressive in the extreme."[10]

Cambodia's communists thus quietly went about developing their revolutionary organization in the jungle, leaving the countryside strewn with corpses as they geared up for a full-scale war to overthrow Sihanouk and his Kingdom of Cambodia regime. Far away in Phnom Penh, however, events were conspiring to transform the situation in ways the Khmer Rouge could not have anticipated. Sihanouk had been struggling for years to insulate his country from the war that had already engulfed neighboring Vietnam and Laos. That balancing act required many compromises, and in one such compromise, Sihanouk had agreed to turn a blind eye to North Vietnamese communist forces who were using Cambodian territory to prosecute their struggle against the American-backed regime in South Vietnam. Some in Sihanouk's government, however, were strongly opposed to that policy. The accumulated resentment over Vietnamese activities in Cambodia became one of the principal reasons that Sihanouk's ministers and advisers decided to overthrow him.

The 1970 coup d'état against Norodom Sihanouk was a watershed event in Southeast Asian history. This act cataclysmically transformed the strategic landscape of the entire region, with catastrophic consequences for Cambodia. Prior to the coup, the Khmer Rouge had struggled alone against Sihanouk's regime, with no assistance from the communist parties of the Union of Soviet Socialist Republics (USSR), the People's Republic of China (PRC), and North Vietnam. These communist nations had viewed the Cambodian communist movement with a degree of contempt, considering its cadre artless in their grasp of doctrine. With the coup against Sihanouk, however, Cambodia's new government suddenly turned against the Vietnamese, demanding that they remove their army to Vietnam immediately. This abrupt change in Cambodian policy prompted an equally abrupt shift by the USSR, the PRC, and North Vietnam. The communists began providing massive amounts of assistance to Cambodia's struggling revolutionary movement. The Khmer Rouge revolution was positioned for explosive growth, and their penchant for murder would soon escalate to epic proportions.

As important as this change of policy in the communist world, however, was the change in the relationship between Sihanouk and the Khmer Rouge. When the Khmer Rouge were beaten to the putsch in their plan to overthrow Sihanouk, the former king suddenly became their most valuable tool in their quest to seize state power. Sihanouk joined the Khmer Rouge in forming the National United Front for Kampuchea (FUNK), calling on the Cambodian people to rally to the fight against those who had overthrown him. Conditioned by centuries of tradition to respect the monarchy, many rural Cambodians flocked to Prince Sihanouk's banner. The battle lines were thus drawn for a vicious five-year civil war that would bring the Khmer Rouge to power. In the process of getting there, the Khmer Rouge would kill friend and foe alike. No one would be safe.

The Khmer Rouge used FUNK to draw recruits to their cause, while Sihanouk and his royal entourage stayed in Beijing, safely distant from the possibility of any real influence. Most of those who joined FUNK were consumed as cannon fodder in the war against the Khmer Republic, but a few potentially talented cases were winnowed from the masses to be shaped for roles in the Communist Party. A few years into the 1970–1975 civil war, the Khmer Rouge began to liquidate their allies inside FUNK, including not only ethnic Vietnamese who were fighting for the revolution but Sihanouk's partisans as well. Very soon Sihanouk would be nothing more than a figurehead, with the Khmer Rouge in control. They accomplished this coup d'état within the Front using a simple yet direct method: mass murder. This systematic killing of allies foreshadowed the grand scale of what was to follow.

When the Khmer Rouge seized power on April 17, 1975, the killing began in earnest. In the first wave, the defeated Khmer Republic's military officer corps, from the top generals right down to the lowliest non-commissioned officer, was targeted for execution. The rank-and-file soldiers would be hunted down and exterminated later. Along with the officers went all the civil servants of the previous regime, no matter how innocuous their role had been in the past or how essential their skills might be for the future. Meanwhile, all residents of the cities were marched into the countryside, where their biographies were repeatedly scoured for signs that they harbored the enemy virus within. Anyone with any education, even wearing eyeglasses, was considered a class enemy and was vulnerable to summary execution. With time, as in so many revolutions, the Khmer Rouge began to feed on their own. The communist movement's leaders and the ranks alike followed ordinary people into the maw of the Khmer Rouge killing machine.[11]

Khmer Rouge violence was not limited to Cambodians, however, and this would ultimately prove to be their undoing. Recently discovered documents from inside the Khmer Rouge military reveal that they imagined themselves as being in a state of war with all three of their neighbors—Vietnam, Thailand, and Laos—from the very moment the Khmer Rouge regime came to power.[12] They acted accordingly, with Vietnam on the receiving end of repeated atrocities.[13] In time, Khmer Rouge attacks against civilian villages in Vietnam became intolerable, and Vietnam resolved that it had been reduced to a single option to deal with the problem. The Vietnamese assembled a small expatriate army from refugees who had fled Cambodia, most of whom were former Khmer Rouge themselves. They attached this ragtag group to their own formidable military forces, and on December 25, 1978, Vietnam attacked. The Khmer Rouge state of Democratic Kampuchea crumbled before the advancing Vietnamese troops, and in a mere two weeks, Cambodia had been "liberated." Rather than being the end of the story, this fateful invasion set the stage for another two decades of war in Cambodia.

Cambodia may have been liberated from the terror of the Khmer Rouge regime, but many Cambodians were not liberated from Khmer Rouge terror. The Khmer Rouge found sanctuary at the Thai border and established military camps on Thai territory. Tens of thousands of civilians were herded into these camps by the Khmer Rouge, where they were subjected to systematic violations of their human rights for more than a decade. "These abuses include denial of food and medical care to those who refuse to fight; use of children in the war; forced labor; exposing civilians to physical danger by making them targets of military attack; and forced *refoulement*, or forcing refugees back into the country from which they fled."[14] And, of course, murder. Vietnamese taken prisoner by the Khmer Rouge, both civilian and military, were subject to summary execution.[15] Cambodian military and civilian prisoners fared little better. Despite the overthrow of the Khmer Rouge regime, the specter of Khmer Rouge terror had not yet been lifted from the Cambodian people.

The war plodded on, and the Vietnamese finally withdrew from Cambodia in 1989, leaving their client regime, the People's Republic of Kampuchea, to fend for itself against the Khmer Rouge and the royalist and republican armies that had allied themselves with the Khmer Rouge. With the inability of the Phnom Penh regime to eliminate the rebels or of the Khmer Rouge to defeat the Phnom Penh regime, the two sides had settled into a stalemate. This stalemate soon became wearisome to the external powers backing the respective combatants, prompting international efforts to broker a peace deal. That deal was consummated in 1991 with the "Agreements on a Comprehensive Political Settlement of the Cambodia Conflict."[16]

Under the terms of the peace agreement, the four principal domestic parties to the war—the Khmer Rouge and the Phnom Penh regime, plus the royalist and republican factions—were to lay down their weapons and compete for power peacefully under the auspices of a United Nations-organized election. At least that was the plan, though it did not quite work out that way. The Khmer Rouge opted instead to renege on the agreements, continuing their familiar patterns of terror and war.[17] The Khmer Rouge also attacked the United Nations itself, actions that resulted in the murder of numerous international peacekeepers.[18] Meanwhile, the Khmer Rouge continued to massacre civilians in Cambodia.[19]

Accustomed to relating to the Khmer Rouge as a member state of the United Nations (UN), the UN was at a bit of a loss as to how to deal with this kind of aggression. "The Khmer Rouge refused to disarm, negotiated in bad faith, shelled UN buildings, shot down [or at least shot up] UN helicopters, [and] murdered UN soldiers, yet the organization took no action."[20] In the end, the UN peacekeepers were reduced to attempting to defend themselves from Khmer Rouge attacks and doing their best to carry on with the plan for an election, now with three main factions participating rather than the original four. That strategy was ultimately successful, insofar as the elections did produce a new government. The new regime was accepted by the international community as a legitimate state, and the UN quickly declared victory and withdrew. The Khmer Rouge continued their long war.

In the wake of the UN intervention in Cambodia, the Khmer Rouge had a new problem. They faced an enlarged enemy in the form of a regime in Phnom Penh that included their own former royalist and republican allies. The Khmer Rouge response was to escalate the violence, adding various new categories of foreigners to the already long list of those who were thought to be in need of torture and execution.[21] For those unlucky enough to live in zones controlled by the Khmer Rouge, treatment of the local population continued to be draconian, including detention in tiger cages, throat slashings, and being burned alive as forms of discipline.[22] In many areas outside Khmer Rouge control, Cambodians lived in constant fear of raids by roving bands of Khmer Rouge guerillas, who often attacked without warning, burning, looting, and killing everything in their path. It sometimes seemed as if this was the only thing the Khmer Rouge knew how to do well, so that is what they did, and they did it for thirty long years. It amounted to one of the most remarkable and destructive crime sprees in modern history.

CRIME WITHOUT PUNISHMENT

Even an abbreviated list of crimes committed by the Khmer Rouge during the Thirty Years War is astonishing. When they accused someone of treason, they killed not only the accused but also his wife and children. The Khmer Rouge effectively enslaved the entire population, dragooning everyone into forced labor gangs and forcing them to work so hard that many dropped dead in the fields from exhaustion. They illegally deported thousands of ethnic Vietnamese Cambodians, murdering any who did not leave quickly enough. The Khmer Rouge engaged in wanton destruction of property, laying waste to villages and cities alike. They carried out institutionalized torture, devising ingenious low-tech methods to inflict pain on helpless prisoners. They destroyed Cambodia's religious and cultural heritage, desecrating temples, mosques, and cathedrals. To this they added religious persecution, targeting religious leaders for execution and carrying out mass murder against entire villages where some had protested the elimination of their faith. The scale of the violence was such that it constitutes war crimes, crimes against humanity, and that ultimate crime, genocide.

Khmer Rouge depredations drove Cambodia's ancient culture to the brink of extinction and resulted in the extermination of approximately one-third of the Cambodian people. But perhaps the most appalling thing about all of this is that twenty-five years after the end of the Khmer Rouge regime, no senior leader of the Khmer Rouge has ever been brought before a court of law to answer for these heinous crimes. The impunity that the Khmer Rouge leadership has continued to enjoy is part and parcel of the reason that so many young Cambodians simply do not believe the genocide ever happened. In such a society, the very concept of justice appears to be nothing but an illusion—and indeed it may well be.

The Peace of Westphalia in 1648 ended the Thirty Years War of an earlier century, but the price of that peace was justice; the treaty forgave the many war crimes that had been committed in the course of laying waste to Europe's German-speaking lands and killing at least a third of its peoples. The Peace of Westphalia also gave rise to the modern system of states, and modern international law gradually formed along with it. In recent years, a new tenet has developed in international law, holding that the punishment of war crimes is necessary to the restoration of peace in the wake of war. Will the crimes of the Khmer Rouge ultimately be punished in the aftermath of Cambodia's Thirty Years War? The answer to that question will reveal to Cambodians whether their country is beginning to emerge as a modern state, or if, on the contrary, it remains locked in the grip of archaic feudal mores.

When Cambodia's Thirty Years War finally ended with the surrender of the surviving Khmer Rouge leaders, hopes were raised among the victims that justice would be done. As one victim put it, "You don't just let them go free after they have killed millions."[23] It was not to be so simple. Some five years later, Cambodia had not yet found peace with justice. If peace in Cambodia is not eventually leavened with justice, then the new order will be erected on shaky pillars of impunity. *After the Killing Fields* is the story of the search for that justice and why it has been frustrated for so long. To tell this story, we begin by returning to that first moment when it appeared justice might be within reach, as the Khmer Rouge regime was toppled and a new government came to power in Cambodia in 1979. Part of the reason that justice has been so long in coming has to do with the nature of the government that replaced the Khmer Rouge and also its own connections with the Khmer Rouge. We now turn our attention to that new government, a regime that came into being during a desperate time.

2

A DESPERATE TIME

The problem of stabilizing an entire country and establishing a new government after a regime-changing invasion is, not to put too fine a point on it, a significant challenge. The United States has recently been reminded of this in Iraq, and Vietnam learned this hard truth in 1979. The challenge was made all the more difficult for the Vietnamese in Cambodia in 1979 by the fact that the Khmer Rouge had almost completely destroyed their own country, having been especially hard on Cambodia's human capital. The invading Vietnamese army inevitably did additional damage, but the Vietnamese had understood clearly prior to their invasion that it was in their interest to establish a new government as quickly as possible. To do so would require some unpalatable compromises.

Thus, a hard fact sometimes overlooked in the story of modern Cambodian politics is that the regime that replaced the Khmer Rouge government in 1979 was heavily populated by former members of the Khmer Rouge. For example, Heng Samrin was a senior military commander in the eastern part of Cambodia during the Khmer Rouge regime and then became one of the most senior political leaders in the successor People's Republic of Kampuchea. Hun Sen, former political commissar for a regiment of troops in one region of eastern Cambodia under the Khmer Rouge regime, went on to become foreign minister and later rose to the post of prime minister in the People's Republic of Kampuchea. Chea Sim was the top political leader in another region of the east during the Khmer

Rouge regime and then became a leader of the National Assembly in the People's Republic of Kampuchea.[1] These men were but a few of the many former Khmer Rouge cadre in the new 1979 party and government.

These Khmer Rouge defectors were balanced in the new regime by another group of non–Khmer Rouge Cambodians who had been trained in North Vietnam and who had either remained in Vietnam or returned there during the war against the Lon Nol regime, prior to the establishment of Democratic Kampuchea. Even so, the presence of numerous former subordinates of Pol Pot suggested a legacy that might well be worrying to the citizens who had suffered so dramatically under the Khmer Rouge. Consequently, the new government faced the urgent task of differentiating itself from its predecessor in the minds of the people. One of their primary mechanisms for accomplishing this objective was to establish the People's Revolutionary Tribunal of 1979.

THE PEOPLE'S REVOLUTIONARY TRIBUNAL

The People's Revolutionary Tribunal would be the world's first war crimes trial since the Nuremberg Tribunal in the aftermath of World War II. On July 15, 1979, the new Cambodian regime promulgated "Decree Law No. 1." This law was the first of a corpus of decrees establishing a post–Pol Pot legal order in Cambodia. It formally established the "People's Revolutionary Tribunal at Phnom Penh to Try the Pol Pot–Ieng Sary Clique for the Crime of Genocide."[2] The law mandated a tribunal that would judge just two Khmer Rouge leaders—Prime Minister Pol Pot, along with Deputy Prime Minister and Foreign Minister Ieng Sary—on charges of genocide.

On a sultry August day barely one month after this decree was issued, an American lawyer sat in a small theater on the banks of the Mekong River in central Phnom Penh, where she faced the judges of the People's Revolutionary Tribunal. The lawyer's task was to defend deposed Prime Minister Pol Pot against the new regime's accusations of genocide. "I have not come from halfway around the world to give approval to monstrous crime or to ask for mercy for the criminals," Hope Stevens began, "No! A thousand times no! Not at all!"[3] Warming to her theme, she continued, "It is now clear to all that Pol Pot and Ieng Sary were criminally insane monsters."[4] Her defense strategy, such as it was, was to argue that the People's Republic of China somehow made Pol Pot commit the crime.

Stevens' Cambodian co-counsel, Dith Munthy, though less theatrical, was similarly dismissive of his client's presumed innocence: "I have no dispute with Comrade Prosecutor regarding the criminal acts and criminal intention of the two accused."[5] It became very clear that the defense co-counsels had no intention of presenting a real defense argument on behalf of their absentee clients. The verdict had already been written into the script in advance.

This general tone of contempt for their client from Pol Pot's defense counsel during the five-day trial is one reason that the proceeding has often been dismissed as a communist "show trial," yet unlike classic Stalinist show trials, this tribunal involved a great deal of legitimate evidence relating to the charges at hand. Affidavits from survivors of Khmer Rouge brutality, field investigations of mass graves and crematoria, analyses of the impact of the Khmer Rouge regime on Cambodian social institutions, excerpts from captured documents, and even a collection of press accounts were all delivered into evidence at the People's Revolutionary Tribunal. They were well on their way to creating a public record of what had occurred during the Khmer Rouge regime. Regardless of the evidence, the outcome of the tribunal was never in doubt.

The evidence compiled by the People's Revolutionary Tribunal presents a litany of horror, such as widespread cannibalism practiced by lower-level Khmer Rouge cadre, the use of pits of crocodiles to exterminate groups of children, and a catalog of torture methods rarely matched in its barbarism. This gratuitous cruelty was foreshadowed on the very first day of the Khmer Rouge regime, as the victorious revolutionaries were emptying Phnom Penh and other Cambodian cities of all their inhabitants. Mrs. Yasuko Naito recounted to the tribunal her evacuation from the capital on April 17, 1975:

Along the way, we met patients who had been forced out of the Calmette Hospital and other hospitals. Some who were weak walked with the help of nurses, having been operated upon only a few hours before. The places where the operation had been performed were still bleeding, with flies swarming around. They all wore hospital clothing. It made me think of a painting I had seen somewhere depicting scenes of hell.

Farther along, I saw the naked body of a man, nailed to a door. On his chest was written in large letters: "enemy." Soldiers of Pol Pot standing by the body watched the people passing it. They broke out laughing and told everyone to open their eyes and look at it. We all worried about the future.[6]

The "painting" she had seen somewhere depicting scenes of hell in fact may well have been a bas-relief at Cambodia's ancient Angkor Wat temple, where in the South Gallery, the "Judgement by Yama, Heaven and Hell" shows a wicked person suffering punishment by being nailed to a wall, in one of thirty-two Hindu hells described in the carving.

Did the evidence presented to the People's Revolutionary Tribunal support the charges of genocide against defendants Pol Pot and Ieng Sary? The prosecution produced no witnesses with firsthand knowledge of the defendants, much less of their having given orders to carry out the crimes. Despite the fact that several leaders of the new regime would have been personally and professionally acquainted with the defendants, it was evidently determined that their testifying at the tribunal might draw unwanted attention to the fact that the new regime largely comprised former Khmer Rouge officials, even though they might have been able to share relevant knowledge on some aspects of the alleged crimes. Aside from the odd reference in captured Khmer Rouge documents to things such as a purported need to kill "from 0.5 to 1 percent" of the population,[7] none of the evidentiary documents directly linked the defendants to the commission of the crimes as charged. Thus, even though there was a large quantity of evidence, the legal case was actually quite weak. That said, it must be noted that on balance the evidence does paint a compelling picture of a regime bent on exterminating huge numbers of people. In a modern judicial context, the top leaders of that regime would not be likely to escape onus for these acts. They were in charge when these crimes were committed, and hence they are responsible under the law for those crimes.

Pol Pot and Ieng Sary alone were tried at the 1979 People's Revolutionary Tribunal, but the verdict of death from the *in absentia* trial was never carried out. Pol Pot escaped it by evading capture until he died in his bed twenty years later. Ieng Sary was pardoned by the Royal Government in 1996 as part of a political deal, which was the beginning of the end of the Khmer Rouge political and military organization. Thus, despite the plea of one People's Revolutionary Tribunal witness "that those responsible should be prosecuted at all levels,"[8] no senior member of the Khmer Rouge has yet had to endure legal punishment for the death of as much as one-third of the Cambodian population during the Khmer Rouge regime. A number of lower-level Khmer Rouge cadre were, however, imprisoned in the wake of the Vietnamese invasion.

Evidence uncovered in the last few years suggests that the Vietnamese occupation authorities played a central role in organizing the People's Revolutionary Tribunal. An aide-memoire dated May 10, 1979, was recently discovered in the archives of the People's Republic of Kampuchea in Phnom Penh. This memo describes a secret Vietnamese decision to "create a Cambodian Judicial Operations Team to assist the Cambodians in convening a court session to try the Pol Pot–Ieng Sary Group."[9] Virtually all of the People's Revolutionary Tribunal trial documents, the originals of which were almost all in the Khmer language, appear on the face of it to have been prepared by various officials of the new Cambodian regime. While it is difficult to determine the extent to which Vietnamese experts may have aided Cambodian officials in designing the People's Revolutionary Tribunal and preparing its documents, this remains an interesting issue. Since the late 1990s, Cambodian Prime Minister Hun Sen has frequently referred to the People's Revolutionary Tribunal in asserting that renewed demands for bringing Khmer Rouge leaders to account should be done in a "Cambodian way." Steve Heder has argued that the People's Revolutionary Tribunal in fact had nothing to do with Cambodian traditions but rather belonged to a legacy of justice flowing from twentieth-century French colonial and Vietnam communist roots.[10]

So, Khmer Rouge chief Pol Pot had been convicted of genocide and sentenced to death, but as he was not in custody, the sentence could not be carried out. Far from it—as the People's Revolutionary Tribunal concluded its deliberations in Phnom Penh, Pol Pot was marshaling his forces and expanding his network of allies from bases in Thailand and along the Thai border in Cambodia's remote western and northern provinces. To what extent the regime's tribunal was successful in distinguishing the new government from the Khmer Rouge is open to question, because the authorities found it a continuing challenge to consolidate their rule over the shattered country, earn the loyalty of their people, and achieve legitimacy in the eyes of the international community.

FACING THE ENEMY WITHIN

The greatest problem facing the Cambodian government was the long-term guerilla war Pol Pot was preparing. How could the new regime defeat this threat and ensure the survival of their government? The new state apparatus was suffused with strongly nationalist personalities who did not want to rely in perpetuity on Vietnamese armed forces for their survival, but until a measure of internal and external security could be achieved, they would have to accept occupation by their neighbor's troops. Paradoxically, the longer they relied on protection by Vietnamese soldiers, the stronger would be the perception that they were not a sovereign entity but rather simply "puppets" of an imperial power. This was particularly problematic for the Cambodian people, because of their long-standing animosity toward the Vietnamese.

The new government's first task was internal security. They needed to identify and deal with individuals still loyal to the overthrown Khmer Rouge regime. The new government adopted a two-pronged strategy to deal with this challenge. First, they issued a blanket invitation for "misled persons" to defect to the Phnom Penh regime's side in exchange for amnesty. Second, captured enemy agents were incarcerated without trial, even those merely suspected of sympathy to the enemy.

From the very inception of the new regime, at their founding congress on December 2, 1978, the guidelines put in place by those who would become the political and military authorities of the regime proclaimed a policy of forgiveness for those who were or had been associated with Pol Pot's Khmer Rouge regime. The first communiqué announcing the formation of the group that intended to overthrow the Khmer Rouge regime called upon the "cadre and personnel of the traitorous state power to return and join hands with the people" and promised "leniency vis-à-vis those who are honest and who understand and sincerely correct their wrongdoings."[11] Soldiers and cadre of Democratic Kampuchea who had "committed crimes against . . . the civilian population" would "benefit from a reprieve" if they surrendered themselves to the new revolutionary authorities.[12] On January 6, 1979, the new authorities elaborated on this promise by announcing that former soldiers of the Khmer Rouge regime would be subjected to only five days of "re-education" and then would be free to return to their lives as peaceful citizens of the nation.[13] Confronted with the need to gather the forces that would be required to staff a new national administration and to defeat the still-substantial Khmer Rouge forces, this policy made practical sense. It also set a precedent for the impunity of those who were involved in genocide and crimes against humanity during the Khmer Rouge regime.

As soon as it appeared that the Khmer Rouge military forces had been decisively defeated, however, the new authorities began to harden their policy of forgiveness. An order dated April 15, 1979, declared:

> Those who directly engaged in the massacre of people or signed such an order must stand before the local revolutionary power, ask forgiveness from

the people, and fully recognize their crimes. To re-educate them, the revolutionary power in various localities may subject them, according to the se-
riousness of their wrong-doing, to a period of re-education lasting from 3
to 5 years in order to turn them into honest people in the national community.[14]

This same directive allowed that those who "served the interests" of the
regime might enjoy a reduction in their "reeducation" sentences but also
specified that the regime would "severely punish" those who continued to
follow the orders of the Pol Pot "clique."[15] In the climate of the times,
such wording might well have been interpreted as meaning execution. As
time passed, these declarations would be applied inconsistently. Some individuals who had committed heinous offenses escaped with very mild
punishments, or even none at all, and others who may have done little or
nothing suffered prolonged extrajudicial confinement. Take You Huy, for
example, a Khmer Rouge cadre who was chief of guards at the notorious
Tuol Sleng prison and who had supervised the murder of thousands of
men, women, and children. During the early 1980s, he surrendered to government authorities, professing his loyalty to the new order and a desire
to return to the national community. He was given a lenient sentence of
one year of reeducation and was then released to return to life as a farmer.[16]

Despite these declared and sometimes actual policies of amnesty, reconciliation, and leniency, in practice there were often strict limits on forgiveness. A Ministry of Interior directive dated February 21, 1984,
described the criteria for deciding which detained persons were eligible
for review under an amnesty declared in honor of the January 7 "National
Independence Day." Those eligible to have their cases reviewed were rank-
and-file nonviolent offenders who had endured at least three years of
"reeducation," as well as those who were detained "for breaking laws in
force, but who have not been tried for specific crimes."[17] Other categories
of individuals who could be considered for the amnesty included "people
who have had contact with the traitorous enemy forces, but who were deceived and have not committed treason, and first offenders."

Those deemed not eligible for review of their cases, however, were listed
as "enemy leaders or those accused of violence," as well as "spies for the
imperialists, Chinese hegemonists, and enemy security forces and police."
Moreover, the directive stated that "core cadre and those trained abroad or
in enemy camps shall not be reviewed for release." This, presumably, would
include all rank-and-file combatants of the Khmer Rouge and their allies,

as they certainly would have been trained in "enemy camps." As a practical matter, then, many captured or suspected enemy soldiers and political operatives, as well as many merely suspected of sympathy toward the Khmer Rouge and their allies, were incarcerated for lengthy periods without the right of trial or review.

The leadership of the Phnom Penh regime was fully aware of this situation. A report to the Council of Ministers in 1985 detailed the widespread violation of rights by the regime.

> Arbitrary searches, arrest, detentions and imprisonment occur practically everywhere. Arrests, detentions and imprisonments are getting more abusive. There are arrests without actual evidence, without a clear investigation, and without a file. Most arrests are followed by imprisonment based only on the report of a single person or merely on suspicion. . . . The arresting and detaining organizations have no intention of sending [detainees] to the organizations responsible for prosecution. Adjudications don't occur, because there are no files and no evidence at all, and [yet] [detainees] are not released.[18]

As the strength and effectiveness of the Khmer Rouge and their allies grew, so, too, did concern within the Phnom Penh regime, leading to ever more arrests.

During the 1984–1985 dry season, Vietnamese and Phnom Penh forces succeeded in crushing most of the major bases of the Khmer Rouge and their allies on Cambodian soil along the Thai border, dispersing them into Thailand. Faced with the loss of these interior bases, the Khmer Rouge shifted from trying to seize and hold territory inside Cambodia to a roving guerilla warfare mode. As one of the militia leaders allied with the Khmer Rouge put it in January 1985, "Now we change everything—tactics, headquarters. We will have to take off from the border. We have to go inside and liberate our country."[19] Later that year, this change of strategy began to pay off as the government began reporting increased insecurity in the vicinity of Phnom Penh, forcing the Vietnamese to divert their own units from confronting the enemy at the border to patrolling the heartland of the country.[20] At the same time, the regime's province-level militia units were finding themselves in combat against enemy forces across a wide range of areas, including Siem Reap, Battambang, Pursat, Kompong Thom, Kompong Cham, Kompong Speu, Kompong Som, Kampot, and Kompong Chhnang Provinces.[21] In addition to hit-and-run military op-

erations by the Khmer Rouge forces deep inside the country, enemy propaganda teams began to circulate in Phnom Penh's base areas.

Within the upper levels of the government's security services and political leadership, suspicion ran deep about the potential for subversion
among the population in their "liberated" areas. After the 1985–1986 dry
season, the government noted that enemy infiltration of its zones was increasing. A March 25, 1986, Council of Ministers and Ministry of Interior
document asserted that the Khmer Rouge and their allies were expanding their forces and carrying out subversive activities all through central
and southern Cambodia, far from their main base areas in the north and
west. Among other things, this document identified "psychological war"
tactics being employed by the Khmer Rouge forces, such as spreading slo-
gans like "Khmer do not fight Khmer."[22] This slogan suggested that all
Cambodians should band together to fight the "real" enemy, the Vietnamese.

In response to these perceived threats, the regime's security services were
directed to combat this infiltration by being suspicious of virtually everyone, describing potential sources of subversion in terms that very much
recalled the language used by the dreaded Khmer Rouge security apparatus, the *Santebal*. Traders, people who attempted to move from district to
district, defectors, and people with relatives living in enemy zones were to
be scrutinized and monitored with secret forces. The list of potential subversive elements to be monitored, as a practical matter, appears to have included virtually everyone except senior officials of the party—though they,
too, were subject to close observation by the party's Monitoring Committee. To many, this level of surveillance would have been an eerie re-
minder of life during the Khmer Rouge regime, when the ruling
apparatus, *Angkar*, was said to have "as many eyes as a pineapple."[23]

THE K-5 PLAN

The survival of the Khmer Rouge after Pol Pot's ouster from Phnom
Penh and the reinvigoration of their military as a potent guerilla force operating from sanctuaries along the Thai–Cambodia border presented a serious challenge to the survival of the People's Republic of Kampuchea.
The government's Vietnamese patrons consequently devised an elaborate
defense plan to contain the Khmer Rouge military threat, so that they
could end their costly military intervention and occupation in Cambodia
with assurances that their new client regime would be able to keep Pol

Pot at bay. This plan was code-named "K-5," but it has been so shrouded in secrecy and so obscured by rhetoric that scholars still do not agree on precisely what it was all about.

The confusion begins with the name itself, as there has been a great deal of speculation regarding what the code designation, K-5, actually means. One possibility is that it derives from the term Vietnamese sources have used to refer to the project, *ke hoach nam*. *Ke hoach* is Vietnamese for "plan," and *nam* can mean either "year" or the number "five," depending upon context. Thus, K-5 could refer to a "plan 5," or possibly to a "five-year plan." By extension, it could be a play on these meanings, incorporating both in a shorthand form. This latter possibility is given more credence by the fact that some analysts argue that the plan included five major phases and was intended to be implemented over a five-year time period. An entirely different possibility is that it derives not from Vietnamese, but rather from the Khmer language. The "K" may refer to the first initial of *kar karpier*, meaning "defense" in Khmer.[24] One analyst thus suggests that K-5 designates the fifth in a series of Cambodian defense plans. Another possibility is that both explanations were true, depending on whom you asked.

Other unclear aspects of K-5 concern exactly when this plan was originally conceived and when implementation of the plan began. Some argue that K-5 was launched in 1984, after the 1983–1984 dry season and in preparation for the following year's dry season.[25] Margaret Slocomb argues that it was initiated by a decision dated July 17, 1984, and also quotes Hun Sen citing 1984 as the start of K-5.[26] However, Prasong Soonsiri, then-head of the Thai National Security Council, told reporters that according to his intelligence information, construction of the K-5 border fortifications had begun in 1983.[27] Another source suggests that the Vietnamese began attempting to implement the plan, or at least conceived it, far earlier than that. Former People's Republic of Kampuchea Prime Minister Pen Sovann has reportedly claimed that on March 27, 1981, Vietnamese leader Le Duc Tho first raised the issue of the K-5 plan with him.[28] Pen Sovann supposedly reacted negatively to this proposal, which, if true, may be part of the explanation for his removal later that year from the powerful posts of prime minister, party secretary, and minister of defense.[29] Despite the uncertainty regarding the derivation of the code name and the precise date of the plan's beginning, one thing is perfectly clear about K-5: at its inception it was an enormously controversial undertaking, and today, many years after it ended, it still remains enormously controversial.

K-5 was a master plan for defending the new government, defeating the Khmer Rouge guerillas and their allies, and securing Cambodia adequately to cover a withdrawal of Vietnamese forces. In this sense, it was in some ways reminiscent of the U.S. plan for "Vietnamization" during the Second Indochina War. Under Vietnamization, the United States bolstered the South Vietnamese army with new training and equipment. At the same time, a combined U.S.–South Vietnamese attack into Cambodia sought to relieve pressure on allied forces in southern Vietnam from Viet Cong and North Vietnamese forces operating from sanctuaries across the border. K-5 was also similar to Vietnamization in the broad scope of its design and the magnitude of the resources required to carry it through to completion. According to some analysts, the K-5 plan aimed to accomplish five integrated tasks:[30]

1. protection of the population in government-held areas from enemy attack;
2. destruction of the enemy base camps on Cambodian territory;
3. construction of a strategic barrier along the Thai border to stop new infiltration;
4. elimination of the enemy guerillas operating inside Cambodia; and
5. creation of a Cambodian military capable of protecting the country by itself.

Whatever the date that K-5 was actually conceived by Vietnamese military planners, it is clear that several elements of this plan were in process shortly after the initial liberation of Cambodia from Pol Pot's Khmer Rouge in 1979. According to Esmeralda Luciolli,

The Vietnamese army had started to enlist Khmer civilians to do strategic work since 1979. Early on, in the autumn of 1982, the population was made to participate in "socialist service." This work consisted of building dams, roads and earthworks near their dwellings and proved to be useful to the inhabitants. But very quickly, this task took a strategic turn and the peasants were ordered to clear the surrounding forests and build protective barriers around the most important dwelling centers. Starting in 1983, the population was made to create fences out of two or three rows of prickly shrubs or bamboo, sometimes lined by mine fields, around the villages. The people were also forced to set up defensive barriers along the railroads, around the bridges and at strategic points of the highways. . . . However, the first chores lasted only a short time and did not require any displacement of the population.

In 1984, a new stage was reached: the population of the country was mobilized for gigantic labors officially designated as "work to defend the fatherland." At the beginning of that year, the Vietnamese authorities decided to seal the Thai border. The dry season offensive of 1984–1985 destroyed the major camps of the resistance located in those areas. To reinforce this victory they had to tightly seal the country against infiltration by the guerrillas and prevent the population from fleeing to the border.

To this end, the decision to set up a "defense line" eight hundred kilometers long was made in Hanoi, in early 1984, by the Vietnamese Communist Party's central committee.[31]

According to this account, then, by the end of the 1984–1985 dry season, with physical security improvements in place around interior population centers and strategic points and enemy bases overrun and destroyed along the Thai border, phases 1 and 2 of K-5 were complete. Now it was time to implement the crucial phase 3 of the plan, attempting to seal the Thai–Cambodia border, before proceeding to eliminate the remaining guerilla forces operating on the Cambodian side of the border defense line. This was the point where K-5 began to run into serious problems in both its conception and its implementation. Unintended consequences created a new set of problems.

The plan to construct a system of fortifications all along the 500-mile length of the Thai–Cambodia border would require a fantastic amount of labor, and it was for this purpose that the Cambodian government in 1984 began requiring that large levies of civilian labor from each province go to the border area to participate in this huge construction effort. Precise numbers are difficult to determine. By Luciolli's estimation, some 100,000 to 120,000 persons were requisitioned in each wave. Their tours at the front typically lasted from three to six months. Citing internal regime documents, however, Slocomb argues that Luciolli's estimates are "exaggerated" and that the total number of civilian workers employed on the K-5 border project for the entire duration of the construction was approximately 380,000.[32] The initial phases of this work were especially difficult, because not only did the labor involve clearing land-mine infested jungle, but these particular jungles were also infested with a strain of malaria against which most lowland Cambodians had no natural immunity. Moreover, at the outset of this gigantic project, inadequate provisions had been made to house and feed the workers, contributing to the high rate of sickness and death in the K-5 workforce. According to several estimates, 80 percent of these workers contracted malaria, and of those, up to 5 percent succumbed to the disease.[33]

According to the plan, only draft-age males 17–45 were supposed to be liable to recruitment for duty building the border fortifications, but factors such as corruption, unavailability of sufficient labor, and the urgency with which the project was viewed by the authorities resulted in some women as well as younger and older men also being sent for K-5 duty. Nonetheless, with so many of the able-bodied men away at the border working "in defense of the fatherland," fewer people were available to grow rice and tend other crops. The beginning of the labor requisitions for K-5 also unfortunately coincided with serious flooding and a subsequent drought that by official estimates ruined half of the 1984–1985 rice crop.[34] These factors, combined with the high level of illness and death among the K-5 workers, caused serious concern in the government leadership about the level of agricultural production.[35] "In 1985, according to an official of the Ministry of Agriculture, only 60 percent to 70 percent of the rice fields cultivated the preceding year were being sown."[36] Thus, the threat of hunger was widespread in Cambodia in 1985 and 1986; nonetheless, K-5 remained the priority.

Another unanticipated consequence of K-5 was its effect on the regime's popularity. In the view of one analyst, government officials initially thought that the K-5 would inspire the people to a defense of their homeland against the dreaded forces of Pol Pot and that with their patriotic instincts thus aroused, there would be ample volunteers for the border fortification duties.[37] This turned out to be a major misreading of the people's feelings. It did not take long for stories of the hardship experienced by K-5 draftees at the border to spread among the people, and such stories were often laced with horror:

"When we arrived," said Touch Saroeun (a participant), "thousands of workers had preceded us. We were maybe ten thousand coming from several provinces. There was no shelter at all. It was useless to seek to build a cabin, because we were moved every day. Some of us had hammocks, others had nothing. They slept on the ground, on bits of plastic sheets or even on the soil." . . .

"We were told that there would be every thing on the spot," says a villager from Takeo. "But once there, there was nearly nothing to eat." . . .

Thory, a young woman from Battambang, said that in her group, "several people died of starvation. It was like under the Pol Pot regime." . . .

Sunnara, from Prey Veng, was obliged to guard the "volunteers." "We did not have any choice, the Vietnamese were after us. The rare persons who tried to escape were recaptured and savagely beaten, then taken to jail. Some have been executed." Sareth, from Pursat, was demining: "Often those who were blown on [sic] the mines were accused of wanting to flee. In fact, these were accidents because we did not know at all where the mines were."[38]

The border regions, of course, were an active war zone, and the Khmer Rouge and their allies were actively opposing the construction of these fortifications. As a result, convoys of K-5 workers were sometimes attacked by the Khmer Rouge guerillas and often hit land mines that had been laid in the road by rebel forces:

In Sitha's convoy, two trucks were disintegrated. Out of the hundred people carried by each truck, more than half of them died and most of the others were injured. In March 1985, on the way to Pursat, a nurse from Prey Veng saw the truck that preceded his blow up. About twenty "volunteers" were killed and another fifty wounded.[39]

So unpopular was the K-5 project with the Cambodian populace that it soon became a potent point of leverage in psychological warfare operations.[40] Forces of the Khmer Rouge coalition operating deep inside government territory propagandized the population on this issue, arguing that the regime was oppressing them by forcing them into K-5 duties, while demonstrating by their very presence the futility of the project. A March 1986 Ministry of Interior report noted this tactic, asserting that the enemy was "exaggerating or distorting, by threatening cadre and people in terms of implementing the task of recruiting soldiers and participating in building the K-5 border defense system."[41]

Eventually, K-5 became extremely unpopular not only with the people but also among cadre of the ruling party itself. In 1989, the Monitoring Committee of the ruling party's Central Committee, responsible for ensuring discipline and enforcing adherence to the party line, issued a set of instructions that aimed to address certain categories of "problem" cadre within the party. Prominent among these were "cadre who avoid the task of conscription, cadre who avoid the task of the K-5, and cadre who avoid the task of building up militia forces for self-defense."[42] This set of instructions further specifies that all such miscreants should be "rounded up, guarded, judged and educated." That the problem of noncompliance with K-5 duties assigned by the party had risen to a level requiring harsh discipline against members of the party itself suggests this program was almost universally loathed within Cambodia. It also provided a fertile ground for Khmer Rouge propaganda.

There was good reason for the resentment of the people against K-5. The death toll among workers was high, and the toll of nonfatal casualties was almost certainly much higher. According to one official from the Ministry of Defense who defected to Thailand, official Cambodian government estimates concluded "in March 1986 that 30,000 people died since the beginning of the labor."[43] What the final total of dead might have been, as well as how many more were maimed by land mines or otherwise seriously injured, we probably will not know until the archives of the government from that period are completely opened for study by scholars. Perhaps we will not know even then.

By the end of the 1987 dry season, construction of the border fortifications was nearing completion. To mark the event, a delegation of East European ambassadors accompanied the Vietnamese ambassador to Cambodia, Ngo Dien, to the northwestern city of Pailin to inspect the ramparts.[44] They were reportedly told that the fence was "very efficient, a reliable protection against infiltration."[45] Along much of the several hundred-mile length of this purported "bamboo wall," in actual fact, it consisted of little more than a fifteen yard-wide trench lined with mines.[46] Unsurprisingly, infiltration continued virtually unabated. While completion of this gargantuan construction project reduced the need to conscript "volunteers" for "wall-building" duties, some teams continued to be requisitioned for maintenance chores along the 500-mile border zone. Those teams continued to suffer attrition, particularly from malaria and land mines, but after much toil and suffering, phase three of the K-5 plan was at an end.

Phase four—the elimination of guerilla forces operating in the interior of the country—and phase five—the upgrading of the new government's military capability to the level of self-sufficiency—were more problematic. Given the ease with which coalition military forces were able to breach the supposedly "very efficient" border defense fortification, penetration of the border zone and resupply of guerillas operating in the interior was not difficult. This increased pressure on the provincial militia to resist and repel attacks by guerilla units, but since the militia units were often defending their home villages and families, their motivation to fight may well have been stronger than that of the regular army units posted to the front lines. Though enemy fighters continued to strike deep into the country, security continued to be maintained at an acceptable level, especially in the areas directly surrounding Phnom Penh. As one analyst expressed it, suppression of "the resistance forces and inland guerrillas was assessed as mixed with the bottom line conclusion that the trends were favorable for Vietnam."[47] With the security situation in the interior of the country thus considered manageable, then, the ultimate effectiveness of the K-5 could now be tested.

Phase five of the K-5 plan was put to the test in 1989. On September 26, the last of Vietnam's main force units withdrew from Cambodia, leaving the newly renamed State of Cambodia and its Cambodian People's Armed Forces to stand alone against the combined forces of the Khmer Rouge and their allies. On that very day, State of Cambodia President Heng Samrin issued a proclamation exhorting the people that "we must concentrate all our forces on preventing the resurgence of Pol Pot's genocidal regime."[48] In preparation for this pivotal moment in the struggle, the previous month the parliament had voted to conscript into the military all men above the age of 16 who had not enrolled in local or provincial militia forces.[49] The Khmer Rouge and their allies formally declared that the Vietnamese withdrawal was a fake and that more than 100,000 armed Vietnamese soldiers remained in Cambodia.[50] On the battlefield, however, the Khmer Rouge knew better and wasted no time probing the mettle of the government defenders.

Sensing the weakness of the regime now that the protective cover of the People's Army of Vietnam was no longer facing them, the combined forces of the Khmer Rouge and their allies launched a full-scale assault with fierce attacks all along the front lines in the western and northwestern areas of the Thai–Cambodia border. The newly independent Cambodian military was initially battered and driven back in a wide arc of territory along the Thai border. On October 22, only a matter of weeks after the Vietnamese withdrawal, the Khmer Rouge army seized the strategic town of Pailin in northwestern Cambodia and threatened to overrun Battambang City, the second largest city in the country.[51] By the beginning of 1990, alarm spread in the regime as their military forces continued to lose ground to the Khmer Rouge, and the tempo of guerilla attacks deep in the interior began to increase dramatically. At this point, the government called on Vietnam to supply forces to back up their faltering troops. Vietnam responded by dispatching a small contingent of combat troops, who had the effect of stiffening the resolve of the Cambodian military.[52] Though they poorly weathered their first test as an independent fighting force, the government's soldiers ultimately held the line.

By 1991, such was the intensity of Khmer Rouge pressure on the government's armed forces that the conscription of new recruits to replace casualties and expand the army became an urgent priority for the regime. Orders went out from the government to local authorities that "youth of the ages from 17 to 30 . . . shall have an obligation to defend the country."[53] A system of city-provincial and quarter-district steering committees was organized to ensure the comprehensive drafting of all able-bodied men who were not otherwise engaged in security duties. Those who attempted to avoid this duty were to be charged with a crime and punished by the court. There were apparently serious concerns about draft dodging and fears that enemy propaganda was encouraging such avoidance, because the same directive also warned local authorities to "take defensive measures to prevent the disastrous activities of enemies who make use of this obligation [to military service] to make psychological war in an attempt to create a split between the people and the authorities." The cumulative demands of the K-5 project over the previous years, however, had already created a split between the people and the authorities. Though the regime had begun with acute sensitivity to the need to avoid coercion in their relations with the Cambodian people, a legacy of the terrible experience under Pol Pot, the urgency of the struggle to prevent the return of the genocidal regime meant that step by step, caution was thrown to the wind as "volunteers" for state-mandated national defense duties were gradually coerced into carrying out ever more onerous and dangerous tasks.

For all of the unpopularity of the K-5 among the Cambodian people and even within the party itself and for the high cost paid by the Cambodian people, what did the K-5 project accomplish? The border fortifications constructed under the auspices of the K-5 plan were a predictable failure, an immense Maginot Line in the jungle that was easily breached by the rebels and may have served little more purpose than to funnel the defenders into predictable kill zones for Khmer Rouge ambushes. Other elements of the K-5 plan were more successful in holding the resurgent Khmer Rouge and their allies at bay for more than a decade. Even though the Khmer Rouge were backed militarily, economically, and politically by China, the United States, the Association of Southeast Asian Nations (ASEAN), and most of the rest of the Western world, this was no small accomplishment, and it did indeed prevent the return of the Pol Pot regime. Cumulatively, though, the coercion that was required to implement the K-5 plan reminded many Cambodians of the excesses of the Khmer Rouge regime, and in this sense it cost the government authorities an enormous amount of political capital among their people. That cost would soon come home to roost as the State of Cambodia faced the most profound challenge in its short history: peace.

WAR BY OTHER MEANS

The story of the labyrinthine, decade-long negotiations in search of a resolution to the Third Indochina War has been exhaustively described elsewhere, so it need not be recounted here in great detail.[54] Though it seemed relatively simple on the surface, with four domestic factions struggling for supremacy over Cambodia, in reality this war was deceptively complex. Not only were there struggles among the four Cambodian factions, but there were also struggles within them. There was a regional rivalry between Thailand and Vietnam for influence over Cambodia; there was a Great Power rivalry for influence in the region that centered on China's ambitions; and there was the Cold War dimension of superpower rivalry, involving the United States and the Soviet Union, along with all of their respective allies. These multiple overlaid dimensions of the Cambodian situation brought into play a maze of conflicting and cross-cutting interests, all of which had to be harmonized in some fashion in order to bring the war to a conclusion.

It is notable, however, in view of the global scope of politicomilitary interests engaged in this war, that more than a decade after the peace negotiations reached a climax in 1991, the same Cambodian leader who was in power at that time—Hun Sen—still controlled the fate of the nation. Given his relative youth and modest education, many had underestimated him. He attended a Phnom Penh high school and learned to read and write. These skills served him well when he joined the Khmer Rouge guerillas in 1969 or 1970. Respected by his largely illiterate peers as a relatively intellectual figure, he quickly assumed leadership positions. Hun Sen was soon selected by the Khmer Rouge for advanced leadership training. He was one to be watched and groomed.

Over the course of the 1970–1975 civil war, however, Hun Sen had come to see the wanton brutality of the organization he had joined. As the Khmer Rouge regime took shape after 1975, he was ordered to lead his troops against domestic "enemies" of the regime. Hun Sen says that he evaded a command to attack an ethnic Cham village in Kroch Chhmar around the end of September 1975 by claiming that he and 70 percent of his men were sick with malaria.[55] He also began to see increasing numbers of his revolutionary comrades being called away by the Khmer Rouge for "meetings," never to be seen again. Before long it was his turn to be called away for a meeting, and it was then, in June 1977, that he made the fateful decision to flee the Khmer Rouge purges for Vietnam. He was initially jailed by the Vietnamese, until Vietnam altered its policy toward Cambodia. Like the Khmer Rouge before, the Vietnamese recognized Hun Sen's leadership potential and began grooming him to lead forces back into Cambodia to fight and topple the Khmer Rouge regime.

After the Khmer Rouge regime was overthrown, the Vietnamese selected Hun Sen as foreign minister of the new regime. He performed well in that role, gaining stature among his colleagues, trust from the Vietnamese whose troops occupied the country, and experience with the international community, in general, and the UN, in particular. Within a few years he was appointed prime minister, a post he clung to through the following tumultuous two decades. His survival in such a lethal environment demonstrated Hun Sen's ferocious competitive drive. He was a natural, an instinctive political animal.

Hun Sen outlasted all of his domestic rivals and defied the efforts of most of the Great Powers of the world to bring down both him and his regime. Hun Sen has cultivated a reputation as a master chess player. In the game of chess, the key to effective play is to be able to plan several moves ahead, positioning one's pieces in a way that simultaneously forecloses your opponent's options and channels him into a vulnerable arrangement. Such foresight characterizes not only Hun Sen's recreational activities but also his management of the state. His statecraft would be put to the test as never before when the international negotiations to find a solution to the Cambodian war finally yielded a consensus document.

The long peace negotiations reached a climactic stage on August 28, 1990, when the five permanent members of the UN Security Council adopted a "Framework for a Comprehensive Political Settlement of the Cambodian Conflict."[56] This document outlined the essential principles upon which the peace process would be based, and it was accepted two weeks later by the four main domestic parties to the conflict in a meeting at Jakarta.[57] The solution called for a UN-supervised electoral competition among the four parties, to be implemented in what would be the largest and most ambitious UN peacekeeping mission ever attempted up to that time. Among the key elements of this plan was the notion that in order to ensure a "neutral political environment" for the election, the UN would assume control of several key administrative organs of the Phnom Penh government, including the ministries concerned with national defense and public security. Though the Phnom Penh government agreed to this arrangement on paper, in practice, they had another idea altogether.

Once the outlines of the political settlement became clear, the State of Cambodia immediately began to organize a secret plan known by the code name "K-990." The purpose of this plan was said to be "to ensure political stability and social order once the political settlement is in progress."[58] The objective of maintaining "political stability" would seem to imply that the Phnom Penh regime would continue to wield power in Cambodia, a goal not necessarily consistent with the outlines of the framework document. In reality, the K-990 plan had to do principally with security matters, a reflection of the prevailing view within the Phnom Penh regime that the peace plan simply represented a continuation of the war by other means. As analyst David Ashley has noted, "It is clear from internal documents obtained by UNTAC's [United Nations Transitional Authority in Cambodia] Control Team missions . . . that the [Phnom Penh regime] viewed the May 1993 elections as part of, rather than marking an end to, the post-1979 civil war."[59]

In order to ensure operational security for the K-990 plan, in February 1990 the Phnom Penh regime established a secret courier network known as "Z-91," which would be "responsible for reporting and transferring information to and from lower to top levels."[60] The Ministry of Interior directed that this national network be organized in classic cell form, so that "only one contact knows one contact," and that the network must "maintain secrecy to the maximum." To this end, instructions from the superior level to field operatives would be transmitted by the courier network in verbal form, eliminating any paper trail for specific operational orders. This arrangement was very effective in maintaining the covert nature of these operations, despite heroic efforts by UN authorities to identify the authors of the political violence that plagued Cambodia during the implementation of the peace plan. Judy Ledgerwood has noted that despite these efforts, UN investigators could never conclusively demonstrate that the ruling party in Phnom Penh, the Cambodian People's Party (CPP), was responsible for the violence. "No evidentiary 'smoking gun' was ever found proving CPP political violence at the local level was conducted as part of a centrally formulated, centrally directed plan."[61]

The centrally formulated and centrally directed nature of these operations might well have been clear enough simply from the welter of code-named covert action units that proliferated in Cambodia just prior to, and during, the UN intervention: intelligence and security units known as Z-91, A-90, A-92, A-93, S-91, and so on were operating on a nationwide basis, and all were identified as being involved with various aspects of "dirty tricks" against the opposition parties during the run-up to the UN-managed election of 1993. These dirty tricks included infiltrating the opposition parties, attempting to influence the planning and policy agendas of the opposition parties, hiring local thugs to disrupt opposition party events, threatening and intimidating opposition party activists, carrying out acts of sabotage against opposition party offices and organizations, and deterring individual citizens from becoming involved with opposition parties, as well as arresting and in some cases murdering opposition political activists. It was a highly organized strategy to create as much chaos as possible among those who were, under the putative protection of the UN, attempting to challenge the entrenched power of the Cambodian People's Party in an open electoral contest. These tactics revealed clearly the fact that the People's Party simply did not accept their former military opponents as legitimate political players. The People's Party operated as if by the credo that, in war by any means, anything goes.

A glimpse of how some of these groups operated was provided in a UN report analyzing documents obtained by UNTAC Control Teams during raids on police posts and other State of Cambodia (SOC) offices in various provinces. One category of operations discussed in this report was known as "reaction groups." According to the report, "Reaction forces are tasked with the overt disruption of legitimate political party activity through verbal and physical harassment of opposition party members and representatives. . . . Reaction forces are hand-picked by SOC security forces from known trouble-makers in the local community. . . . What is clear is that the SOC security forces are fully apprised of the implications of their activities, and are under instruction to conceal all SOC/CPP [State of Cambodia/Cambodian People's Party] links with reaction forces."[62] These "reaction groups" were organized in such a way as to ensure deniability of any connection to the government, while providing local teams of thugs who could be assigned to intimidate activists attempting to or-

ganize for the elections. Another section of this report discussed the so-called A-92 groups:

> The A-groups, in particular the A-92 groups, are charged with the covert disruption of legitimate political activity through the infiltration of political parties. Their mission is to subvert political parties through such tactics as exacerbating internal disagreements. The profile of A-groups is at the other end of the social spectrum to reaction forces. According to a central level document, "A" groups are recruited from among people of high standing such as professors, monks, medical practitioners and "persons with influence among the ranks of the popular masses."[63]

According to the UNTAC analysis, the targets of this infiltration activity are "all political organizations inside and outside the country, all parties and associations." The "A" groups were all under the command of the Ministry of National Security.[64] Thus, the regime had implemented a countrywide network of overt and covert intelligence units designed to attack efforts by their political opposition to organize and compete in the elections, all centrally coordinated by the highest authorities of the state.

In front-line provinces such as Battambang and Siem Reap, where local authorities had faced the Khmer Rouge in battle for a decade, such activities developed a more direct and violent character. UNTAC found that special intelligence units in these provinces under the command of the Ministry of Defense were assassinating the Phnom Penh regime's political opponents. A unit that adopted the code name "S-91" in 1991, presumably in preparation "to ensure political stability and social order once the political settlement is in progress," engaged in the "arrest, detention and execution of political and non-political targets" during the period of the peace process implementation.[65]

Laying the groundwork by organizing these types of intelligence operations, the Phnom Penh regime began preparing, well before the peace process had even been finalized, to meet their opponents on a new battlefield, the field of "peaceful" political competition. Cambodian politics has often been described as a particularly ruthless enterprise, and the People's Party demonstrated an aptitude for strategic deception, clandestine operations, covert manipulation, and violent repression well suited to such an environment. Such behavior did not, however, augur well for the UN's hopes to bring peace and democracy to Cambodia while fostering national reconciliation.

CRIMES IN A DESPERATE TIME

Strategies such as the People's Revolutionary Tribunal, the K-5 plan, and the K-990 intelligence operations gave some people the sense that the People's Republic of Kampuchea/State of Cambodia regime was nothing more and nothing less than a different shade of Khmer Rouge. This sense was heightened by the fact that the people who made up the Phnom Penh regime viewed their own organizational heritage through the same prism as did the Khmer Rouge, as both groups traced their lineage to the breakup of the Indochinese Communist Party in 1951.[66] Despite the feelings of some Cambodians that the government was just another form of the Khmer Rouge regime, it is clear that the People's Republic of Kampuchea was a very different creature than Pol Pot's Democratic Kampuchea.

The pragmatism of Hun Sen and his colleagues did much to assist in the rehabilitation of the shattered country following the utter devastation of the Khmer Rouge regime. The most xenophobic and extreme traits of Pol Pot's rule were quickly eliminated by the new government. In the area of civil and social rights, freedom of movement was restored—though it was later to be restricted once again due to civil war security requirements. The observance of Buddhism and Islam was once again permitted, albeit in restricted forms, and once the Vietnamese withdrew, Buddhism once again was declared the state religion. Communal dining and state-regimented labor were abolished, except for the programs of work "in defense of the fatherland." The practice of state-arranged marriages was ended, as were the bulk of the other most onerous aspects of the Khmer Rouge regime.

On the economic front, money and markets were reintroduced. The change of regime from the People's Republic of Kampuchea to the State of Cambodia saw the country opened to free market reforms, though this also had its downside. Frontier capitalism and attendant corruption quickly stripped state enterprises of their assets, which were sold off at fire-sale prices in an anarchic privatization process.[67] Another negative consequence of the late 1980s liberalization of the economy was the collapse of the state-supported social safety net and the consequent erosion of communal mutual support systems that had evolved during the hard-pressed years of recovery from the destruction of the "Pol Pot time." These changes in socioeconomic relations had the most serious impact on the most vulnerable members of society. Despite these difficulties, however, on balance there can be no question that the quality of life for the Cambodian people improved immensely after the 1979 ouster of the Khmer Rouge and then

improved again when the government abandoned socialist economic policies in 1989. For example, one former Khmer Rouge economic cadre in
Takeo province argued that conditions improved for the majority in his
commune when the late-1980s privatization policies were put in place:
"People in general had more food to eat during the State of Cambodia.
The standard of living was a little better than what it was during the People's Republic of Kampuchea."[68]

That said, it is also clear that serious human rights abuses were committed under the post–Khmer Rouge regime, including arbitrary detention and extrajudicial execution. Perhaps the most egregious human rights
abuses during the new regime were in connection with the K-5 program.
Given that the forced labor component of that program required huge
numbers of civilian Cambodians to engage in "work in defense of the fatherland" against their will, it is difficult to characterize this policy as anything other than indentured servitude on a mass scale. This policy violated
any number of international covenants to which Cambodia was a state-
party.[69] Moreover, regardless of any treaties by which Cambodia may have
been bound, and regardless of whether or not the new regime amounted
to a "competent authority" for purposes of upholding international treaty
commitments, this forced labor also appears to have been a violation of
customary international law, which applies to all states under all circumstances. Experts on international law suggest that the K-5 forced labor program therefore may be said to have constituted a war crime, and some go
so far as to argue that it was a crime against humanity.[70] The Charter of
the International Military Tribunal defined enslavement as a crime against
humanity, when "committed against any civilian population" in the context of an international war—and this war clearly was international in character.[71] The argument might be made that the authorities were compelled
to implement the K-5 labor program by the necessity of preventing the
return of a genocidal regime, but that does not justify carrying out another form of crimes against humanity—all the more so in view of the
fact that the border fortifications were generally ineffective in fulfilling
their avowed purpose of preventing infiltration by enemy forces. The fact
that government authorities may have felt compelled either by moral necessity or by the force majeure of Vietnamese military occupation to carry
out this program does not change the fact that it was a serious violation
of the human rights of the Cambodian people.

The Charter of the International Military Tribunal defined war crimes
as including "deportation to slave labor or for any other purpose of civil-

ian population of or in occupied territory."[72] Cambodia was occupied at that time by Vietnamese troops. Though the government's leadership may have had no choice given the influence of the Vietnamese over their security policy, nonetheless, acting in a capacity as the agents or surrogates of Vietnam, the government was responsible to avoid any such behaviors as deporting civilians from their home provinces to engage in compulsory labor in hazardous areas without remuneration. The exceptions to the general prohibitions on forced labor in international human rights law require that the workers not be removed from their residences, that they not be subjected to dangerous working conditions, that they be required to work for not more than sixty days per year, and that the workforce be limited to males between the ages of 18 and 45. All of these prohibitions appear to have been routinely violated in the course of the K-5 border defense project, thus depriving Cambodian citizens of their liberty—and, in some cases, of their lives. Such acts not only invited the condemnation of the international community for serious violations of human rights but also squandered the most precious asset the regime had, the gratitude of the Cambodian people for the overthrow of the Pol Pot regime.

Pragmatic politician that he is, Hun Sen recognizes the political damage inflicted on the regime by the K-5 program, but he responds to these charges by saying, in effect, "We had no choice." "If the US had not supported the Khmer Rouge," he told an interviewer, "there would have been no K5."[73] In terms of its impact on the Phnom Penh regime's political prospects, the ultimate evaluation of this program may be that, to paraphrase a famous Frenchman, K-5 was worse than a crime; it was a blunder.

The popular resentment engendered by the K-5 abuses and the ubiquitous internal security surveillance imposed on the people would come back to haunt the Cambodian government during the UN intervention in Cambodia. In turn, fear of popular support for opposition political movements as well as a sense among government authorities that there could be no such thing as a legitimate opposition to their rule led them to institute a covert apparatus designed to subvert all opposition movements, both the democratic alternatives and the totalitarian Khmer Rouge alike. Faced with a regime that felt it necessary to resort to such activities, and the Khmer Rouge, which had a record of cultivating allies and then exterminating those allies, the UN peacekeeping operation would find it a monumental challenge indeed to bring peace and national reconciliation to this war-torn nation.

3

AFTER THE PEACE

U.S. Secretary of State Warren Christopher described the 1993 UN-organized elections in Cambodia as "the triumph of democracy."[1] Charles Twining, the U.S. representative in Cambodia and soon-to-be U.S. ambassador to Cambodia, mocked the Khmer Rouge after the election: "This leaves the Khmer Rouge in the forest."[2] One year after the elections, U.S. Deputy Assistant Secretary of State Peter Tomsen told the House Foreign Affairs Subcommittee on East Asia and the Pacific, "UNTAC was a stunning peacekeeping success."[3]

In the wake of the UN's Cambodian peacekeeping operation, it seemed that the UN Secretariat, the international media, and many others agreed with these upbeat U.S. assessments of the accomplishments of the mission. Most professional Cambodia-watchers, however, were less sanguine. Cambodians themselves—from the four parties to the peace, as well as the Cambodian public—all appeared to be somewhat distraught about the outcome of the peacekeeping mission. King Norodom Sihanouk succinctly summarized local perceptions of the UN peace process: "It was a waste."[4]

Members of ASEAN exhibited a more nuanced view of UNTAC's outcome than either the sunny optimism of the United States and the UN or King Sihanouk's glum perspective. Vietnam voiced reservations about the results of the peace process, in part because Khmer Rouge forces had encroached closer to the Vietnamese border than at any time since 1989. Numerous European Community countries—France, Belgium, Holland,

and Germany, for example—were also not entirely satisfied with the out-come, perhaps having been somewhat nonplussed by the ruling party's strong-arm response to its electoral defeat. There were other reasons for all this grumbling, as well.

In 1994, Cambodia was on the verge of anarchy. Unresolved problems following the withdrawal of the UN mission to Cambodia were festering and growing unchecked. There was little or no effective governance in the territories controlled by the Royal Government, and the zones controlled by the Khmer Rouge had again grown through military conquest. The people were angry about it. On a visit to Cambodia early in 1994, nu-merous times when some Cambodian citizen inquired about my profes-sion, I would summarize by saying, "It is my job to put Pol Pot in jail." The response was often something like, "Well, don't stop there; the gov-ernment is full of criminals, from top to bottom."

Peace, stability, and national reconciliation were not among the accom-plishments of the UN peacekeeping operation in Cambodia. Moreover, besides peace, stability, and reconciliation, there were many other key goals of the peace agreements that the UN had failed to accomplish in Cam-bodia. How could it be that there was such a disjuncture between the plau-dits accruing to the UN peacekeeping mission from the UN, the United States, and elsewhere and the negative assessments by almost everyone liv-ing in the region?

UN PEACEKEEPING IN CAMBODIA

The Paris Peace Accords on Cambodia adopted in October 1991 com-mitted the UN to what was at that point the largest, most expensive, and most interventionist peacekeeping operation in its history.[5] Idealists argued that the goal of the accords was to bring peace to a land that had suffered two decades of war and genocide. Realists argue the primary purpose was to remove the "Cambodia Problem"—the long, stalemated, and increas-ingly pointless Cambodian war supported by most of the states of the re-gion and powers of the world—from the international agenda. In either case, the Agreements on a Comprehensive Political Settlement of the Cam-bodian Conflict[6] were being touted as a model for collective security in the post–Cold War world order.[7] Consequently, it is essential that we have a clear understanding of exactly what these agreements did—and did not—accomplish.

The peace process did achieve numerous significant objectives. The Cambodian conflict was decoupled from superpower geopolitical conflict, and Chinese military aid to the Khmer Rouge was terminated.[8] Cambodia's two decades of international isolation ended.[9] 362,000 refugees left the camps in Thailand and returned to Cambodia.[10] The three-faction rebel coalition challenging the Cambodian government was reduced to a single recalcitrant faction—the Khmer Rouge. The fragile beginnings of political pluralism were put in place. A free press began flowering in Cambodia as never before.[11] Indigenous human rights groups were founded and growing rapidly. Ninety percent of eligible Cambodians registered to vote, and 89 percent of those voted in 1993's free and fair elections, despite Khmer Rouge threats to kill anyone who participated.[12] A liberal constitutional monarchy was promulgated, and a coalition government began functioning, more or less. These were huge accomplishments, a tribute to the skill and dedication of the international civil servants who risked and in some cases sacrificed their lives in Cambodia. It was $3 billion well spent.[13]

At the same time, one must be clear-headed in assessing the impact of the UN in Cambodia. The Comprehensive Settlement laid out numerous central objectives above and beyond the elections. First, a cease-fire was to be implemented and maintained among the combatants. Second, all outside assistance to the warring factions was to be terminated. Third, the several contending armies were to be returned to their barracks, disarmed, and demobilized. Fourth, the utterly destroyed Cambodian economy was to be rehabilitated. Fifth, the demobilized soldiers, internally displaced persons, and repatriated refugees were to be reintegrated into civil society. Sixth—and crucially—a "neutral political environment" was to be established; that is, state institutions were to be decoupled from the organs of the theretofore ruling party. Not a single one of these central objectives of the UN peace plan in Cambodia was achieved.[14]

These requirements were defined in the Comprehensive Settlement as integral elements of the peace process and necessary precursors to the conduct of the elections. When they failed to materialize, the UN deftly redefined its mandate on the fly from peacekeeping—since there was precious little peace to keep—to election-holding. The elections were indeed held, and a new government was established, though that process turned out to be rather messy, with the defeated ruling party tenaciously maintaining its grip on power despite the verdict of the electorate. The UN then declared victory and somewhat precipitously withdrew, leaving the Cambodians to their own devices.

Thus, Secretary Christopher's assertion that the elections were "the triumph of democracy"[15] was hyperbolic, to say the least. One UN-administered election does not make a democracy, particularly when the results of the election are implemented in as desultory a fashion as happened in Cambodia. The transitions to stable, liberal democratic systems in Western Europe, in Latin America, and in the emerging democracies of East Asia all make clear that the development of democracy is a long process. It depends upon a variety of social and economic conditions, such as strong labor movements and a powerful middle class, capable of bargaining with the landed and capital-holding sectors of society. These conditions did not remotely exist in Cambodia, and thus one could confidently conclude that it was quite premature to predict the consolidation of democratic rule in Cambodia. To be completely fair, critics of the UN operation in Cambodia should not have ascribed such a goal to the operation. Partisans of the UN operation should have avoided claiming to have achieved that goal.

So, with what was at best a protodemocracy stumbling ahead, the war in Cambodia raged on. Cambodian battlefields saw their heaviest fighting since 1989, and the new Royal Army was not necessarily getting the best of the fighting.[16] Poorly planned assaults and temporary seizures of the main Khmer Rouge bases at Anlong Veng in the north and Pailin in the west dissolved into disasters for the government, as the insurgents transformed the Royal Army's Pyrrhic victories into death traps. After these initial fiascoes at Anlong Veng and Pailin, one might have thought the government would have been chastened, but it was not. The Royal Government immediately began to plan the retaking of the Khmer Rouge stronghold at Pailin, this time without waiting for the dry season. Thus, the UN intervention in Cambodia had not terminated the war, despite what Secretary Tomsen termed the UN's "stunning peacekeeping success."

THE INTERNATIONAL SITUATION

In the aftermath of the UN Transitional Authority in Cambodia, the involvement of the Great Powers in Cambodia had undergone a dramatic transition. In Moscow, Cambodia became a nonissue. In one of the few statements on Cambodia to issue from the Russian Federation in the immediate aftermath of the peace process, the Russian Foreign Ministry supported the outlawing of the Khmer Rouge by the Cambodian National Assembly in July 1994 and called for Cambodia's neighbors to "contribute to the cause of protecting peace" by blocking aid to the Khmer Rouge.[17] One measure of the degree to which Cambodia had fallen off the agenda in Moscow was found in comparing the pledges for economic assistance at the International Conference on the Rehabilitation and Reconstruction of Cambodia in June 1992. The Russian Federation pledged US$1.8 million, which was approximately 10 percent of the amount pledged by Canada and less than 1 percent of the amount pledged by Japan.[18]

Likewise, in Washington, at least according to one off-the-record Central Intelligence Agency (CIA) source, it was being said that "the Cambodian issue was dead." As far as U.S. domestic politics was concerned, this was certainly true, notwithstanding a continuing proprietary interest in Cambodia on the part of some elements of the Washington bureaucracy, as well as the signing into law of the Cambodian Genocide Justice Act (CGJA) in 1994.[19] Among other aims, the CGJA required the U.S. State Department to put forward a U.S. proposal for an international genocide tribunal to judge Khmer Rouge crimes against humanity. Many viewed such a tribunal as an essential prerequisite for national reconciliation in Cambodia, while others—particularly among the Khmer Rouge—argued that it would make national reconciliation impossible.

In direct response to the CGJA, the Khmer Rouge announced on October 1, 1994, that they were establishing a "Commission to Review the U.S. War of Aggression to Massacre the Cambodian People between 1970 and 1975."[20] A principal motive for this decision, according to a broadcast over Khmer Rouge clandestine radio, was that the United States had been "conducting all manner of activities to oppose national reconciliation." This Khmer Rouge "commission" later announced that it had "convicted" the head of the U.S. State Department's Office of Cambodian Genocide Investigations, career diplomat Alphonse La Porta, of war crimes and genocide. The Khmer Rouge "sentenced" La Porta, along with three Yale University academics working under the auspices of the CGJA, to death *in absentia*.[21]

The United States did, however, put in place a variety of economic, diplomatic, and military support programs for the new Cambodian government. In 1994, the Clinton administration threatened a long-standing U.S. ally, Thailand, with military sanctions over the issue of continuing relations between the Thai military and the Khmer Rouge.[22] Early in the tenure of the newly elected Royal Government, the Pentagon dispatched several dozen military advisers and trainers to assist in the reorganization of the Royal Cambodian Armed Forces. The United States also provided nearly $1 million in nonlethal military assistance in 1994 and sent a succession of military delegations in subsequent years to study lethal aid requirements.[23] The U.S. Agency for International Development initiated a rural development and democratization program in Cambodia on the scale of $25–30 million per year, including projects to assist with the reintegration of defecting Khmer Rouge soldiers into society. Despite these modest, if welcome, initiatives, Cambodia was no longer a foreign policy priority in Washington.

Beijing, on the other hand, remained deeply interested in Cambodia. In an August 1994 letter to the co-prime ministers of Cambodia, People's Republic of China Premier Li Peng affirmed that China had maintained its cutoff of assistance to the Khmer Rouge, adding that "China will continue to render support and assistance to Cambodia's national reconciliation and reconstruction."[24] The Chinese backed this assertion by providing a variety of assistance to the Cambodian Royal Armed Forces and greatly increasing their bilateral aid and foreign direct investment in Cambodia. Chinese state-industrial firms even negotiated to build a large industrial center in Cambodia—which never happened—but China did provide a wide variety of other direct subventions to the government.[25]

Having recently grown to be the third-largest economy in the world, China continued to pursue a massive rearmament program reflecting its economic stature. China's aggressive behavior on such issues as Tibet, the Spratly Islands, Hong Kong, and the Missile Technology Control Regime spurred growing fears among its Southeast Asian neighbors. For centuries, China has regarded Southeast Asia as properly its exclusive economic and political sphere, and there were emerging signs that China might one day soon be willing to employ force to back up those claims. Even though the Chinese had distanced themselves from the Khmer Rouge, Beijing thus remained a major factor in the Cambodian crisis. The Chinese were determined to cultivate close relations with the new Cambodian regime and seemingly spared no effort in their attempt to bring Cambodia into their sphere of influence.

Regional powers also remained closely involved. ASEAN countries began to show strains in the solidarity they had demonstrated on the Cambodian issue through the 1980s, as Cambodia's Co-Prime Minister Hun Sen maneuvered to split Malaysia and Indonesia from Thailand. Vietnam, which had paid a dear price for its Cambodian invasion and occupation, continued to maintain a hands-off policy in hopes of achieving full normalization of relations with the United States. The Vietnamese, however, could not remain indifferent to events on their western border. Vietnamese intelligence sources indicated that they believed the Royal Government was failing, and they feared the Khmer Rouge might once again menace their border.

Thailand, by contrast, had successfully destabilized the pro-Vietnamese Cambodian government, while largely ignoring UN attempts to curb Thai infringements on Cambodia's sovereignty and territorial integrity. Thailand also engaged in a massive investment program in Cambodia, coming to dominate the tourism, banking, transportation, and natural resource extraction sectors of the Cambodian economy. The scale of the Thai program prompted one commentator to remark that Thailand was treating northwestern Cambodia as the seventy-fourth province of Thailand.[26] Thai foreign minister Prasong Soonsiri argued that any "interference" in Cambodia by outside powers would only prolong the war, but his protestations in this regard were not persuasive.[27] The Paris Peace Accords on Cambodia had required Thailand and all other signatories to cease any economic or military relations they might have with the Khmer Rouge guerillas. Every signatory of the Comprehensive Agreement honored this requirement, except for Thailand. After the Comprehensive Agreement was signed in October 1991, Foreign Minister Prasong Soonsiri insisted, "The Thai people have never supported the Khmer Rouge."[28] After the Royal Government of Cambodia was formed in September 1993, Soonsiri asserted, "Thailand no longer supports the Khmer Rouge."[29] When the Cambodian National Assembly formally outlawed the Khmer Rouge in July 1994, Soonsiri promised that Thailand "would cease" its support for the Khmer Rouge.[30] With Thai rhetoric on their relationship to the Khmer Rouge traversing from "never" to "no longer" to "would cease," all in the space of eighteen months, it was not difficult to trace the roots of Thailand's tattered credibility on the issue of interference with Cambodia's sovereignty and territorial integrity.

THE MILITARY SITUATION

When the UN protectorate finally departed from Cambodia in late 1993, the Khmer Rouge held or dominated broad swaths of territory, as much as 20 percent of the country.[31] They also controlled a significant minority of Cambodia's population, perhaps 600,000 or more people. While the size of the Khmer Rouge military forces remained a matter of some dispute, its continuing support by Thailand was clear.[32] The Khmer Rouge enjoyed sanctuary in Thailand, as well as its diplomatic, political, economic, and military support.[33] The Khmer Rouge had seized the initiative.

As of mid-1994, then, developments in Cambodia were worrying. A senior U.S. diplomat who was ordinarily quite optimistic simply told me, "The situation is not good." The day I arrived for a visit, April 19, 1994, the Khmer Rouge recaptured their base at Pailin, which had been taken by troops of the Royal Army one month earlier. It was a humiliating defeat for the government, a defeat predicted by the king, who worried that it could lead to the collapse of the Royal Government. Indeed, the defeat at Pailin quickly turned into a rout as government troops fled in disarray and the Khmer Rouge rolled over the hapless government defenders. In an impressive display of conventional warfare tactics, the Khmer Rouge seized areas of the country they had not controlled since 1980. Everyone was shocked, sowing panic across the northwestern quadrant of Cambodia.

A year earlier, following a March 1993 visit to Cambodia, I had prepared a report that raised a range of concerns about the effectiveness of the UN peacekeeping operation in Cambodia and the prospects for achieving the fundamental goals expressed in the Agreements on a Comprehensive Political Settlement of the Cambodian Conflict, including the ceasefire, disarmament, political integration, human rights protections, social stability, and economic development.[34] The tone of my 1993 report was sharply at odds with official UN assessments that the process was proceeding very well indeed. The contradictions between my analysis and official reports became even more acute after the surprisingly smooth conduct of the May 1993 elections. The conclusions from my 1993 assessment remained outside the official consensus view a year later.

When I visited Cambodia in March 1993, near the climax of the UN intervention, I toured UN and government military (CPAF) bases in Battambang Province. What I found there was unsettling, particularly with respect to the disposition of military forces in northwestern Cambodia. After briefings by UN and government military commanders, I became concerned that government forces were dangerously exposed to possible Khmer Rouge counterattack. In the report I prepared after that tour, I suggested:

> The sequence of events since the beginning of this dry season bears an eerie resemblance to the dry season of 1971. Twenty-two years ago, Lon Nol's Republican army advanced up Route 6, deep into Khmer Rouge territory, in an attempt to relieve the besieged garrison of Kompong Thom and to

open a land-line between Battambang and Kompong Cham. The operation was dubbed Chenla-II, and it proceeded at first with little resistance. Twenty battalions of the Republican army's best troops were eventually stretched out along a thin and indefensible line through many miles of hostile territory. Then the communists attacked, and more than half of the Republican army was killed or captured by the Khmer Rouge and their allies. It was the military turning-point of the 1970–75 war. Now, in 1993, once again the Khmer Rouge have Battambang virtually surrounded. Once again they have drawn their opponent deep into their territory, showing little resistance. CPAF has exposed long lines of logistics and communications, while Khmer Rouge forces in the area have secure interior lines of communication and logistics. The similar experience of commanders on both sides of this CPAF–NADK [Cambodian People's Armed Forces–National Army of Democratic Kampuchea] confrontation will probably prevent the situation from becoming another Chenla-II. But I find troubling the parallels in northwestern Cambodia between 1971 and 1993.[35]

My optimistic conclusion that Chenla-II would not be repeated in the 1990s foundered on a fatally flawed assumption that the Royal Government army was competently commanded at both the military and political echelons. In Phnom Penh, the military command opposed the proposal to attack the Khmer Rouge stronghold in Pailin. A former republican commander, General Sak Sutsakhan, argued at the highest levels of the Royal Government that another assault on Pailin would be folly at that time, but his arguments were overridden by the political leadership. General Sak would die of natural causes on April 29, 1994, ten days after the collapse of government forces at Pailin.[36]

Despite their misgivings, the Royal Army commanders saluted smartly and proceeded to carry out their orders. Their plan for taking Pailin was creative and bold. The main "highway" to Pailin, Route 10, was impassable due to years of neglect and mining, so they would cut a brand-new road to Pailin from the north. When the new road was quickly mined by the Khmer Rouge army, yet another new road was cut through the swamps and mountains of western Battambang Province. While this activity proceeded, the Khmer Rouge organized an orderly evacuation of Pailin, removing their civilian population to Thailand and dispersing their troops to the jungles and hills around the town—precisely the tactics they and their Vietnamese allies had applied two decades before in response to the Chenla-II offensive. Along the new road, the Khmer Rouge engaged in hit-and-run attacks to keep government troops off-balance. But the Khmer Rouge made no attempt to defend the town itself from the elite commando units sent to seize it. The government armed forces waltzed into Pailin unopposed, save the occasional harassing small arms, mortar, and artillery fire.

Once Pailin was taken, however, there followed a gross failure of military discipline and command. Officers who swept into town on the heels of the vanguard force organized a systematic looting of the town and then evacuated with their booty. The soldiers who did the dirty work were not allowed to share the spoils. This was a blunder, insofar as government troops had not been paid for several months. There were complaints from the troops about lack of food and water and their inability—by air or ground— to evacuate their wounded. Losses from malaria were also significant. The morale of government troops at Pailin deteriorated dramatically; reports of troops "fragging" their officers began to circulate. It was beginning to look like a repeat of the debacle at Anlong Veng, where the government's capture of that Khmer Rouge base had proven to be short-lived and costly.

According to press, military, and diplomatic observers who visited the captured town, evidently there were no competent military officers in charge. The troops were not made to dig in or construct any manner of fortification. There were no patrols of the surrounding area, which was still heavily infested with Khmer Rouge soldiers. Feeble efforts to take Khmer Rouge gun emplacements on the dominating hills were not successful. The Khmer Rouge soon confirmed that they could effectively interdict resupply by air through the expedient of mortar fire. The new road to Pailin was constantly harassed, and, unsecured by checkpoints, it became an effective kill zone for Khmer Rouge ambushes. Most observers believed the Khmer Rouge would retake Pailin as soon as the monsoon rains began in June. Observing the weaknesses of the defenders, the Khmer Rouge saw no reason to wait for their friend, the rain. They launched a major offensive, retook the remote town, and then advanced into more heavily populated areas toward Battambang City, a regional citadel that they had not held since 1979. This military disaster only exacerbated an already serious political crisis.

THE POLITICAL SITUATION

Partially as a result of Khmer Rouge battlefield successes but primarily as a result of its inherent weaknesses, the Royal Government of Cambodia was in chaos. As King Sihanouk expressed it in May 1994, "There is a civil war between the Khmer Rouge and royal armed forces, civil war within FUNCINPEC [National United Front for a Cooperative, Independent, Neutral, and Peaceful Cambodia], civil war everywhere."[37] If there was any honeymoon for the new coalition partners of the Royal Government of Cambodia (RGC), it was over. Intra- and interparty struggles were proceeding full bore, often in the open.

The royalist party, FUNCINPEC, was indeed in civil war. The principal princes—Ranariddh, Sirivuth, Sirirath, and Chakrapong—were at each other's throats, but the split was not merely royal rivalry for power, or the question of royal succession. Their differences were also grounded in serious substantive disputes on policy issues such as corruption, Thailand, the Vietnamese question, how best to handle the Khmer Rouge, land reform, investment regulations, the press law, party development, and even the very nature of market systems. These legitimate differences in the royalist party may have been magnified by Khmer Rouge agents provocateurs who had infiltrated the party during its partnership with the Khmer Rouge in the 1980s and by Cambodian People's Party agents provocateurs infiltrated into the royalist party during the UN intervention.[38]

Within the Cambodian People's Party, there was also much turmoil. The supposedly "moderate" wing of the party under Hun Sen made stunning gains during and after the 1993 elections and the ensuing succession crisis. The supposedly "hardline" faction under Chea Sim regained much of its advantage in the subsequent year. This should not have been surprising, given the continuing control of the security forces by cadre loyal to Chea Sim. Yet, Hun Sen was soon able to weaken that advantage, arranging for the purge of several key Chea Sim supporters on apparently trumped-up charges of an attempted coup d'état. The long knives were always out within the People's Party.

The Royal Government had been set up according to a unique coalition scheme. Prince Ranariddh, representing the royalists, was first prime minister, while Hun Sen, representing the CPP, was second prime minister. Similarly, positions in each ministry and in each provincial administration were also shared, with ministers and secretaries of state at the national level and governors and vice-governors at the provincial level. If the objective was to share power, it was not working very well—neither in terms of power-sharing nor in terms of governance. Everybody knew that the People's Party still held all the power, despite the royalist election win.

On my spring 1994 visit, I interviewed senior ministers and secretaries in several key ministries; their level of invective against their counterparts from the opposite parties was sharp and personal. Most of the royalist ministers had not brought their families to Cambodia from France or the United States, or wherever they hailed from before joining the government. That was beginning to look as if it had been a shrewd decision.

The Royal Government of Cambodia did indeed feel threatened by Khmer Rouge military pressure, but more important than the threat of outright conquest was the political effect of Khmer Rouge military gains. The Cambodian people were sick of war and would give just about anything for peace. This popular mood was suggested by the fact that Prince Ranariddh's FUNCINPEC party had campaigned on a peace platform during the election; on the promise that he would bring an end to the war through negotiations, the voters gave his party a plurality, but after he became first prime minister, the prince was converted to Hun Sen's view that the only solution was more war. This gave the Khmer Rouge a distinct political advantage, as they continued to demand the rights that had been conferred upon them by the UN peace plan; however, if the Royal Government permitted the Khmer Rouge to join the governing coalition without the Khmer Rouge first agreeing to disarm and surrender control over their zones, the government feared this might well eventually lead to a Khmer Rouge return to undisputed power.

Consequently, it was no surprise when peace talks in North Korea between the Royal Government and the Khmer Rouge in May 1994 turned out to be a farce. Khmer Rouge spokesman Khieu Samphan told the meeting, "To achieve genuine national reconciliation . . . all of us should compromise and make mutual concessions,"[39] but neither the Khmer Rouge nor the government was interested in compromise. Both sides began with an opening stance that the other side was illegitimate and should dissolve itself immediately. With both sides calling for the preemptive surrender of the other, there was little ground for "mutual concessions." Unsurprisingly, they found little to agree on. This resulted in a somewhat bizarre final communiqué from the failed peace talks; the only thing the two sides could agree on was something that was not true: they affirmed that Cambodia was undivided and indivisible.

The government responded by adopting the "Law on the Outlawing of the Democratic Kampuchea Group," formally placing the Khmer Rouge outside of society and imposing new legal sanctions on members of the group.[40] For their part, the Khmer Rouge formally proclaimed a provisional resistance government and, from their "liberated" base areas, renewed offensive military operations.[41] These developments appeared to many to be the final deathblow to the UN's plan for bringing peace and national reconciliation to Cambodia. These events transpired less than one year after the UN had declared its Cambodian intervention a resounding success and had withdrawn its forces from the country.

In summary, as of mid-1994, it was clear to all disinterested observers that while the UN intervention in Cambodia had certainly transformed the nature of the conflict, that conflict was far from over. The Royal Government was performing very poorly in virtually all fields of governance, and the Khmer Rouge were keen to press what they saw as a new strategic advantage.[42] A proactive campaign by Khmer Rouge intelligence networks in Australia, France, Canada, and the United States to forestall the possibility of foreign military aid for the Royal Government of Cambodia indicated that the guerillas were not suffering from overconfidence and were attempting to neutralize this potential danger to their plans from the international community.[43] The Khmer Rouge believed the Royal Government was slowly disintegrating. All they needed to do was to keep up the military pressure, and the ripe jack fruit would eventually fall into their hands. The Khmer Rouge organization had altered its outer appearances, but the essence of the party was unchanged.[44]

A VERY HOT PEACE

The Comprehensive Settlement sought to transform the basis of political interaction in Cambodia from armed conflict to peaceful competition for political power, but the UN intervention failed to alter the habits of Cambodian politicians. Khmer Rouge habits, in particular, had not been changed by the UN intervention. They still sought to seize state power by force and resume their interrupted revolution.[45] They were also still employing criminal methods.[46] Beginning in the early 1980s, the Khmer Rouge revisited the approach that had brought them to power in the 1970s: they formed a united front, infiltrated the allied organizations, and then proceeded to liquidate their partners within the united front.[47] The payoffs were manifest. From the vantage point of 1994, it was not at all clear when the war would end, or who would be on top when it did.

The United States, China, and Russia had financed the war in Cambodia and sustained it through their diplomacy. But with the end of the Cold War, this proxy contest became an irrelevant irritant to Great Power relations, and so the Great Powers fashioned the peace process to extricate themselves from their "Cambodia Problem." That their solution took little account of the realities in Cambodia was itself irrelevant to the issue of Great Power concord. The authors of the peace plan, however, could hardly just come right out and say so. Thus, political necessity motivated the United States and other key member States of the UN to overreach in their claims regarding the effectiveness of the UN intervention in Cambodia. The UN's implementation of the Cambodian peacekeeping operation did transform the external and internal conditions of the Cambodian conflict. These new dynamics would inexorably transform the shape of Cambodia's political and military battlefields, but those changes would be long and hard in coming.

For Cambodians, however, no amount of political hyperbole could obscure the fact that neither peace nor democracy had been consolidated in their country. King Sihanouk lamented in January 1994 that "20% of Cambodian territory is today occupied and exploited by an armed and independent, that is, secessionist faction . . . the Khmer Rouge."[48] The king would have wished the Khmer Rouge goal was secession from Cambodia, but unfortunately, that was not what they had in mind. Whether one took the idealist view that the goal of the UN intervention was to bring peace to Cambodia or the realist view that the goal was to remove the "Cambodia Problem" from the international agenda, neither goal had been definitively accomplished. The Khmer Rouge were continuing to make war on the new government, and that government was looking increasingly fragile. The Cambodia Problem would remain on the international agenda.

In this environment, the international community was increasingly coming around to the point of view that what the Khmer Rouge were continuing to do—not to mention what they had done when they were in power—was not merely an unfortunate by-product of legitimate political struggle but rather was plainly criminal in nature. Before anyone could contemplate prosecuting the crimes of the Khmer Rouge, however, those complex and poorly understood violations of international criminal law and international humanitarian law would have to be carefully documented. It is to this issue that we now turn.

4

Documenting Mass Murder*

Many theories have been advanced over the years to account for the massive death toll during the Khmer Rouge regime of Democratic Kampuchea between 1975 and 1979. Most of these theories have centered around the general idea that Pol Pot was the architect of a "genocide" in Cambodia. My objective in this chapter is not to declaim on the complex technical question of the degree to which the mass killing in Cambodia may or may not qualify under various definitions of the term "genocide." Instead, we examine a scientific project that was undertaken in an effort to discover what kind of evidence might be brought to bear to confirm or refute such an assertion.

One thing that can be said about theories of the Cambodian genocide is that for nearly twenty years they were largely unsupported by empirical evidence. Other than a now-substantial and persuasive set of refugee and other interview data, there was not a great deal of independently verifiable empirical evidence regarding what happened during the Pol Pot regime. As a result, scholarly speculation about the

---

*This chapter is an adapted version of an earlier work entitled "Achieving Accountability and Reconciliation in Cambodia," by Craig Etcheson, in Diane Hiscox and Johanne Levasseur, eds., *Globalism: People, Profits and Progress*, pp. 1–26. © 2002 Kluwer Law International. Reprinted/Adapted by permission from Kluwer Law International.

Cambodian genocide remained largely in the realm of hypothesis. There was little or no physical evidence that would explicate the specific mechanism through which the Khmer Rouge could have carried out such large-scale killings, nor was there much hard evidence demonstrating that the Khmer Rouge leadership in fact had been in command of any such bureaucratic apparatus.

This "data vacuum" on the Cambodian genocide is now a thing of the past. During more than ten years of fieldwork and other research, the Cambodian Genocide Program and the Documentation Center of Cambodia have collected a wide variety of empirical evidence conclusively demonstrating the existence of a nationwide bureaucratic apparatus dedicated to mass killing under the Democratic Kampuchea regime. The new data also show that Pol Pot exercised effective command and control of this bureaucratic apparatus. The Khmer Rouge internal security apparatus, known as the *Santebal*, was charged with the liquidation of all enemies of *Angkar* ("The Organization," the chillingly modern alias Pol Pot chose for the Communist Party of Kampuchea). This chapter reviews the work of the Cambodian Genocide Program and the Documentation Center and introduces the new evidence gathered through these research efforts.

ORIGINS OF THE PROJECT

Following a three-year advocacy campaign spearheaded by the Campaign to Oppose the Return of the Khmer Rouge,[1] the U.S. Congress passed the "Cambodian Genocide Justice Act" in April 1994.[2] In May 1994, U.S. President Bill Clinton signed the measure into law. The Cambodian Genocide Justice Act made it "the policy of the United States to support efforts to bring to justice members of the Khmer Rouge for their crimes against humanity committed in Cambodia between April 17, 1975 and January 7, 1979." The legislation directed the U.S. Department of State to contract with private individuals and organizations for an expert investigation into violations of international criminal law and international humanitarian law during the Democratic Kampuchea regime between April 17, 1975, and January 7, 1979.

Attorneys Jason Abrams and Stephen Ratner were commissioned by the State Department to prepare a legal analysis of the potential culpability of members of the Khmer Rouge on charges of war crimes, genocide, and other crimes against humanity. Their study concluded, in part, with respect to charges of genocide: "We find *prima facie* culpability for acts against religious and ethnic groups, such as the Cham, Vietnamese and Chinese communities, and the Buddhist monkhood."[3] Similarly, they found *prima facie* culpability for war crimes and other crimes against humanity.

Also under the authority of the Cambodian Genocide Justice Act, after a competitive bidding process, the U.S. State Department concluded a cooperative agreement with Yale University's Cambodian Genocide Program, providing funds for Yale University to carry out documentation, research, and training related to the prospective establishment of an accountability mechanism to address Khmer Rouge crimes.[4] What was initially designed as a two-year research program eventually expanded into a more than decade-long effort in an attempt to cope with the wealth of new evidentiary materials discovered in the course of the work.[5] The Cambodian Genocide Program, in cooperation with the Documentation Center of Cambodia, has assembled a remarkable collection of materials clearly implicating the entire top leadership of the Communist Party of Kampuchea in directing the mass terror in Cambodia between 1975 and 1979.[6]

The Documentation Center of Cambodia was founded at Phnom Penh in January 1995 as the field office of the Cambodian Genocide Program. Until the conclusion of its mandate with the Cambodian Genocide Program in December 1996, the Documentation Center coordinated all operations in Cambodia concerning the Cambodian Genocide Program's three main objectives: documentation, historiographical research, and legal training. The Documentation Center became an autonomous Cambodian research institute in January 1997 and is now funded from a wide variety of international sources.[7] It is operated entirely by Cambodians, with support from scholars and experts in North America, Europe, Australia, and Asia. As of January 2004, the staff level at the Documentation Center was forty-five persons, with some 100 volunteers. This institution continues as a legacy of the Cambodian Genocide Program and as a permanent center for the study of genocide in Cambodia.[8]

MATERIALS ACQUISITION

The Cambodian Genocide Program originally set out to catalog all known primary and secondary sources of information pertaining to the Cambodian genocide. Initially, this seemed like a relatively manageable task. What the leaders of the Cambodian Genocide Program did not immediately understand, however, was that an enormous quantity of previously unknown primary material lay hidden in various caches around Cambodia and that an extraordinary range of additional types of evidentiary materials also existed and was in dire need of preservation, cataloging, and analysis. This must be counted as one of the crucial lessons learned by the Cambodian Genocide Program; none of this vast quantity of new material was known to the world's leading scholars of the Khmer Rouge prior to the beginning of the Cambodian Genocide Program's work in December 1994.[9] Thus, it should never be assumed that sources relevant to a given instance of mass atrocity do not exist simply because scholars or other investigators have not yet discovered them.

For the last ten years, the Documentation Center has continuously acquired new and previously unknown primary documents dating to the Khmer Rouge regime, many of them from within the top-secret Khmer Rouge security services, known as the *Santebal*. These documents reveal the story of how the Khmer Rouge implemented mass murder in Cambodia, and thus they constitute an irreplaceable historical and legal resource. The archive now numbers more than 1 million pages of primary documentary holdings, along with some 25,000 photographs and many other types of materials relating to the Cambodian genocide. It constitutes the world's premier resource on the Khmer Rouge and continues to grow as new materials are acquired on a regular basis.[10] These materials are being systematically cataloged and entered into a series of computer databases, including bibliographic, biographic, photographic, and geographic databases.

THE CAMBODIAN GENOCIDE DATA BASES

Yale University's "Cooperative Agreement" with the U.S. Department of State specified that the Cambodian Genocide Program was to construct a computerized PC DOS-compatible index of documents relevant to the Cambodian genocide. The Cambodian Genocide Program's management team construed this task as the central element of the entire undertaking but felt constrained by a very limited budget and a short implementation time frame; originally, the entire project was to be completed within just two years. It was therefore deemed necessary to employ inexpensive, off-the-shelf, and ready-to-deploy software as the engine for the computer databases. The database software selected for this task was CDS/ISIS. This package is "freeware" distributed by the UN to libraries around the world. Originally designed for mainframe systems, it has since been ported to midrange and microcomputers, and hence it conformed to the Cambodian Genocide Program's contractual requirements. The package supports coding in both the English and Khmer languages, as well as having the capability to support records in a vast range of languages and orthographic systems, allowing the recording of source materials in Russian, Japanese, Chinese, and so on.[11] A custom software patch supports image files, which can be attached to individual records, permitting display of scanned documents and photographs. Cambodian Genocide Program staff and consultants quickly mapped out a data structure and converted some preexisting records, creating the prototype version of the first bibliographic database within less than two months after the initiation of the program.[12] Since that time, the databases have expanded dramatically, and they continue to be enhanced.[13]

BIBLIOGRAPHIC DATABASE

The Bibliographic Database represented an attempt to compile records on all known primary and secondary sources of documentary information on gross violations of human rights under the Khmer Rouge regime. This task was rendered more challenging by the discovery of several large, previously unknown archives of primary documents produced by the Khmer Rouge "bureaucracy of death" between 1975 and 1979. The Documentation Center has also discovered a wide variety of additional documents pertinent to any attempt at determining the facts of state-organized violence during that regime. As an example of this type of material, between 1979 and 1983, the successor regime to Democratic Kampuchea carried out a large-scale research project to interview every family in Cambodia about their experiences under the Khmer Rouge, resulting in a collection of documents said to bear more than 1 million individual signatures or thumbprints.[14] Though this particular archive consists largely of standardized *pro forma* loyalty oaths to the new regime, some interviewees did append statements that may still have legally probative value today. These records have been obtained by the Documentation Center.

All documents acquired by the Documentation Center are first meticulously cataloged, recording bibliographic data regarding their source, origin, author(s), length, date, condition, contents, persons mentioned, and so on—a total of fifty different fields of data. Once the documents have been properly cataloged, the bibliographic data are entered into a computerized system known as the Cambodian Genocide Bibliographic Database. The Bibliographic Database currently contains records for some 3,300 primary and secondary documents, articles, and books pertaining to the Cambodian genocide, and a major upgrade will soon increase this total to more than 17,000 records. In many cases, the database includes digitally scanned images of the original document. This painstaking cataloging work is done on an ongoing basis at the Documentation Center.

Biographic Database

The Biographic Database represents an attempt to delineate the chain of command through Khmer Rouge political and military organizations by documenting the personal histories of all members of the Khmer Rouge. In this effort, the Cambodian Genocide Program and Documentation Center assembled biographical histories for Khmer Rouge leaders at the center, zone, region, and district levels and, in some cases of particular interest, at the subdistrict (or commune) and village levels. The Biographic Database contains up to seventy different fields for each record, allowing the inclusion of data on subjects such as aliases, family connections, education, superiors and subordinates, alleged victims, classes of human rights violations alleged (based on the industry-standard Huridocs human rights coding system), and so on. The fully indexed system thus provides a powerful tool to examine and track the behavior of individual members of the Khmer Rouge and to analyze events in the Khmer Rouge regime across a wide range of topics, such as events in particular regions, connections with particular leaders, or even particular types of human rights violations.[15]

One set of primary archives recovered by the Documentation Center appears to represent, for want of a better term, the records of the Khmer Rouge "human resources" department, that is, the personnel records of the Communist Party of Kampuchea. This material includes, among other things, the detailed autobiographies that party cadre were periodically required to write and rewrite. This cache has proved an excellent source of data with which to construct personal histories for the Khmer Rouge political cadre and military officers, adding significant depth to the Biographic Database. According to various estimates, in the late 1970s, the Communist Party of Kampuchea had a membership of some 14,000–40,000 persons. To date, the Biographic Database has entries for some 10,412 members of the Khmer Rouge, including many who were purged from the organization during the regime stage, 1975–1979. The Documentation Center hopes to carry this work through to completion, ideally making this biographical compilation comprehensive, though it is likely that it will not be possible to find data on each and every member.

GEOGRAPHIC DATABASE

The Geographic Database represents an attempt to construct an exhaustive inventory of prisons and "Killing Fields" dating from the Khmer Rouge era. This particular project has turned out to be one of the most astonishing single efforts of the entire program undertaken by the Cambodian Genocide Program and the Documentation Center. When this effort was first launched, we had no idea of the magnitude of the task we had set for ourselves. As the work proceeded, it soon became clear that we were faced not with hundreds or even thousands, but rather tens of thousands of mass grave pits. Based on data from thirty-four districts collected during the first two years of work on this project, on our understanding of the patterns of violence during the Khmer Rouge regime, and on population densities in various parts of Cambodia, in 1997, I estimated that we would find a total of approximately 20,000 mass grave pits in all of Cambodia.[16] As the project has now proceeded into a tenth year of fieldwork, it has become apparent that this was not an overestimate.

The methodology employed in the mass grave surveys is a combination of high technology—global satellite position mapping—and old-fashioned human fieldwork, with investigators trudging across the Cambodian countryside, village to village, searching for the Killing Fields.[17] With the help of local informants as well as the records of the Khmer Rouge secret police, mass grave sites have been discovered in virtually every district visited by Documentation Center field researchers. Once the field investigators reach the location of a Democratic Kampuchea prison or mass grave site, they employ the Global Positioning System (GPS) to accurately fix the geographical location of the site.[18] The information thus generated is then fed into a computerized Geographic Information System (GIS), allowing the researchers to create very precise maps of the Killing Fields.[19] In addition to the GPS/GIS technologies, the Cambodian Genocide Program attempted to employ remote sensing technologies such as satellite imagery and side-scanning, ground-penetrating radars in this work, though with less success, primarily due to budgetary limitations.[20]

The mapping reports compiled by Documentation Center researchers in the course of this work constitute the most comprehensive resource ever assembled on the mechanism of Khmer Rouge mass murder.[21] At most of the sites the field researchers have visited, they have also identified local witnesses who claim to remember the types of victims killed at each mass grave site and who also recall the identities of the Khmer Rouge officials in charge of each particular security center. Thus, this data set includes not only precise geographical coordinates of the prison, execution, and burial sites but also statistics on the number of mass grave pits, victims, and memorials, as well as witness accounts by both survivors and perpetrators, photographic documentation, and other information such as documents acquired from local archives and physical artifacts like the iron shackles (or *knoah*) often used to restrain Khmer Rouge prisoners.

Between 1995 and 2004, the Documentation Center mapped the overwhelming majority of the 170 districts throughout Cambodia. In the course of this work, the Documentation Center located more than 660 "genocide sites." At these sites, mapping teams found 19,521 mass grave pits, containing the remains of an estimated 1,100,000 victims of execution by the Khmer Rouge security services.[22] This estimate exceeds the most expansive previous analytical estimates of the number of executions carried out by the Khmer Rouge.[23] Some of the digital maps constructed in the course of this work are available on the Yale and Documentation Center Web sites.[24] With continuing deterioration over time, the physical genocide sites are gradually disappearing. The mapping project preserves the factual details of every single genocide site investigated, serving as a crucial source for both historical research and legal inquiry.

PHOTOGRAPHIC DATABASE

Finally, the Photographic Database originally represented an attempt to collect and preserve all known photographs taken in Cambodia during the Democratic Kampuchea regime. This effort, too, has proven to constitute a substantial challenge. Far more photographic material from the Khmer Rouge era has surfaced than we ever imagined existed.

For the initial thrust into the area of photographic documentation, the Documentation Center scanned the entire surviving collection of prisoner "mug shots" from the notorious Tuol Sleng torture and execution center. This collection of nearly 6,000 victim and staff portraits is now mounted on the Cambodian Genocide Program Web site, where any interested person may peruse the photos. Most of the victims pictured in these photos are unidentified. The Cambodian Genocide Photographic Database Web site includes an interactive response form, so that Cambodians and others examining the collection can inform the Cambodian Genocide Program should they recognize any of the victims pictured. Only a small trickle of suggested identities has been forwarded to the Cambodian Genocide Program, but it is hoped that with time, identities can be restored to at least some of these anonymous victims of the Cambodian genocide. In addition to these victim images, the Documentation Center has assembled a large collection of photographs, including leadership galleries, depictions of the destruction of cultural and religious infrastructure, mass forced labor gangs (*chalat*), and other aspects of daily life in Democratic Kampuchea, totaling some 25,000 images to date.

With the final collapse of Khmer Rouge military and political organizations early in 1999, a number of photographic archives held by Khmer Rouge cadre and military officers have become available, greatly enhancing the depth and range of the photographic evidence available to researchers. However, aggressive collection of these photographs by journalists and media organizations has created a bidding environment often unsuitable to acquisition by a nonprofit organization such as the Documentation Center. Nonetheless, cooperative agreements with some media organizations, such as the *Phnom Penh Post* newspaper, have allowed the Documentation Center to access some of the collections accumulated by private organizations.

The Documentation Center has also launched an effort to obtain motion picture and video materials related to the Khmer Rouge period. However, in a dynamic similar to the situation with still photographs, competition with private media and documentary film companies has created an unfavorable acquisition environment. Moreover, in this particular arena, certain political complications have stymied operations. A collection of some 100 motion pictures made by the Khmer Rouge between 1975 and 1978 was whisked out of the country in May 1998, only one week before the Documentation Center was scheduled to take possession of the cache from the Royal Government's Ministry of Culture. This most interesting archive of films was subsequently deposited with a private commercial organization in Paris. The public explanation for this seeming expropriation of Cambodian public property was that it was intended to "protect the king," who is evidently shown in some of these films in the company of senior Khmer Rouge officials. Private explanations for the spiriting away of this cache of evidentiary materials have suggested that it was an effort to shield the reputation of Prime Minister Hun Sen, who is rumored to appear in at least one of the Democratic Kampuchea-era films. Efforts continue to recover this cache of important materials and arrange its deposit at the Documentation Center of Cambodia in accordance with the center's agreement with the Royal Government of Cambodia, but more than six years after the films were removed to France, those efforts had not yet been successful.

FORENSIC DATABASE

The Documentation Center for many years sought funding to support a detailed forensic archaeology project, aiming to exhume a sample set of the mass graves in order to compile a database of forensic information confirming the times and causes of death of those interred in the mass graves. This work will provide a fourth leg to the three-legged stool of evidence assembled so far in the mass grave mapping project, consisting of eyewitness testimony, physical evidence collected or recorded by the mass grave mapping teams, and documents from within the Khmer Rouge security services that make reference to the system of execution centers. The Documentation Center finally secured funding for an initial forensic survey and implemented that project in early 2002.[25] This work was completed in early 2004.

USES OF THE INTERNET

All four of the primary research databases constructed under the auspices of the Cambodian Genocide Program and the Documentation Center have been mounted on the Internet and are online at http://www .yale.edu/cgp. The Documentation Center is in the process of constructing its own Web site to offer a Cambodian portal for this information, supplementing the Yale site.[26] In addition, a second edition of a CD-ROM has been published, containing versions of the bibliographic, biographic, and photographic databases; the CD-ROM is available through the Documentation Center of Cambodia.[27] These information-age multimedia technologies are ideal for organizing and disseminating the large quantities of data accumulated in the course of the work to scholars and legal researchers, as well as governments, private individuals, and other interested parties.[28]

The Cambodian Genocide Program Web site has proven to be quite popular. When the site was initially unveiled in January 1997, user traffic was at a far higher volume than we had anticipated, reaching as many as 4,500 "hits" per day. As word of the Web site spread through the media and as political tensions increased in Cambodia over the course of 1997, the volume of hits on the Cambodian Genocide Program Web site rose to an average of 20,000 per day.[29] Thus, hundreds of thousands of people all over the world have accessed the Cambodian Genocide Data Bases and other information presented on the Web site. This level of interest was not expected when we originally committed to build the Web site, and it serves to indicate the value of Internet technologies in making information on human rights abuses easily and cheaply available to a global audience. This is another lesson of the Cambodian Genocide Program.

Another crucial use of the Internet in the Cambodian Genocide Program has been for communication and data interchange. Personnel associated with the Cambodian Genocide Program and the Documentation Center of Cambodia operate across wide expanses of the globe, in Asia, Europe, Australia, Africa, and North America.[30] To maintain communications with these far-flung personnel by telephone would have been prohibitively expensive; for example, overseas direct dial toll charges to and from Cambodia are as high as eight U.S. dollars per minute. Thus, e-mail was absolutely essential to support the communications infrastructure of such a multi-disciplinary international research enterprise. Moreover, electronic data in the gigabyte range of volume are regularly exchanged between the Documentation Center and its overseas partners, as well as among research centers assisting in various aspects of the work. The Cambodian Genocide Program could never have achieved the accomplishments that it did, and the Documentation Center of Cambodia could not exist in its present form, without recourse to these modern information technologies.

PRESERVATION STRATEGIES

Document preservation closely follows the documentation project. The twenty- to thirty-year-old documents the Documentation Center has been acquiring are in very poor condition and in serious danger of further deterioration. These documents are of crucial importance to the history of Cambodia and must not be lost. They are also of crucial importance in any accountability process that may eventually be mounted to bring the Khmer

Rouge leadership to justice for their crimes during the Democratic Kampuchea regime. Consequently, the Documentation Center is systematically photocopying, microfilming, and digitally scanning its archives, duplicating the archives and depositing them in secure locations abroad. This procedure not only serves to preserve the documents but also provides multiple points of access to the material for scholars, legal researchers, and other interested parties.

Moreover, digitally scanned images of key documents are being compiled in computer databases. Scanned material is then posted to the Internet and distributed on CD-ROM, providing further ease of scholarly access and additional security in the event that some harm should come to the originals. This continuing work ensures that the Documentation Center's entire archive will eventually be deposited in multiple international repositories, foiling those who may wish to destroy the archive in order to protect themselves from the information contained therein. Even dedicated pursuit of a range of preservation strategies, however, cannot stop the inexorable emergence of gaps in the historical and evidentiary record.

GAPS IN THE HISTORICAL RECORD

Although the Cambodian Genocide Program and the Documentation Center have discovered far more evidence of Khmer Rouge abuses on the ground in Cambodia than we ever believed we would find, at the same time, nearly thirty years after the Khmer Rouge began their genocide in earnest, we have also clearly come to understand the fragility of the nature of the remaining evidence. A huge historical tide is gradually washing away that evidence. Threats to the physical integrity of the remaining evidence come from a variety of sources, including deliberate destruction of records, accidental destruction of records, and environmental degradation of other evidentiary materials. Thus, we have been motivated by the imperative to preserve the remaining evidence of the genocide from various sources of threat, or at least to record the remaining evidence before it is destroyed.

The original sources are disappearing at an alarming rate, beginning with the humans themselves. Many witnesses—both perpetrators and surviving victims—have died or have reached an age where their memories are no longer reliable. We have also learned from surviving witnesses that as the Khmer Rouge regime was in the process of being overrun by Vietnamese troops in 1979, they destroyed a great deal of documentary evidence before they fled Phnom Penh to resume guerilla warfare from the jungles.

The protracted civil war, which lasted from 1979 until 1999, also resulted in the destruction of an unknown, but undoubtedly a great deal, of evidence. For example, in 1998, we learned of at least two caches of documents that were destroyed in Banteay Meanchey Province during military attacks that year, one by the Khmer Rouge and one by a rebelling faction of the royalist party.[31] When the UN peacekeeping forces flooded into Cambodia in 1992, the UN troops requisitioned and/or rented hundreds of private homes and government buildings, some of which, we later learned, much to our dismay, had contained caches of primary documentation on the genocide, which were carted out back unexamined and burned as rubbish to clear the way for UN personnel.

We have also experienced political interference with our acquisition of evidence, such as the case mentioned earlier in which film records of the Khmer Rouge regime were removed from the country and secreted abroad on grounds that they allegedly were potentially harmful to either His Majesty the King or Prime Minister Hun Sen, depending upon whose version one chooses to believe. In addition, there are many cases where local villagers have destroyed structures employed by the Khmer Rouge as part of their nationwide extermination apparatus, at first destroying some of them in rage in the aftermath of the fall of the Khmer Rouge regime and later dismantling some of them simply to obtain building materials.

In another seemingly benign activity, thousands of temples, mosques, and churches that had been deliberately destroyed or desecrated by the Khmer Rouge in their zeal to exterminate religion have been rebuilt and reconsecrated by believers anxious to restore the symbols of their faith but not always cognizant of the importance of carefully documenting the destruction prior to restoration. In a particularly poignant and ongoing religious situation, several Buddhist temples in Thailand have been paying peasants to retrieve human skulls from genocide memorials and mass grave sites in Cambodia, so the Thai monks can perform the proper ceremonies over the cremated bones, thus releasing the spirits of the victims from their purgatory so they may move on to the next life. Though this is done with the best of religious intentions, each such action destroys potentially probative evidence of genocidal crimes.

Mass graves are particularly vulnerable to destruction both by humans and by the environment. We have seen hundreds of cases where mass grave evidence has been disturbed or destroyed by grave robbers seeking jewels or other valuables that may have been hidden in the clothing of the victims placed in the pits. We also know of hundreds, if not thousands, of mass graves that have been erased by impoverished, landless farmers, desperate to reclaim paddy land on which to eke out their meager existence. At the opposite end of the wealth ladder, the richest businessman in Cambodia decided to build a cement factory on an important genocide site in Takeo Province, oblivious to our pleas that he take measures to secure the evidence of crimes before proceeding with construction.

Livestock poses an unexpected threat to mass grave evidence, as well. Many a time we have observed cows and pigs consuming human bones that have been placed in open, unsecured genocide memorials. Even the earth itself passively consumes the evidence of genocide. The soils in much of Cambodia are highly acidic, and they rapidly dissolve the remains of victims in mass graves, including the bones of those interred in the graves. The simple environmental encroachment of rats, insects, mildew, seedlings, rust, and rot in the extremely humid tropical environment takes a fearsome toll not only on paper records and human skeletal remains but also on more durable artifacts such as torture devices and shackles and even permanent structures like thatch, wooden, and even concrete or brick buildings. Finally, in Cambodia, there is annual flooding over a great portion of the country—which is essentially one gigantic floodplain for the lower Mekong River basin—and thus we have seen numerous instances where mass graves have been washed away by the erosion of wandering rivers as they eat into riverbanks.

All in all, these factors point up another crucial lesson in the documentation of gross abuses of international humanitarian law: it is essential to move early and move fast to gather the evidence of genocide and other crimes against humanity from the field. Humans, animals, and the environment itself, by omission or commission, deliberately or accidentally, by neglect or design, or simply by the natural decay processes omnipresent in the universe, gradually and inexorably consume the evidence of violations of international humanitarian law.

LEGAL TRAINING AND OTHER TRAINING INITIATIVES

Beyond documentation activities, a second major thrust of the Cambodian Genocide Program involved a variety of training initiatives. The Documentation Center, in conjunction with the Cambodian Genocide Program, the Yale Law School, and the University of San Francisco School of Law carried out a pair of consecutive summer legal training courses in

1995 and 1996. The aim of this process was to help prepare Cambodian personnel to participate in a trial or truth commission for the Khmer Rouge. The students in these courses were primarily young judges from the Royal Cambodian Government's Ministry of Justice but also included officials from various other government agencies, such as the Ministry of Interior and the National Assembly, as well as human rights workers from nongovernmental organizations. The course work focused on international humanitarian law and international criminal law and covered the basic outlines of international law relating to war crimes, genocide, and other crimes against humanity.[32] Additional training sessions were presented on such topics as criminal procedure, evidence, and due process issues, as well as a particularly valuable section on Cambodian law. Various approaches to accountability for international human rights violations were discussed at length and illustrated through moot exercises, including international criminal tribunals, domestic criminal tribunals, and truth commissions.

The legal training courses were augmented with a conference hosted by the Documentation Center and the Cambodian Genocide Program, the 1995 "International Conference on Striving for Justice: International Criminal Law in the Cambodian Context." This conference was presided over by the Cambodian Co-Prime Ministers Samdech Krom Preah Norodom Ranariddh and Samdech Hun Sen. A wide range of government personnel attended two days of sessions, listening to presentations from several international legal scholars and genocide experts and debating options for accountability processes appropriate to Cambodia's situation.

In 1997, the Documentation Center, in cooperation with the Yale Law School, conducted a legal survey on various approaches to seeking justice for the Khmer Rouge, aiming to discover which options might suit the Cambodian context and best serve the Cambodian people's interests.[33] The survey showed that 75 percent of the respondents desired criminal prosecutions of the top leaders of the Democratic Kampuchea regime, with the overwhelming majority of those preferring an international criminal tribunal on the model of the ad hoc international tribunals for the former Yugoslavia and Rwanda.

In cooperation with the Cambodian Genocide Program, both Yale University and the University of New South Wales in Sydney, Australia, have also hosted a number of Cambodian students for training programs in documentation, information systems management, international politics, and other topics. The Canadian government has also recently begun to sponsor overseas training programs for Documentation Center staff. Students enrolled in these training programs have earned certificates of completion and, in a few cases, graduate degrees. The Documentation Center also carries out a continuing in-house training program, developing staff expertise in scientific research methodologies, computing technologies, geographical information systems, archival studies, and other modern research techniques.

The Documentation Center is in the process of launching a new project dedicated to systematic legal research and training.[34] The complexity of international and Cambodian law and jurisprudence regarding genocide and crimes against humanity requires detailed work on the Documentation Center archives if the true nature of the crimes committed is to be uncovered and the individuals responsible for those violations are to be properly identified. This project aims to bring international legal specialists to the Documentation Center to assemble individual criminal cases, with a view to providing support for private individuals who may wish to seek legal redress for crimes against members of their families, as well as to the prosecutor of any judicial body that may assert jurisdiction over the crimes attributed to the Khmer Rouge.[35] These international specialists will also train Cambodian legal professionals to help bring the Cambodian bar up to international standards.

RESEARCH

In addition to documentation and training, a third principal thrust of the work of the Cambodian Genocide Program and the Documentation Center of Cambodia concerns research. There were many areas where, in the judgment of the Cambodian Genocide Program's management, the existing scholarly literature did not adequately address historical issues concerning the Khmer Rouge regime. Consequently, numerous historiographical studies have been produced under the auspices of the Cambodian Genocide Program and the Documentation Center, including monographs on the Western, Northwestern, and Northeastern Zones of Democratic Kampuchea and on the Chinese and Cham minorities, women, and Buddhist monks under the Khmer Rouge.[36] Further studies currently in progress at the Documentation Center include the Eastern Zone, Southwestern Zone, the Vietnamese, Chinese and Hill Tribe minority groups, and children, young Khmer Rouge cadres, women, genocide memorials, and medicine in Democratic Kampuchea.[37]

The Documentation Center has also published a wide variety of monographs compiling materials on historical, analytical, and legal topics concerning human rights violations under the Khmer Rouge regime. In addition, the center has carried out a great deal of translation work, including translating approximately 1,500 pages of Khmer Rouge secret documents from Khmer into English.[38] In a complementary arena, the Documentation Center has been hosting international research specialists on the Khmer Rouge who are preparing a number of book-length studies based in whole or in part on Documentation Center archives.[39] The Documentation Center has also provided support to U.S. government investigators affiliated with the search for U.S. soldiers missing in action from the Second Indochinese War, more commonly known in the United States as the Vietnam War.

PUBLIC SERVICE

The Documentation Center has organized a variety of public service projects aiming to assist the Cambodian people. One of the most unique public services provided by the Documentation Center is its Family Tracing File system. Virtually every single family in Cambodia had loved ones disappear during the course of the Khmer Rouge revolution, never to be seen or heard from again. This left a gaping void in the lives of millions of people. Some of these victims of the Cambodian genocide no doubt died anonymous deaths, unrecorded and unremembered by anyone. Many of them, on the other hand, were formally processed through the Khmer Rouge internal security system, which kept records in sometimes astonishing detail. Over the course of the first decade of the Documentation Center's work, many individuals with such lost family members have requested information about their missing relatives. The Documentation Center estimates that in approximately 80 percent of these cases, it has been able to locate information regarding the fate of the missing family members.

A second notable aspect of the Documentation Center's public service activities is found in its monthly magazine. In January 2000, the Documentation Center published the inaugural issue of *Searching for the Truth*, a Khmer-language periodical designed to help inform the Cambodian people about life under the Democratic Kampuchea regime. This publication also aims to educate Cambodia's citizens regarding the preparations for, and conduct of, any criminal tribunal that may be established to seek redress for the crimes of the Khmer Rouge. The magazine includes a variety of sections concentrating on different topics every month. Each issue features articles describing documentation activities at the Documentation Center, historical feature articles, legal analysis from international scholars, a public forum for debates on issues related to genocide justice in Cambodia, and a family tracing column describing the efforts of the Documentation Center to locate information about missing family members. Up to 5,000 copies of *Searching for the Truth* are distributed free of charge each month at the district level throughout the country. The magazine is also available for purchase at the Documentation Center.

LEGAL ACCOUNTABILITY FOR GENOCIDE

Perhaps the most significant area where the Documentation Center aspires to perform a public service role concerns preparations for a criminal tribunal or other formal accountability mechanism to deal with the crimes of the Khmer Rouge regime. In one sense, the Documentation Center was designed from the outset to be ready to deploy its staff and resources to support a tribunal and/or a truth commission, if and when such a body or bodies are created to seek legal redress for the crimes committed during the Khmer Rouge regime. With the apparently increasing likelihood that criminal proceedings against leaders of the Khmer Rouge may be launched in the near future, the Documentation Center began in late 1999 to seek funding to support the complex task of assisting in the prosecution of genocide and crimes against humanity. Shortly thereafter, it launched the "Promoting Accountability" project, designed to consolidate information of potential probative value to prosecutors of a criminal tribunal.

Such activities had been in progress at the Documentation Center for some time already. During the official investigation carried out by the UN Group of Experts, appointed by the UN secretary-general to determine whether or not sufficient cause existed to recommend the establishment of an international tribunal, UN officials visited the Documentation Center in November 1998 to examine evidentiary materials and to consult with the staff of the center.[40] Since then, in the protracted negotiations between the UN and the Cambodian government over the formation of a tribunal, UN officials have repeatedly visited the Documentation Center to confer on various aspects of the process. This series of official contacts underlines the legal significance of the Documentation Center's archives and other research and the consequent political sensitivity of those archives. It is a continuing challenge to balance the need to retain a certain degree of confidentiality for potentially probative materials that implicate certain individuals in criminal acts with the need to provide open access to scholars. Providing a reasonable degree of transparency to the local and international media, as well as to governments that provide funding to the Documentation Center, further complicates these challenges. It has not always been obvious how to strike an appropriate balance among these competing and directly contradictory requirements.

For example, when former Democratic Kampuchea deputy prime minister and foreign minister Ieng Sary was in the process of defecting from the Khmer Rouge to the Cambodian government in 1996—and not incidentally, negotiating for a royal amnesty for his death sentence dating from 1979—the officers of the Cambodian Genocide Program came under tremendous pressure both from the media and from international human rights groups to release all the data we had accumulated that might implicate Ieng Sary in war crimes, genocide, and other crimes against humanity. At that time, we chose to refrain from intervening in the internal Cambodian political process in this way. In part we refrained because that was not our mandate. More strategically, however, it was clear to us that a successful defection of Ieng Sary—along with the majority of the Khmer Rouge troops who were loyal to him—would seriously cripple the ability of the Khmer Rouge to continue their armed resistance and hence could materially hasten arrival of the day when the Khmer Rouge leadership might be brought to trial. Another consideration was the fact that we judged that such sensitive information should for the time being remain confidential and be reserved for the office of the prosecutor of a duly constituted judicial body that might eventually assert jurisdiction over these alleged crimes.

The situation has evolved substantially since 1996. Early in 1999, after the final collapse of Khmer Rouge political and military organizations, the most notorious of Khmer Rouge military commanders, General Ta Mok, and the chief of the Khmer Rouge secret police, Duch, were taken into custody by the Royal Government and subsequently charged with genocide. They remain in custody, pending the outcome of the international negotiations on the form of a tribunal to judge the charges against them and others. Meanwhile, both government investigators preparing charges against this pair, as well as their respective defense counsels, have approached the Documentation Center seeking evidence concerning the accusations against them. It is the policy of the Documentation Center to cooperate with both the prosecution and the defense in any such cases, providing to both sides copies of all relevant primary documentary materials accumulated by the center. The Documentation Center has also developed a body of analytical materials potentially relevant to prosecution of certain members of the Khmer Rouge; this latter category of materials will be provided to the prosecution alone and will be released to defense counsel pursuant to whatever concept of discovery is eventually embodied in the rules of procedure for the court that eventually asserts jurisdiction over these cases. These kinds of issues remain tremendously complex, existing on a shifting ground of ethical, moral, and legal questions. It is not easy to know how to proceed, because all of these questions are embedded in a morass of political considerations.

POLITICAL CONSIDERATIONS

As suggested in the previous section, one of the underlying objectives of the Cambodian Genocide Program and the Documentation Center of Cambodia has been to support activities leading to an official accountability process for the crimes of the Khmer Rouge regime, whether in the form of a truth commission or other truth-telling mechanism, a domestic tribunal, an international tribunal, or, as now seems likely, a new form of mixed domestic/international judicial proceeding. These matters are inherently submerged in a political context, and thus any organization involved with such matters will also find itself swimming in a turbulent political sea. Given the origins of the Cambodian Genocide Program in an explicitly political advocacy effort,[41] the officers of the Cambodian Genocide Program were fully aware of the political character infusing their otherwise largely scientific undertaking. This stands out clearly as another lesson of the Cambodian Genocide Program that should be noted by others who undertake similar projects: documenting serious violations of international humanitarian law and international criminal law is a process that inevitably involves political elements.

In this respect, we may not have been fully prepared for the extent to which the aphorism "Live by the sword, die by the sword" would apply to our research project. Initially, some observers close to our enterprise believed that the most significant political obstacles to our research would be erected by Cambodian officials. This suspicion was natural enough, considering the extent to which all factions in Cambodian politics are to one extent or another compromised by involvement with the Khmer Rouge. In the event, however, this turned out not to be the case.

One of the first objectives of the Cambodian Genocide Program (CGP) was to negotiate an agreement with the Cambodian government that would permit unrestricted research inside the country. In a series of meetings with Co-Prime Ministers Norodom Ranariddh and Hun Sen, as well as Deputy Prime Minister and Minister of Interior Sar Kheng in January and February 1995, the CGP program manager secured an agreement that authorized us, in effect, to go anywhere and seize any object that we deemed relevant to our investigation. At the time, we felt that it was highly unlikely the government would actually honor this agreement, once they realized how literally we intended to apply the provisions. Nonetheless, the Royal Government has in fact honored this agreement to a significant degree, permitting our investigators to repeatedly penetrate some of the most sensitive precincts of the government.

Exceptions to this generally cooperative attitude from the Cambodian government include a few cases such as the archives of political organs of the ruling Cambodian People's Party and private archives held by certain senior political figures, which have thus far remained off-limits. Even so, though it is perhaps odd to say, we got infinitely more open cooperation from Cambodian intelligence agencies than we did from the intelligence agencies of the U.S. government, even though that government initially was the primary sponsor of our research.[42] Other than occasional death threats from the Khmer Rouge and our judgment that it was unwise to venture into areas occupied by the Khmer Rouge military, we have encountered few impenetrable obstacles to access anywhere in Cambodia.

Perhaps surprisingly—or then again, perhaps not—the most significant political challenges to our research in fact emanated from the United States itself. The trouble began on April 17, 1995 (which, not coincidentally, was the twentieth anniversary of the Khmer Rouge rise to power), with publication of an op-ed article in the *Wall Street Journal* attacking the director of the CGP as an inappropriate choice to lead the federally funded project. These objections appeared to be based primarily on the fact that some twenty years previously, as an Australian student, the director had published writings opposing the U.S. intervention in Cambodia and supporting the

Khmer Rouge revolution. A second version of the article appearing in the *Asian Wall Street Journal* was even more strident, arguing that the choice of Yale University to lead the project "disgraces American honor and spits upon the graves of more than a million Cambodians."[43] This led to a long series of letters to the editor in the newspaper, generating much heat but precious little light,[44] but this was only the beginning.

As the controversy sparked by this original article escalated, the U.S. Congress entered the fray. On May 3, 1995, Congressman Martin R. Hoke of Ohio began circulating a "Dear Colleague" letter titled "Pull State Dept. Grant from Khmer Rouge Apologist," demanding that the grant be withdrawn from Yale.[45] Over the following months, the situation began to get serious. On August 7, 1995, six senior Republican U.S. senators wrote to Secretary of State Warren Christopher, challenging the award of the State Department grant to Yale University and calling the decision "unconscionable."[46] The U.S. State Department responded to the senatorial letter with a spirited reply in September, informing the concerned legislators that the department "maintains confidence in Yale University to uphold the highest standards of integrity and operational effectiveness" and dismissing the eight specific concerns raised by the senators with detailed refutations.[47] Managing such political damage seemed to consume the majority of the director's time. Meanwhile, the rest of the officers and staff attempted to remain focused on carrying out the mandate of the program.

That was not to be the end of it. Early in 1998, Republican congressman Tom Campbell of California had another go at the CGP, reportedly complaining on behalf of one of his constituents to the U.S. secretary of state about alleged financial misconduct involving the State Department grant to Yale. This accusation triggered a formal investigation by the inspector general and resulted in close official scrutiny of the program. By the end of that year, the investigation had found "no evidence of wrongdoing" and was terminated.[48] This suggests yet another important lesson from the CGP for other human rights documentation projects: the crucial importance of strict financial accounting procedures. Even for projects like the CGP that operate in good faith, when challenged by donors, if you cannot prove that every penny has been spent for legitimate purposes, then you may find yourself with a serious problem. The CGP's rigorous and exacting business manager at Yale University often wearied program officers with her relentless demands for financial documentation, but eventually that burden turned out to have been a critical safeguard against politically inspired attacks.

THE DOCUMENTATION CENTER OF
CAMBODIA AS A MODEL

The Documentation Center of Cambodia provides a model for future documentation of massive social trauma resulting from gross violations of international humanitarian law. In 1996, the government of Rwanda approached the CGP and requested that Yale apply the model developed for Cambodia to the 1994 Rwandan genocide. Unfortunately, however, despite encouragement from the good offices of the U.S. Institute of Peace, funding was not forthcoming to support this endeavor. Nonetheless, it has subsequently been suggested that precisely such an undertaking may still have merit.[49]

In early 1998, the author also met with the Office of the Special Prosecutor in Addis Ababa, Ethiopia, to explore the possibilities for applying a similar documentation protocol to the masses of evidence accumulated there for the ongoing genocide trials against senior officials of the Derg regime. Unfortunately, though there was keen interest on the part of Ethiopian officials, no funding could be secured to support a project in Ethiopia similar in scope to that undertaken in Cambodia.

In April 2000, Dr. Helen Jarvis, at the time an associate professor at the School of Information Systems, Technology, and Management at the University of New South Wales and a consultant to the CGP, traveled to Indonesia to discuss applying the lessons of the CGP to documentation of the Indonesian massacres of 1965 and 1966.[50] However, the political climate in Indonesia militated against launching such an undertaking at that time.

There have been several other instances of interest in the Documentation Center model, as well. The British charity Oxfam UK sponsored a delegation of officials from East Timor to visit the Documentation Center in July 2000 to study methods for documenting gross violations of human rights.[51] Though the Documentation Center model was not implemented in East Timor, some of the techniques developed by the CGP were eventually applied there.[52] In October 2000, a Palestinian academic approached the Documentation Center proposing to use that organization's experience as the basis for a project to document alleged Israeli violations of international humanitarian law.[53] There has been no follow-up from this inquiry. Interest in the Documentation Center model was also expressed during 2003 and 2004 by civil society organizations in Burma, Iraq, Afghanistan, and the former Yugoslavia.[54]

Thus, it appears that the model developed by CGP and the Documentation Center of Cambodia may well have applications to many other situations. Without any question, however, the lessons learned by the CGP certainly do apply to other efforts in the documentation of serious violations of internationally protected human rights. The CGP and the Documentation Center of Cambodia made it possible for analysts to move from theories to facts about the Cambodian genocide, and so it would appear a relatively easy matter to soon advance the case from the facts to the law. We now turn to a more detailed examination of some of those facts and what they tell us about how particular individuals may be implicated under the law in Cambodia.

5

CENTRALIZED TERROR

In my 1984 book on the Khmer Rouge revolution, *The Rise and Demise of Democratic Kampuchea*,[1] I discussed at length questions surrounding the sources and extent of violence during the Democratic Kampuchea regime. In that work, I wrote that it "is open to serious question . . . just how systematically, thoroughly, and deeply the post-victory purification pogrom affected the lower levels of the civil service, intellectuals, and bourgeoisie."[2] After reviewing the known data available on this question up until that time, I argued that "these facts alone do not prove that the KCP [Communist Party of Kampuchea] instituted a program of class genocide."[3] I concluded that scholars had been handicapped in assessing this question by the fact that the various schools of thought on the matter remained "unsupported by solid, independently verifiable evidence concerned with the alleged mass atrocities," particularly as regards the sources and extent of the violence. Still, the lack of data did not stop scholars from exploring this question—far from it. In fact, the scholarly debate about how the mass killing in Cambodia unfolded became the central issue in the historiography of modern Cambodia.

The scholars in this debate represent schools of thought about genocide, and their various approaches form the intellectual corpus of the new field of genocide studies. The debate over the root cause of mass killing during the Khmer Rouge regime evokes that other great historical debate about genocide, the German *Historikerstreit*, which concerned the rela-

tionship between the Holocaust and German culture and national identity.[4] Were the Cambodian people somehow Pol Pot's "willing executioners," with the violence of the Khmer Rouge regime reflecting an
underlying cultural trait of the Cambodian people, historically unique to
the time and place it occurred?[5] Or did the violence of the Khmer Rouge
regime emanate from some more broadly distributed ideological origin,
therefore rendering it amenable to comparison? Perhaps the Khmer Rouge
mass killing arose from the same tenets of communism that brought about
the mass killing of Stalin's Russia and Mao's China but that was, by ab-
solute numbers, much less *evil*. Or perhaps the killing in Cambodia can
be understood as a response to the perceived threat from Vietnam, as the
Khmer Rouge themselves have argued at some length. These same themes
and issues lay at the heart of the *Historikerstreit*, and they also are part and
parcel of genocide studies.[6]

In the scholarly literature on the Khmer Rouge regime of Democratic
Kampuchea, there have been two principal schools of thought regarding
the nature of the violence that took so many lives in such a short period
of time. One school of thought holds that the primary locus of the violence was local and that it was largely the result of the spontaneous excesses of a vengeful, undisciplined peasant army. A prominent proponent
of this school of thought is Michael Vickery.[7] A second school of thought
holds that the locus of the violence was centralized and that it was largely
the result of a carefully planned and centrally controlled security apparatus. Several observers have proposed this explanation of the violence in the
Democratic Kampuchea regime, including, for example, the recently retired U.S. ambassador to Cambodia, Kenneth Quinn.[8] It can be argued,
however, that until recently there was an inadequate amount of data to
make an unambiguous determination on this question.

A wide range of new evidence uncovered by the Documentation Center of Cambodia over the course of the last ten years has done much to
resolve this controversy. In particular, data on the frequency, distribution,
and origin of mass graves, combined with data gleaned from newly discovered Khmer Rouge internal security documents, have given us new insight into the question of the economy of violence within Democratic
Kampuchea. The data lead inexorably to the conclusion that most of the
violence was carried out pursuant to orders from the highest political authorities of the Communist Party of Kampuchea. In this chapter, I briefly
review some of the new evidence that so strongly suggests this new and
now well-documented conclusion.

Two classes of evidence are particularly compelling in concluding that the bulk of the political violence in Democratic Kampuchea was centrally directed. The first class of evidence is a large collection of official documents discovered only in the late 1990s, consisting of the bureaucratic records of the region, zone, and central internal security services of Democratic Kampuchea. This evidence illuminates the chain of command inside Democratic Kampuchea, the lines of command and control in the security apparatus of that state, and the individuals involved in the mass killings both as victims and as perpetrators. The second class of evidence consists of the results of an ongoing satellite mapping survey of Cambodia, which aims to create a comprehensive inventory of the prisons, execution centers, and mass graves dating from the Democratic Kampuchea regime. This evidence suggests that a centralized execution system operated at high efficiency over the entire course of the Democratic Kampuchea regime, resulting in more than 20,000 mass graves dating from the Khmer Rouge period. Combined, these two classes of evidence constitute a compelling case for the proposition that the violence in the Democratic Kampuchea regime was centrally directed by the highest state authorities. The mass grave evidence is treated in Chapter 7. The present chapter offers a brief overview of some of the new documentary evidence.

DOCUMENTARY EVIDENCE

One type of newly uncovered evidence bearing on the question of the sources of violence during the Democratic Kampuchea regime is internal security documents from the Democratic Kampuchea regime itself. This evidence is contained in several large collections of official Democratic Kampuchea documents, consisting of bureaucratic records from the region, zone, and central internal security services of Democratic Kampuchea.[9] Although scholars have not yet had the time required to carefully tease out the full implications of this treasure trove of documents, some of the meaning has already become clear. Moreover, surprisingly, confirmation of the meaning of some of these documents has come from within the ranks of the Khmer Rouge itself. In August 1996, news organizations in Cambodia received a press release from a Thai public relations adviser to senior Khmer Rouge official Ieng Sary, defending the latter's record and purporting to identify those responsible for mass violence during the Democratic Kampuchea regime. The Ieng Sary statement asserted,

At the same time, a secret "national security committee" already in place before the liberation of Phnom Penh [sic], was functioning in Phnom Penh in charge of arresting, torturing and executing all people, most of them cadres and leaders suspected of being "traitors." This committee is instrumental in consolidating Pol Pot's "reign of terror." It is composed of:

- Nuon Chea, Deputy Secretary General of the Party (Known as Brother No. 2), President of the Committee
- Son Sen, Deputy Prime Minister in charge of National Security, Member of the Committee
- Yun Yat, Son Sen's wife, Assistant of the Committee

This committee is answerable to Pol Pot and Pol Pot alone.[10]

The balance of this statement can easily be dismissed as a self-serving attempt to improve Ieng Sary's public image in the wake of his 1979 conviction on charges of genocide, in anticipation of the royal pardon that would soon materialize to reward his defection from the Khmer Rouge to the government. Even so, Ieng Sary's comments on the composition of the "secret national security committee" were a revelation to researchers at the Documentation Center of Cambodia.[11] Upon reading this press release, a lightbulb immediately went off in Program Officer Youk Chhang's head. He directed his research staff to focus on a set of recently discovered Khmer Rouge archives. This particular collection of documents contains a large amount of material concerning leadership directives regarding the handling of various prisoners at the Tuol Sleng Prison, headquarters of the S-21 internal security apparatus.

The Documentation Center staff began by scrutinizing the list of offices and individuals to which the documents had been distributed, often written in the corner of the cover pages of so-called confessions—confessions that had been extracted under torture from prisoners of the S-21 bureaucracy. These confessions include many bizarre and improbable "admissions," such as simultaneously being an officer of both the KGB and the CIA. It immediately became apparent to researchers that the cover sheets of many of these confessions had at least one, and in some cases all three, of the names mentioned in Ieng Sary's August missive.[12] "At," "Khieu," and "Nuon" were often handwritten on the distribution list in the corner of the cover sheets of these forced confessions. "Nuon" was the name used by Nuon Chea on internal Khmer Rouge documents; "Khieu" was the nom-de-guerre of Son Sen; and "At," that of Son Sen's wife, Yun Yat.

Many of these cover sheets also include instructions to "Duch" (aka Kang Keck Iev, the director of the Tuol Sleng Prison and chief of Khmer Rouge secret police) regarding the handling of individual prisoners. Some of the documents also include comments to or from "Angkar" and "870," the first a commonly used alias of Pol Pot and the second the code for Pol Pot's central office. Thus, Ieng Sary's assertions regarding the command structure for internal security in Democratic Kampuchea were entirely consistent with independently verified primary source materials. This drove Documentation Center researchers to conclude that the "national security committee" probably functioned more or less as stated by Ieng Sary. Scholars of genocide—as well as prosecutors, should a court ever be established to address the crimes in question—may now assert, with two independent sources that corroborate one another, that the top level of the chain of command for internal security matters during the Khmer Rouge regime was constituted as Ieng Sary has claimed.

A cursory sampling from the archives uncovered by the Documentation Center illustrates the circulation of "confessions" among the top leaders of the Khmer Rouge regime. Mostly from 1977, this sample suggests that Pol Pot and the "security committee" closely followed the progress of Tuol Sleng interrogations, evidently on an almost daily basis. For example, a handwritten note on a confession dated January 16, 1977, shows a commentary from Duch to "Brother," perhaps referring to "Brother Number 1," aka Pol Pot, or to Nuon Chea, who was known as "Brother Number 2."[13] Another confession cover sheet contains a note, dated March 24, 1978, from Duch to "Khieu," aka Son Sen.[14] A confession cover sheet dated July 6, 1977, shows the circulation of "confessions" through the "security committee" from Son Sen to "At," aka Yun Yat.[15]

Two similar examples dated November 10 and 11, 1977, show notes from Son Sen to Nuon, aka Nuon Chea.[16] Another more extensive note dated October 5, 1977, from Khieu (Son Sen) to Duch concerns interrogation methods for prisoners.[17] In very similar handwriting is an October 9, 1977, note to "Angkar" (Pol Pot), presumably from Son Sen.[18] An interesting counterpart to this is another undated note from "870" (almost certainly Pol Pot) to Khieu (Son Sen) regarding the proper use of the term "Angkar."[19] A final example of the top leadership internal security communiqués concerns the confession of one San Eab, in which a letter to "870" (Pol Pot) is annotated "Angkar responds" and "follow up."[20] Collectively, these materials clearly suggest that Pol Pot, Nuon Chea, Son Sen, and Yun Yat were personally involved in directing the activities of S-21, the nerve center of Khmer Rouge terror. They personally controlled the extermination policies of the regime.

Also included among the bureaucratic traces of organized terror obtained by the Documentation Center are detailed personnel files on the security cadre of the *Santebal*, the Khmer Rouge secret police. Utilizing these files, Documentation Center researchers have constructed an organization chart exhibiting the staffing of S-21, the headquarters of the Khmer Rouge secret police.[21] The Documentation Center is in the process of constructing similar organization charts for other nodes in the nationwide network of interrogation and extermination centers.

S-21 AND THE PROVINCES

The relationship between S-21 headquarters at Tuol Sleng and the network of zone and regional security centers is necessarily more complex than that between S-21 and the top leadership, as are the relationships among the zone and regional security centers. Yet, the archives obtained by the Documentation Center also contain a wealth of information on the daily operations of this far-flung network of security centers.

One such document indicates the type of communications that occurred among region-level security centers and lower levels of the organization. Dated July 8, 1977, it is a reply from the leader of Region 13 (in Takeo Province), responding to an inquiry from a local security center, "105," ordering "105" to "destroy" a particular person.[22] Another document from a local security office, "Prison 105," dated April 15, 1978, and found among the papers at S-21, is a request to higher authority listing twenty-two people for whom permission is sought for "cleansing," a Khmer Rouge euphemism for execution.[23] This document specifies in some detail the charges that have been laid against the prisoners; one of the prisoners was being held for execution on accusations of having made a sarcastic remark.

A pair of examples illustrates the widespread authority exercised by the S-21 director, Duch, over security matters in both the military and civilian spheres. The first is a letter dated June 1, 1977, from Battalion 502 to Duch, forwarded with a note from Duch to an interrogator, with instructions to question a particular military prisoner.[24] The second example is from a provincial security center in Kampong Thom, also dated June 1,

1977, and also annotated with instructions from Duch ordering an interrogation of a civilian.[25]

Confronted by journalists in 1999 with similar records from the Documentation Center archives illustrating his work at S-21, Duch freely admitted his role in implementing the Khmer Rouge system of centralized terror, confirming the authenticity of the documents, and helpfully identifying the scripts of his superiors. "This is the handwriting of Nuon Chea," he told Nate Thayer when shown one S-21 document, "You see his handwriting is square; mine is more oval, like Son Sen's."[26] Duch noted that although he operated under direct orders from Nuon Chea and Son Sen, the mass killings were carried out by authority of the most senior levels of the Khmer Rouge. "The decisions to kill were made not by one man, not just Pol Pot, but the entire central committee. Nuon Chea, he was the principal man for the killings. . . . Pol Pot knew about S-21, but did not direct it personally. He left that job to Nuon Chea as No. 2 in the party and to Son Sen as head of the army and police."[27] These comments from the Khmer Rouge secret police chief echo those of others, such as Khmer Rouge Deputy Prime Minister Ieng Sary, who have also implicated Pol Pot, Nuon Chea, and Son Sen as being responsible for the Khmer Rouge bureaucracy dedicated to mass murder.

A final example of the S-21 archives discovered by the Documentation Center is more mundane, yet poignant and telling. This particular document is of a type we refer to as an "execution log," a daily record of executions at a given security center, in this case, at Tuol Sleng itself. Dated July 23, 1977, it is signed by You Huy (a chief of guards) and authorized by Hor, the deputy director of S-21. The typewritten form lists biographical details on eighteen prisoners executed that day and, almost as an afterthought, in Huy's handwriting a note at the bottom adds, "Also killed 160 children today for a total of 178 enemies killed."[28] This chilling glimpse into the Khmer Rouge internal security services is but a tiny example of the tens of thousands of documents discovered by the Documentation Center of Cambodia.

Once these archives of the Khmer Rouge secret police have been fully analyzed, they will tell a large part of the story of violence during the Democratic Kampuchea regime. Already, it is clear to Documentation Center analysts and other experts who have examined the archives that the works of Democratic Kampuchea's internal security apparatus were ubiquitous across the territory of Cambodia and that these works were centrally controlled by the top leadership of the Communist Party.[29] The evidence suggests that they used this system to expand their control over the entire country, in the process liquidating all perceived enemies of *Angkar*. The list of offenses that might result in one being defined as an enemy seemed to grow inexorably, ultimately reaching the point where a single sarcastic remark was deemed to be a crime punishable by death.

CENTRALIZED TERROR

The new data sources reviewed in this chapter—documents from within the Khmer Rouge internal security bureaucracy—demonstrate graphically that the senior leadership of the Communist Party of Kampuchea was in control of a nationwide coercive apparatus designed to physically eliminate all stripes of possible opposition to the policies of the party. These new data strongly support one of the schools of thought regarding the sources and nature of the mass violence of the Democratic Kampuchea regime presented at the outset of this chapter, namely, that the terror in Democratic Kampuchea originated under the central direction of the highest levels of the Communist Party. The small sample of documents presented here is not sufficient to show that the span of control exercised by the Communist Party political leadership eventually became nationwide, but this issue is revisited with a second and even more compelling class of evidence in Chapter 7.

Moreover, the new data allow us to further refine this conclusion, introducing nuance into the general pattern of central control. The Documentation Center's archives also illustrate the fact that not all of the killings during the Khmer Rouge regime were directly ordered by the central leadership.[30] Authority to kill certain categories of individuals was delegated to local administrations, and they used this power liberally. Once the central directives to exterminate certain categories of "enemies" had been disseminated, and the bureaucratic apparatus became fully engaged with the task, local officials sometimes misinterpreted the leadership directives as requiring an even greater scope of killing. Others used the authority they had been granted to pursue personal agendas, taking revenge for slights felt in local disputes.

In terms of the broader historical debate about the sources of violence under the Khmer Rouge regime, the data presented here sound a note of caution. The unequivocal conclusion that much or most of the violence was centrally directed, as Kenneth Quinn argued, does not entirely invalidate the argument presented by Michael Vickery, because there were also elements of indiscipline and spontaneity in the mass killing. The fact that there were both generalized ideological motivations as well as particularized idiosyncratic or cultural motivations underlying the mass killing of the Khmer Rouge regime suggests that the Cambodian version of the *Historikerstreit* may not have yet run its full course.

In summary, the evidence reviewed in this chapter tends to support three propositions. The first supported proposition is that the highest officials of the Communist Party of Kampuchea were in control of the Democratic Kampuchea security apparatus. The second supported proposition is that the Democratic Kampuchea security apparatus was national in scope and constituted a highly organized bureaucracy. The third supported proposition is that this security apparatus directed the extermination of a still unknown, but significant, percentage of the population of the country. Overall, the data strongly support the conclusion that a high proportion of the mass death during the Democratic Kampuchea regime resulted from a centrally organized and carefully controlled plan to exterminate large numbers of Cambodians and that the leadership of the Democratic Kampuchea regime was intentionally responsible for these deaths. We now turn to the question of the extent to which there may have been variations in the intensity of the killing over time and in different regions of Cambodia during the Khmer Rouge regime.

6

TERROR IN THE EAST

A recurring issue in contemporary Cambodian politics has been the question of whether or not the government that replaced the Khmer Rouge regime was really that much better than the Khmer Rouge themselves.[1] As noted in Chapter 2, a large part of the reason that this question has endured arises from the fact that so many of the key leaders of the new government had been officials of the previous Khmer Rouge regime. One way to examine this issue is to look back at how those who came to power after the Khmer Rouge carried out their official duties during the Khmer Rouge regime.

Some scholars have argued that levels of political violence were relatively constant across all political factions and geographical regions of the Khmer Rouge regime. Others argue that extreme violence was a characteristic only of those regions controlled by factions loyal to the supreme Khmer Rouge leader, Pol Pot, and that levels of repression tended to be less extreme in regions outside the control of the central political leadership. Because many top leaders of the post–Khmer Rouge regime had been officials in the eastern regions of Cambodia during the Khmer Rouge regime, we have a potential method for exploring this question. We frame the question by asking, Was there any difference in the overall levels of violence in a given region when it was under the control of those who later superseded the Khmer Rouge regime, as opposed to when it was under the authority of Pol Pot? We examine this question using primary docu-

ments and other evidence uncovered in recent years by the Documentation Center of Cambodia. The answer to this question explains a great deal
about the lack of trust many Cambodians continue to have in their government today.

OVERVIEW

When the "Khmer Rouge" came to power in 1975, it was not a tightly
unified organization. In fact, the Khmer Rouge circa 1975 is more accurately viewed as a coalition of revolutionary groupings who had been
united largely by the common goal of overthrowing the U.S.-backed Lon
Nol regime. Even before that common goal was finally achieved, however,
another struggle—in many ways a much more desperate struggle—began
with a deadly serious aim: control of the revolution. Within the revolutionary movement, there were many tendencies. Some Cambodian revolutionaries traced their lineage to the revolution in Vietnam; others tended
toward sympathy for allies in the People's Republic of China; still others
were motivated by a strongly nationalistic ideology or were more interested in returning Prince Norodom Sihanouk to the position of power
snatched from his grasp by Lon Nol. Imposing unity and central control
over this fractious collection of tendencies was the task set by Pol Pot, the
chairman of the Central Committee of the Communist Party of Kampuchea (CPK).

Cambodia had been divided into "zones" of control during the war of
1970–1975, defined in large part by whose troops controlled which areas
of the country. Over the course of the war, CPK Chairman Pol Pot formed
a close alliance with the infamous Ta Mok, CPK secretary for the Southwest Zone, whose ferocious military forces were feared throughout the
revolutionary organization. In the eastern areas of Cambodia, troops under
the command of Eastern Zone CPK Secretary So Phim attempted to pursue a policy of cooperation and friendship with Vietnamese communist
forces, who had done so much to help the Cambodian revolutionaries in
the early stages of their war against Lon Nol. This fact alone made So Phim
and his Eastern Zone forces suspect in the eyes of Pol Pot and his allies,
who viewed Vietnam as the historic enemy. Through a complex series of
maneuvers, forces loyal to Pol Pot staged a creeping coup against personnel loyal to So Phim, gradually purging region-level cadre and replacing
them with cadre chosen by Pol Pot and his inner circle of confidants. This
series of aggressive maneuvers culminated in Eastern Zone Secretary So

Phim's death in May 1978 and the military rout of his remaining Eastern Zone forces.[2]

This chapter examines human rights abuses in one region of the Eastern Zone during the period when the zone was under So Phim's control and compares that to the human rights situation in the Eastern Zone after the seizure of control by troops who had Pol Pot's unquestioned confidence. The particular region I examine was known as *Damban* 23, or Region 23, which was almost exactly contiguous with Cambodia's Svay Rieng Province.

As previously discussed, there are two general views in the literature regarding the intensity of human rights violations in areas controlled by Pol Pot versus areas controlled by other Cambodian revolutionary forces. According to one view, the levels of violence were more or less the same throughout all of Cambodia during the Khmer Rouge regime; according to the other viewpoint, there were significant differences in the levels of violence in different areas—particularly in the Eastern Zone, where it has been argued that repression was less severe than elsewhere. I employ arguments advanced by two prominent analysts of the Khmer Rouge regime to elaborate these perspectives.

KIERNAN VIEW

In reference to the Eastern Zone, Ben Kiernan argued in his 1996 book that "despite some exceptions large-scale deaths in detention do not appear to have occurred before late 1976."[3] He continued, "Large numbers of people were imprisoned in 1975, but the information available—from three of the five Eastern Zone regions—suggests the vast majority were released after a brief detention. This distinguishes the East from the other Zones of Democratic Kampuchea."[4] The data underlying Kiernan's assertion of this conclusion include information from Svay Rieng, or Region 23. Kiernan, then, maintains that the incidence of gross human rights violations in the Eastern Zone in general and Region 23 in particular was relatively lower than that in other regions of Democratic Kampuchea, until the Eastern Zone was brought under the direct political control of forces loyal to Pol Pot in late 1976 or early 1977. His evidence comes largely from a collection of interviews carried out between 1979 and about 1993.

Kiernan does acknowledge that extremely brutal prison conditions existed in the Eastern Zone. For example, he cites the case of a prison in Meanchey Thmey District of Region 23, presumably still under the control of Eastern Zone forces, where a high rate of death in detention is reported by witnesses. He recounts that in this particular security facility, "after three hundred inmates died in five months from lack of medicine and overwork, the remaining sixty-four prisoners were released on 30 September 1975."[5] This represents a death-in-custody rate among prisoners of more than 82 percent over the course of five months, hardly what one could characterize as humane incarceration. This, of course, is even before considering the rationales for the incarceration of these prisoners, which seem to have been based principally on political, social, and class criteria, rather than commission of any particular criminal acts. Still, Kiernan maintains that such examples were the exception and that the Eastern Zone authorities can be distinguished from their counterparts in other zones of Democratic Kampuchea by their relatively less harsh security practices prior to the imposition of control over the Eastern Zone by Pol Pot's forces.

LOCARD VIEW

A very different analysis was offered by Henri Locard in 1995. "A few researchers, investigating the country mainly in the early years of the Heng Samrin regime," Locard argued, "demonstrated that, in the East Zone in general (Prey Veng, Svay Rieng and Kompong Cham), from which most leaders of the pro-Vietnamese regime originated after January 7, 1979, living conditions were distinctly more humane. Apart from some northeastern districts in Kompong Cham, I found no evidence to support this theory—at least as far as repression and the prison network are concerned."[6] Locard continued:

> Contrary to my expectations (having read so much about regional variations), and again apart from the Northeast, I found that a closely interconnected three-tier prison network crisscrossed and enmeshed the entire territory. There was first an infinite number of smaller detention centers at the level of the khum, or commune, some the equivalent of our police stations, where suspects were detained and interrogated for a short period of time. . . .
>
> The next tier is the district prison: there was at least one in each of the some 150 districts or so of the country. These institutions were permanent and had been established everywhere in the early months of the regime, while others had been opened from 1972–73 in the areas controlled by the

revolutionaries. . . . Many more populated districts, as in Svay Rieng, Kompong Thom, or Takeo provinces, for instance, had up to two or three or even four prisons per district. . . .

The third kind of prison was the zone prison—there were some thirty zones under the KR, provinces having disappeared from their administrative reorganization of the territory.[7]

In Locard's view, then, the level of human rights violations was relatively constant across all regions of Democratic Kampuchea, with the exception of one unique area in the remote, rugged, and sparsely populated northeast, where conditions tended to differ from those of all other regions of the country during the Khmer Rouge regime. Locard's evidence is presented in the form of a reconstructive narrative about a nationwide network of "prison-torture and extermination centers," which operated continuously across the country over the entire course of the Pol Pot regime.

I attempt to shed light on these opposed interpretations from Kiernan and Locard by examining new evidence uncovered by the Cambodian Genocide Program and the Documentation Center of Cambodia. In particular, I examine one region of Democratic Kampuchea—Region 23, or *Damban 23*—which was located at the southern end of Democratic Kampuchea's Eastern Zone.

POLITICAL AUTHORITY IN REGION 23

Given the extreme secrecy that was characteristic of the Communist Party of Kampuchea, it has always been difficult to establish the facts of leadership within the organization. With the introduction of the Cambodian Genocide Program's Biographical Database on the Khmer Rouge, however, it is now becoming easier to identify lines of command and control within Khmer Rouge organizations and to track changes in leadership across time.[8] There remain uncertainties and substantial gaps in the information presented in this database, but combined with other information that has recently become available, it is possible to discern the outlines of political authority in Region 23 over time.

Within the Khmer Rouge organization, leadership was arranged according to the classic communist cell structure, with a three-person committee in charge of affairs at each level of the organization.[9] Thus, for example, in Region 23, the region party leadership committee was composed of a secretary, a deputy, and a member. One step down the line at the next level of organization, the district level, there would be an identically structured committee of three, and so on, down through the commune and village levels.

In Region 23, I can identify at least five and possibly six different Khmer Rouge officials who occupied the post of region chair or region secretary at various points. Three of these held this post over the course of the Democratic Kampuchea regime, that is, between 1975 and 1979. Beginning in 1975, presumably soon after, or even prior to the April 17 fall of Phnom Penh, a cadre named Chan Sovan was named secretary of Region 23.[10] Sometime in late 1975 or early 1976, Sovan was replaced by a cadre named Sin So.[11]

According to Kiernan, Sin So was purged by Southwest Zone forces loyal to Pol Pot in March 1977, presumably indicating that he had failed to maintain Pol Pot's confidence.[12] However, in a confession extracted at the S-21 prison from the party secretary of Region 22, Meas Chhuon, Chhuon says that So was arrested by the party in March 1978.[13] Moreover, several witnesses interviewed by Kiernan in Cambodia also seem to indicate that Sin So was not purged until 1978. According to three different informants, Sin So's replacement, Seng Hong, was not promoted to the post of Region 23 secretary until 1978.[14] Consequently, we can conclude that around March 1978, Seng Hong took the position of party secretary for Region 23.[15]

From all of this, one may also infer that Pol Pot was focused on asserting his authority over Region 23 by March 1978, in the wake of the Vietnamese military incursion into the region in the previous year.[16] This was not, however, the end of the purges of Region 23. There is evidence that the number two and three officials in the region were sent to Tuol Sleng torture center in Phnom Penh for interrogation and execution in April 1978.[17] Thus, this information gives us a benchmark to identify the collapse of Eastern Zone political autonomy in Region 23 and the installation of personnel who were more responsive to the authority of Pol Pot. Consequently, we will examine the intensity of human rights violations in Region 23, both before and after March/April 1978.

These leaders ruled over a highly simplified, ideologically constructed class structure. There were only three classes of citizens in the Khmer Rouge state. The foundation of Democratic Kampuchea society was a class of citizens known as "full-rights" persons, also called "Old People" or "Base People." The Base People were those of lower socioeconomic status, meaning that they were from the poorest strata of the peasantry and that they had lived in areas controlled by the revolutionary forces prior to the final victory on April 17, 1975. A second class of citizen was the "Candidate," that is, a person who was theoretically qualified to rise to the status of a full-rights person through service to the revolution, military, or otherwise but whose biography was marred by dint of a questionable socioeconomic background, such as having come from a less-than-impoverished peasant family. Finally, there were the "New People." The New People were those who lived in or fled to the cities during the civil war and who did not "join" the revolution until the cities fell to revolutionary forces on April 17, 1975. For this reason, the New People were often called the "April 17" people. The official designation for this lowest class was "Depositee," an apt term insofar as immediately after the April 17 victory, all city dwellers were evacuated from the cities and "deposited" in rural areas. These "New People"—including many poor peasants who had fled to the cities to escape the violence of the war—were all suspected as traitors and enemies, because they had remained in the enclaves of Lon Nol's Khmer Republic and had failed to rally to the Khmer Rouge until it was forced upon them through the victory of the revolution. It appears that the central authorities of the Democratic Kampuchea regime had very little sympathy indeed for the New People and that if they did not explicitly plan to simply kill most of them, bit by bit, over time, then they certainly did nothing to prevent exactly that from happening.

PRISONS AND KILLING FIELDS IN REGION 23

According to a report prepared by the People's Republic of Kampuchea (PRK) Information, Culture, and Press Center in Svay Rieng Province in 1981, there were seventy-four "genocide sites" in Svay Rieng Province dating from the Democratic Kampuchea regime.[18] The term "genocide sites" generally refers to detention, interrogation, and torture facilities, as well as mass grave sites (popularly known as "Killing Fields"). The 1981 PRK report does not give an exhaustive listing of these alleged sites, so one is left to reconstruct the particulars from other sources. In the work completed to date by the Documentation Center of Cambodia, information on these sites remains incomplete. Nonetheless, the Documentation Center's Mass Grave Mapping Project has assembled a good deal of data, enough to construct a partial inventory of sites.

Based on these various sources, I have identified a total of forty-two "genocide sites" in Region 23. Of these, twenty-six were the locations of Khmer Rouge detention, interrogation, and torture facilities, hereafter referred to as prisons. In addition, we have identified at least sixteen sites in Region 23 that contain mass grave pits dating to the Khmer Rouge regime. The twenty-six prison sites are distributed across every district in Region 23, but not in every commune.

Therefore, we cannot confirm Locard's hypothesis that there were prisons in every commune, reporting to higher-level prisons in every district. Still, it appears that there may have been at least an approximation of this system of organization, given the high density of prisons in the region. Even barring the unlikely situation that no additional sites remain to be discovered, this constitutes a rather large number of prisons for such a relatively small region.

Table 6.1 lists the Prison and Mass Grave Sites that I have been able to identify in Region 23. It illustrates the large number of prisons in the region, as well as the numerous mass grave sites located at or near those prisons. In addition to the tabular data, Map. 6.1, of Svay Rieng Genocide Sites, indicates the locations of some of these prisons and mass graves in Svay Rieng Province.

It appears that most of these prison facilities were already operating at the beginning of the regime on April 17, 1975, and hence that many of these prisons were established some time prior to that date. In only a few cases are we able to identify prisons that were either established or disestablished after the seizure of state power by the Khmer Rouge. One specific case is mentioned by Kiernan of a prison at Svay Prohout that was closed in April 1976.[19] Another change in the prison system is the reported relocation of a prison from Region 23's Chantrea District in 1978; since Chantrea is surrounded on three sides by Vietnam, this change was most likely connected to border tensions with Vietnam at that time.[20] The prison at Wat Svay Tateum in Region 23's Romeas Hek District is reported to have been built in 1976.[21] Another is the Wat Beong Rai Prison in Kruol Kou commune of Region 23's Svay Chrum District, said to have been built in 1977.[22] Finally, one witness reports that construction of the security center called Khtoap Khschach in Bos village of Chantrea District began in 1974 but was not completed until after the April 17 victory in 1975.[23]

From the substantial amount of witness commentary discussing killing rates during early 1975 at other prisons in Region 23, it is safe to assume

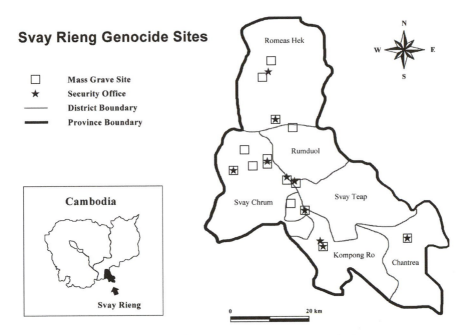

Map 6.1. Based on data from the Documentation Center of Cambodia.

that the majority of the facilities were in operation from early 1975 or before. Thus, it seems clear that there was an elaborate network of prisons and interrogation centers in operation in Region 23 long before the Pol Pot's forces consummated their quest for total control of the region in March/April 1978. We can conclude, then, that So Phim's Eastern Zone Khmer Rouge forces constructed and operated these security facilities-cum-extermination centers prior to the time that Pol Pot asserted direct control over the eastern portions of Cambodia.

A quick inventory of the seven districts in Region 23 illustrates the ubiquitous nature of the Khmer Rouge security services and their works, even at the outset of the revolution in April 1975. In Romeas Hek District of Region 23, we believe that we can identify eleven prisons and four sites containing mass grave pits. According to one witness, a 48-year-old man who was a Base Person in the area during the Khmer Rouge regime, people were imprisoned in Romeas Hek District on charges of "immorality," of stealing food, or of "talking arbitrarily."[24] "Victims taken to be confined here had to work one or two days, and then somehow disappeared." Where they "disappeared" to was the "Killing Fields." One of the Romeas Hek Killing Fields, at Tuol Akream, is somewhat larger than the

TABLE 6.1. PRISON AND MASS GRAVE SITES IN REGION 23

#	District	Commune	Site Name	Site Type	Source
1	Kompong Ro	Svay Teou	Tahnor	Graves	DC–Cam Mapping Data, Renakse Doc. #5
2	Kompong Ro	Svay Teou	Tahnor	Prison	DC–Cam Mapping Data
3	Kompong Ro	Prey Thom	Wat Russei Sang	Prison	DC–Cam Mapping Data, DC Cam Doc. #657
4	Kompong Ro	Prey Thom	Wat Russei Sang	Graves	DC–Cam Mapping Data, DC–Cam Doc. #657
5	Kompong Ro	Ponlear	—	Graves	Renakse Doc #6
6	Kompong Ro	Ponlear	—	Prison	CGDB BIB Rec. #D00371
7	Svay Chrum	Tlork	Tlork (site 1)	Graves	DC–Cam Mapping Data
8	Svay Chrum	Tlork	Tlork (site 2)	Graves	DC–Cam Mapping Data
9	Svay Chrum	Tlork	Tlork	Prison	DC–Cam Mapping Data
10	Svay Chrum	Svay Ang	Wat Svay Phem	Graves	DC–Cam Mapping Data
11	Svay Chrum	Svay Ang	Wat Chas	Graves	DC–Cam Mapping Data
12	Svay Chrum	Kroul Kou	Wat Boeng Rai	Graves	DC–Cam Mapping Data
13	Svay Chrum	Kroul Kou	Wat Boeng Rai	Prison	DC–Cam Mapping Data, CGDB BIB Rec. #D00366, Renakse Doc. #364
14	Svay Teap	Sang Kur	Wat Kdey Rumdoul	Graves	DC–Cam Mapping Data
15	Svay Teap	Sang Kur	Wat Kdey Rumduol	Prison	DC–Cam Mapping Data
16	Svay Teap	Koki Saom	Wat Prey Trachheak	Prison	Renakse Doc. #6, Renakse Doc. #363
17	Rumduol	Kompong Ampil	Khpoap Ampil	Graves	DC–Cam Mapping Data
18	Rumduol	Popok Vil	Tuol Popok Vil	Graves	DC–Cam Mapping Data
19	Rumduol	Popok Vil	Tuol Popok Vil	Prison	DC–Cam Mapping Data
20	Svay Rieng	—	Kruos	Prison	Renakse Doc. #357
21	Svay Rieng	Chhoeu Teal	Wat Sla	Prison	Renakse Doc. #364
22	Svay Rieng	Chhoeu Teal	Chheou Teal Forest	Prison	Renakse Doc. #364

23	Svay Rieng	Chhoeu Teal	Tuol Prich	Prison	Renakse Doc. #364
24	Svay Rieng	Chhoeu Teal	Angkor Vong	Prison	Renakse Docs. #364 & 357
25	Svay Rieng	Chhoeu Teal	Prey Rokar	Prison	Renakse Doc. #364
26	Svay Rieng	Kruol Ko	Russie Dom	Prison	Renakse Docs. #364, CGDB BIB Rec. #D00366
27	Svay Rieng	Sangkat	Chong Prek	Graves	DC–Cam Mapping Data
28	Romeas Hek	Chrey Thom	Prey Rumdeng	Prison	Renakse Docs. #356 & 352, CGP Mapping Data
29	Romeas Hek	Trapeang Sdao	Wat Svay Torteum	Prison	Renakse Docs. #356 & 352, CGP Mapping Data
30	Romeas Hek	—	Prey Dorn Ok	Prison	Renakse Docs. #356 & 352
31	Romeas Hek	—	Tuol Sangam	Prison	Renakse Docs. #356 & 352
32	Romeas Hek	—	Reus Kabass	Prison	Renakse Docs. #356 & 352
33	Romeas Hek	—	Chamkar Kor Ky	Prison	Renakse Docs. #356 & 352
34	Romeas Hek	—	Trapieng Elate	Prison	Renakse Docs. #356 & 352
35	Romeas Hek	—	Phum Ansoang	Prison	Renakse Docs. #356 & 352
36	Romeas Hek	Chrey Thom	Prey Bos Thnoat	Graves	DC–Cam Mapping Data
37	Romeas Hek	Chrey Thom	Tuol Akream	Graves	DC–Cam Mapping Data
38	Romeas Hek	Trapeang Sdao	Wat Svay Torteum	Graves	DC–Cam Mapping Data
39	Chantrea	Cheas	Kaoh Kor	Prison	Renakse Docs. #360
40	Chantrea	Samrong	Tuk Meas	Prison	CGDB BIO Rec. #Y00142 & #Y00099
41	Chantrea	Mestgnork	Bos	Prison	Renakse Docs. #6 & 360, CGP Mapping Data
42	Chantrea	Mestgnork	Tuol Kantuy Chhke	Graves	DC–Cam Mapping Data

Legend:

DC–Cam = Documentation Center of Cambodia

CGDB = Cambodian Genocide Data Bases

Renakse = A cataloging category in the DC–Cam archives

CGP = Cambodian Genocide Program

BIB Rec. = The CGDB Bibliographic Database

BIO Rec. = The CGDB Biographic Database

median Cambodian mass grave site, with about eighty mass grave pits. Other Killing Fields of particular note in Remeas Hek include Prey Bostnoat with fifteen pits and Wat Svay Torteum with twelve.

In Rumduol District, we have identified the location of one Khmer Rouge prison and two sites containing mass grave pits. In Rumduol, the Killing Field at the Tuol Popok Vil is unusual. The Documentation Center's mass grave mapping fieldwork suggests that the average number of victims in a mass grave pit is slightly above fifty (see the next chapter, "Digging in the Killing Fields"). The Tuol Popok Vil Killing Field has 400–500 mass graves, but the data suggest that the average number of victims per mass grave here is perhaps little more than five. Thus, the smaller, but quite numerous, mass graves at this particular location suggest a more careful and deliberate selection of victims than do those sites with hundreds or thousands of persons per mass grave.

In Svay Teap District, we know the location of two Khmer Rouge prisons and one mass grave site. At the Wat Kdey Rumduol Prison in Sang Kur commune, an individual who was classified as a Base Person during the Khmer Rouge regime recalls seeing victims marched in a line from the prison to the Killing Fields near the temple. They did not return. According to this witness, many of these victims, particularly early in the Khmer Rouge regime, were provincial officials from the Lon Nol regime.[25]

In Chantrea District, we have found three Khmer Rouge prisons and one mass grave site dating to the Khmer Rouge period. In Chantrea we also find an unusually large number of the smaller-type mass grave pits, suggestive of a more drawn-out, deliberate process of killing. The topography of Chantrea, with its low-lying land, most of it intensely cultivated rice paddies, is not conducive to the preservation of mass grave sites. Nonetheless, hundreds of mass grave pits are still recognizable. According to a local farmer, in the rice paddies adjacent to the remaining obvious sites, it is common to find human remains while tilling the fields there.

In Kompong Ro District during the Democratic Kampuchea regime, according to a PRK research report, there "were six pagodas transformed into detention centers and another twelve detention centers, one in each commune."[26] So far, the Documentation Center's research has uncovered three prisons and three mass grave sites in Kompong Ro dating from the Khmer Rouge era. At the prison site Wat Russei Sang, one witness who had been imprisoned for a minor offense said that he "saw many people being moved from that prison to other prisons as it filled."[27] Another witness said of the Killing Field associated with this particular prison that "when he was about 14 years old, he saw fifteen prisoners buried up to their necks in the fields nearby, and others tied to a bamboo tree to die. Two other boys who were walking past and saw this were shot by Khmer Rouge soldiers."[28]

Svay Chrum District is especially interesting given that it is adjacent to Svay Rieng provincial town and district. Here we have located two Khmer Rouge prisons and four mass grave sites associated with Democratic Kampuchea mass violence. Both of the prisons are notable. The prison at Wat Beong Rai was said to be the second largest prison in Svay Rieng Province.[29] The other known Khmer Rouge prison site in Svay Chrum District is at Tlork and was known as the "Tuol Sleng" of Svay Rieng Province.[30] Tuol Sleng, of course, was the Phnom Penh headquarters of the Khmer Rouge secret police. We may infer, then, that Tlork and Wat Beong Rai, along with Tuol Prich in nearby Svay Rieng provincial town, may have formed the backbone of internal security operations in Region 23.

Finally, in Svay Rieng District, the capital of Svay Rieng Province, we believe that we know of seven prisons and one mass grave site dating to the Khmer Rouge time in power. One of these Svey Rieng city prisons—the facility at Tuol Prich—was known as the "hot prison" and a "main killing center."[31] This suggests that the prison was part of the headquarters complex for state security in Region 23. Besides Tuol Prich's location at the provincial seat and its reputation as a "main killing center," another factor suggests its importance. The designation of Tuol Prich as a "hot prison" recalls the name of an elite group of interrogators—the "hot group"—at Khmer Rouge security services headquarters, Tuol Sleng Prison in Phnom Penh, who were specifically charged with carrying out torture.[32] Not far from Tuol Prich is Tlork Prison, called the "Tuol Sleng" of Svay Rieng. Moreover, "there was reference to prisoners being brought from the district prisons to Tlork for interrogation and execution."[33] This information would appear consistent with at least some of the hypotheses put forward by Henri Locard regarding the structure of the security system in the Khmer Rouge regime.

WITNESSES TO TERROR

What were the patterns of operation for these prisons before and after March 1978, that is, before and after forces loyal to Pol Pot ousted the indigenous Khmer Rouge from the east? This is a difficult question, but we can gain some insight based on interviews carried out by Documentation

Center Mass Grave Mapping Teams with witnesses who observed the operation of prisons and Killing Fields in Region 23. Several witnesses have testified about Khmer Rouge state-organized killing in Romeas Hek District of Region 23. One man, now graduated from Phnom Penh University, described his family's ordeal there. On April 17, 1975, his entire family was evacuated from Phnom Penh and settled in Tnoat village, Chrey Thom commune, Romeas Hek District, quite close to the Vietnam border.

> My mother was told [that] my grandmother was taken to be shot dead along with many other people in a pit, and the slaughter[er]s left the bodies on the ground like those of animals. It was afterwards, in 1977, that a new chief of the Phum [village] came in charge and at the time there were lots of youth escaping from the place to live in Vietnam as the place was close to Vietnam—just a passage as far as a canal, and one other kilometer walk from the canal—then there was safety. As many tried to escape, some were caught and taken to be killed. But not all members of the family were killed, as in the former chief's time. . . . Then the previous chief including all members of his family were taken to be killed, and a new chief was put in place. This was in fact the second renewed suffering burden.[34]

This witness testifies to varying degrees of brutality by successive leaders of his village, beginning with a high level of killing in 1975 and 1976, changing to a less brutal village chief in 1977, and then, after another purge and a new chief, a return to very high levels of killing in 1978. The first chief in 1975–1976 followed the Khmer Rouge policy of "root and branch," whereby when one member of a family was accused of wrongdoing, the entire family was executed. Apparently there was a brief respite under a new village chief in 1977, during which only those directly accused of wrongdoing were executed, rather than the entire family of anyone accused. Then with another change in village leadership, the policy reverted to "root and branch."

In 1997, a 56-year-old man from Romeas Hek District told of a different Killing Field, this one at Prey Bos Thnoat, Thmey village, Chrey Thom commune, Romeas Hek District.[35] "Every day, around forty to fifty victims were ordered by the killers to walk in lines. They were people from Svay Rieng and many others from Phnom Penh during 1975–76." Another man, a 41-year-old from Romeas Hek, discussed the Killing Field at Prey Akrien, Ansoang village, Chrey Thom commune, Romeas Hek District.[36] This witness says he saw victims being taken there to be killed.

"Most of the victims were male members of the 17 April people evacuated from Svay Rieng and the city. Other victims were people chosen through their biographies, and those taken from the security office in Prey Romdeng village, Chrey commune, and from the security office at Veal Svay. . . . In 1977, victims were brought to dig pits in Prey Akrian. In 1978, lines of 40 to 50 victims were taken to be killed there during the nighttime." The "biographies" mentioned here were the autobiographies that all citizens were periodically required to produce and through which the Khmer Rouge identified "enemies" who should be eliminated. Like previous witnesses, this individual noted that while there was much killing during 1975, 1976, and 1977, the violence increased in 1978.

Another Romeas Hek witness, a 67-year-old male, told us what he witnessed at Svay Tateum village in Trapaeng Sdao commune.[37] He said he saw "victims being walked in lines, taken from everywhere, especially from Srok Romduol. Approximately fifty to sixty persons walked the victims to Wat Svay Tateum, where the killers waited, received and temporarily put the victims in prison. During the following days, victims were interrogated and taken to be killed gradually during the night." This witness testified that the terror at Svay Torteum began in 1976 but that by "late 1977 and 1978, all the victims were killed; there were no survivors." Another witness to events at this same facility, a 60-year-old male, said, "Victims taken to be killed in the prison in Wat Svay Torteum included military police, soldiers, policemen, civil servants, teachers, and students during 1976 and 1977. Until 1978, it was a mass and cruel killing."

From Rumduol District, there is similar testimony. Speaking of a killing site at Khpoap Ampil, through the gateway of Wat Kampong Ampil, one witness told us that "victims taken to be killed here included soldiers, civil servants, teachers, students and intellectuals. They were people of both sexes and all ages. In 1975, during a period of two to three months, victims evacuated from Phnom Penh were taken to be killed here. It was the first phase of killing." Two other witnesses at this same location recalled the names of cadre responsible for killing at this site and noted that these perpetrators still live in the area today.

Elsewhere in Rumduol District, at Tuol Popok Vil, a 58-year-old witness described ruses used by the Khmer Rouge to select who would be the first "enemies" to be executed:

All the victims were taken both from the security office and the prison at
Tuol Popok Vil, as well as from Trapaeng Veng in Phum Tuol Chres, Khum

Chork. Among the victims were civil servants evacuated from the city and from all the collectives throughout Romduol District. In 1976, people were moved from one commune to another throughout the district. At that time, people were selected to be killed in accordance with the rule that anyone who was a soldier, second lieutenant, or first lieutenant was the first to be killed; subordinates, policemen, military police and spies were preferably the first to be killed. Although civil servants, teachers and students were deceived into thinking that they were assigned to plant potatoes and bananas, and would be allowed to have enough to eat, they instead were taken to be killed one by one gradually.[38]

Yet another Rumduol District witness, a 65-year-old male, described the Killing Fields where the Tuol Popok Vil victims were taken for disposal: "There are nine big pits and some 400 to 500 small pits. Each victim family of four to six members were put in the small pits, while forty to fifty victims were buried in the big pits. To sum up, there were around 2,000 to 2,500 people killed in the period of 1975–1977; the number of killings increased in 1978."[39] Once again, we see the pattern of large-scale killings up through 1977 and then an escalation of the violence in 1978.

A final example of recently collected witness testimony comes from Chantrea District. This witness, 48 years old at the time of the interview, had been a student at the time. He was imprisoned at Bos village, Mesthnork commune, for five months in 1975.

There were six security offices and prisons built with tile roofing during 1974–75. The building was used to detain students, policemen and military police. Civil servants in 1975 were the kinds of people evacuated from the city and Svay Rieng. . . . When interrogated, victims were all forced to confess, contrary to the truth, that they were second or first lieutenants. Those victims who readily confessed to being lieutenants, as they were forced to do, were the first taken to be killed. Anyone who denied to answer was kept aside for some reason for a while. Every day, people were forced to do manual labor, such as building dikes, digging canals, or digging ponds. If anyone could not fulfill their work, they were taken to be killed one by one. The killing lasted from 1975 to 1978. After this time, the prison was relocated.[40]

Thus, we see that in the earlier days of the Region 23 prison system, incarceration did not inevitably mean death. Still, this witness points out about the Killing Fields at Tuol Kantuy Chhke, which serviced the prison in which he was held, "There are hundreds of pits, big and small."

Beyond this witness testimony about the high levels of killing in Region 23 before 1978, there is also evidence that the Eastern Zone prisons were functioning as elements of an integrated national security system. People from Region 23, both "New People" and "Base People," were arrested and transported to Tuol Sleng Prison in Phnom Penh for processing. Among the forced confessions of prisoners at Tuol Sleng is one from Sa Son, a 31-year-old Khmer man, born in Tanor village, Svay Rieng commune, Svay Rieng District. Working as an engineer for the Lon Nol regime's Ministry of Information before April 17, he was sent out from Svay Rieng City to a farm in Region 22. On May 28, 1975, barely six weeks after the revolutionary victory, Sa Son was arrested and sent for interrogation and execution at S-21.[41]

Not only were personnel of the defeated regime persecuted, but also revolutionaries were already falling under suspicion of the new regime. An example is the forced confession of Kul Thai, a 44-year-old Khmer male.[42] Kul Thai was born in Ta Suos village, Tros commune, of Region 23. Both before and after April 17, 1975, he served in a Khmer Rouge military logistics force. He was arrested at South Boeng Trabek on November 14, 1975, and transferred to S-21, where he was interrogated, tortured, and then executed.

Finally, in addition to the routine arrests and executions, in 1978 a very large-scale mass execution of Eastern Zone citizens was carried out. The indiscriminate 1978 slaughter of Eastern Zone people has been well documented in previous scholarship,[43] but one example illustrates this development. During the 1979 People's Revolutionary Tribunal in Phnom Penh, a witness described his own culpability in carrying out some of these massacres. Siv Samon recounted that "on 12 August 1978, the Mean Cheay Security [a local security office] issued a circular of the Communist Party of Kampuchea to purge away lives of the people. We had 8 people altogether [assigned to the death squad]. We were assigned to kill 250 people of Krosaom Ark. . . . they were clubbed on the back side of the head with bamboo pipes and kicked into pits. I myself killed 20 of those people."[44]

The prosecutor of the tribunal pressed this line of questioning: "What type of people were killed? What were the accusations? How were they killed?" The witness answered, "We used [an] iron bar to kill them, so the victims did not scream and we didn't cut their limbs. They were people from Svay Rieng and they were under the accusations of being associated with Vietnam. The order was that those who had connection with Vietnam had to be exterminated." It appears that a "connection with Vietnam" became defined as anyone who lived in Eastern Zone regions along the border with Vietnam.

RECONSIDERING THE VIEWS OF KIERNAN AND LOCARD

Kiernan's conclusion that a large-scale execution of prisoners did not occur before late 1976 in the Eastern Zone cannot be sustained in light of the new data on Region 23. Based upon data concerning the structure and operations of the prison system, the provenance of the mass grave sites, and witness statements, it now appears that the Khmer Rouge security authorities were implementing a plan to eliminate all types of people who could be associated with the previous regime—military and police, teachers and students, intellectuals and urban dwellers, and their families—and that Khmer Rouge officials in Region 23 were carrying out these killings by early 1975, long before Pol Pot's forces achieved effective political control of the region. Indeed, because it appears that many of these Khmer Rouge security centers were established well before the victory of the revolution on April 17, 1975, mass killing by Eastern Zone Khmer Rouge authorities may well have been in progress before the Khmer Rouge achieved victory over the *ancien régime*.

By the same token, it appears that Kiernan *is* correct in his contention that the level of violence increased substantially after Pol Pot asserted control over Region 23, which by our reckoning occurred in early 1978. Numerous witnesses also confirm that some individuals in targeted categories survived detention by Eastern Zone authorities. Once they had completed their purge of Eastern Zone authorities in Region 23, Pol Pot's security forces rectified this oversight by seeking out and liquidating these remaining individuals and their families. Pol Pot also appeared to expand his list of official enemies, first, by adding all Khmer Rouge political and military cadre of the Eastern Zone and, finally, by defining all residents of the Eastern Zone as enemies with "Khmer bodies but Vietnamese minds." Thus, to summarize, it seems clear that lethal violence against the civilian population in Region 23 was an ordinary affair and that this violence was sustained at a high level under Eastern Zone CPK Secretary So Phim's leadership. After So Phim's forces were liquidated by Pol Pot, however, the violence reached even higher levels.

Likewise, Locard's conclusion that there were no variations in violence does not appear to be completely supported by the data. Witnesses are virtually unanimous in recalling that violence in Region 23 became much worse in 1978, after the purge of the Eastern Zone Khmer Rouge forces by military forces loyal to Pol Pot. This suggests that there were some variations in the intensity of violence in at least one region of Cambodia, depending upon the particular sort of revolutionary cadre who were in charge at a given time.

On the other hand, Locard's hypotheses concerning the structure of the Khmer Rouge prison system in the Eastern Zone, while not completely confirmed by the new data on Region 23, are also not inconsistent with those data. It is clear that many communes in Region 23 did contain Khmer Rouge detention and interrogation facilities and that most of these prisons were in operation well before 1978, when Pol Pot's forces took over the region. It is also clear, as Locard maintains, that at least several of the districts in Region 23 had "up to two or three or even four prisons."

Moreover, there is evidence indicating that this regional prison system was an integrated part of a centralized national internal security apparatus, feeding suspects up the chain of command to security headquarters in Phnom Penh prior to Pol Pot's imposition of control of Region 23 in 1978. Transfer of prisoners from commune-level to district-level prisons, from district-level to region-level prisons, and finally from region-level facilities to prisons controlled by officials reporting directly to Pol Pot, does not appear to have been unusual, either before or after the imposition of Pol Pot's authority in Region 23. Widespread arrests based on class, religious, political, and other criteria, high rates of death in detention, and compelling evidence of mass executions suggest that it is not unreasonable to characterize human rights abuses in Region 23 as extreme, even prior to the takeover of the eastern parts of Cambodia by Pol Pot's forces.

TERROR IN THE EAST

This case study has examined only one region of one zone in the Khmer Rouge state of Democratic Kampuchea. It is perilous to generalize on the basis of such a small sample. Moreover, the proximity of Region 23 to Vietnam placed it on the front line of a central nexus of Cambodian history, Cambodian–Vietnamese conflict. Therefore, it is possible that Region 23 is not a typical region of the Eastern Zone, in particular, and that it is not typical of regions originally outside the control of forces loyal to Pol Pot, in general. A more thorough study that looks in detail at other regions of the Eastern Zone and at regions in other zones—such as the west, the northwest, and the north—is required to resolve this uncertainty.[45]

Despite these remaining uncertainties, the evidence presented in this chapter affords insight into the differing interpretations of the relative levels of violence in Democratic Kampuchea offered by Locard and Kiernan. It seems clear that at least some authorities in So Phim's Eastern Zone were largely cooperating in a plan to liquidate many members of the class of Cambodians labeled as "New People." Virtually all of the witnesses say that those imprisoned and killed before March 1978 were primarily "New People." As Pol Pot's forces seized control of the east, a new class of victims arose: Eastern Zone Khmer Rouge cadre and military personnel. With time, it appears, this class of victims was expanded to include all residents of the east; they were seen as complicit in the "rebelliousness" of Eastern Zone authorities and as fatally compromised by their physical proximity to Vietnam.

Thus, Kiernan is correct in that levels of repression and extrajudicial execution escalated significantly after the seizure of power by Pol Pot's forces in Region 23. Pol Pot's policy appears to have evolved toward the annihilation of all living persons in Region 23, the ultimate indicia of state terror. By the same token, Locard is correct in that the levels of violence in Region 23 were already extreme prior to the ouster of the Eastern Zone authorities by forces loyal to Pol Pot. Although it evolved through distinct phases and gradually grew worse over time, we can conclude that during the Khmer Rouge regime, terror in the Eastern Zone was continuous and ubiquitous.

It is therefore incorrect to suggest that the Eastern Zone Khmer Rouge cadre who escaped Pol Pot's purges and who later returned under the cover of the Vietnamese invasion to build the successor regime to the Khmer Rouge regime were in no way complicit in the mass terror that characterized Democratic Kampuchea. It is clear enough that this successor regime ended many of the most egregious human rights violations that existed under the Khmer Rouge regime. Even so, it is no wonder that many Cambodians, seeing many of those who had persecuted them under Pol Pot returning to positions of power after Pol Pot was overthrown, would have doubts about the integrity of their new government, even as the full extent of Pol Pot's atrocities was revealed when the new government began to uncover Cambodia's many Killing Fields.

7

Digging in the Killing Fields

In April 1994, the U.S. government was quietly considering whether or not to extend military assistance to the recently established Royal Government of Cambodia. Reflecting the surprisingly effective organizational and intelligence capabilities of Khmer Rouge support organizations in the United States, the Khmer Rouge mounted a small public demonstration—involving no more than a score of people—in Washington's Lafayette Park on Pennsylvania Avenue in front of the White House, to protest against the possibility of military aid to the Phnom Penh regime.

At that time I was executive director of the Campaign to Oppose the Return of the Khmer Rouge, and in that capacity I attended the demonstration with the objective of identifying and photographing the Khmer Rouge cadre directing the protest. I soon found myself engaged in a conversation with the individual who appeared to be the leader of the small band of protesters, a man who called himself Bun Than Eng. Eng was the publisher of a pro–Khmer Rouge newspaper in Lowell, Massachusetts. After asking him about the purpose of the demonstration and who was supporting their protest, I commented to Eng that I had heard of something called the "Killing Fields," where the Khmer Rouge had killed many people. He fixed me with a steely glare and hissed, "The Killing Fields is a fiction. It never happened."

If nothing else, the Khmer Rouge deserved some credit for their discipline in consistently denying the reality of the massive slaughter they carried out in Cambodia with such black-hearted efficiency. Until Ieng Sary's 1996 defection, Khmer Rouge officials had always denied that their murderous policies existed and denied that they had littered Cambodia's landscape with the grim remains of countless victims deemed unnecessary to their xenophobic and chauvinistic utopia. This obsessive secrecy served as their shield against the obtrusive glare of truth, and the isolation of Cambodia from the international community through the 1980s and into the 1990s inadvertently aided the Khmer Rouge in keeping the whole truth from coming into the light of the world outside Cambodia.

Denial of genocide is an evil thing, in some ways perhaps even more offensive than genocide itself, for it abuses the dignity of the victims for yet a second time. Scholars have noted that denial of genocide by perpetrators and by their ideological heirs is one aspect of genocidal violence that seems to be common across virtually all instances of mass killing.

Why do genocidists and other mass killers deny? There are several reasons.[1] The simplest reason may be guilt: many of them may realize that mass killing is terribly wrong, and they do not wish to be implicated in wrongdoing, especially on so massive a scale as that involved in genocidal atrocities. There are more pragmatic reasons, as well. The most compelling of these may be the impulse to avoid responsibility, to evade judgment and punishment either of themselves during their lifetimes or of their reputations in the eyes of history.

There is a darker reason for the denial of genocide. Common to all genocidal situations is the dehumanization of the victims, the declaration that these "enemies" are not worthy of membership in the human race, that they are animals or even lower creatures, parasites whose extermination is a thing to be positively valued. Thus, denying genocide is the final stage in the debasement of the victims: denial of their ontological status, a positive affirmation that the victims, perceived as not worthy of existing, in fact never did exist. Thus is denial of genocide the final, most insulting phase of this evil phenomenon.

The most effective way to combat the evil inherent in the denial of genocide is thorough documentation of the crimes. Documentation of genocide involves collecting evidence of the real lives of both victims and perpetrators, in the form of documents, witness testimony, and physical evidence such as photographs, concentration camp buildings, instruments of torture, and mass graves, as well as other forms of information about the historical reality. This kind of work is the mission of the Documentation Center of Cambodia.

THE "NUMBER"

Many Cambodians believe, almost as an article of faith, that the Khmer Rouge killed more than 3 million people during the Democratic Kampuchea regime. When this estimate of the Khmer Rouge death toll was first publicized in 1979, commentators in the West almost universally dismissed it as a product of Vietnamese propaganda, an invented figure designed strictly for political purposes.[2] In later years, more sober analysts examining this 3 million figure also discounted it, basing their much lower estimates of the death toll on interview data, demographic analyses, and other statistical methodologies.

Yet, the 3 million figure was not a complete invention. In the early 1980s, the authorities of the People's Republic of Kampuchea carried out what amounted to a national household survey, aiming to interview every head of household in the entire country about what had happened to their families during the Pol Pot regime. On July 25, 1983, the "Research Committee on Pol Pot's Genocidal Regime" issued its final report, including detailed, province-by-province data. Among other things, their data showed that 3,314,768 people lost their lives in the "Pol Pot time."[3] But that report was quickly forgotten inside Cambodia, and it never became known outside Cambodia—until 1995.

More than a decade after this report was published, researchers working at the Documentation Center of Cambodia discovered many of the records from this remarkable research project. Those records permitted investigators to reconstruct the methodology employed by the research committee, exposing some flaws in their research design that would tend to lead to an overestimation of the total casualty figure. The research committee interviewers of the early 1980s had gone from village to village, collecting death tolls from heads of household.[4] It appeared, however, that they did not adequately account for the fact that extended families are usually spread out across more than one household or village, and therefore double counting of some victims could occur based on reports from different households belonging to the same extended family.

There were other flaws in the research design, as well. For example, in addition to the household survey, research committee investigators devoted a significant amount of effort to examining mass graves from the Khmer Rouge era. In many cases, the committee sponsored the exhumation of mass graves that had been discovered in various locations, providing a hard count of bodies interred in the pits and other types of graves. These numbers were added to the count derived from the household interviews to yield the 3.3 million number. However, it would have been difficult—if not impossible—to identify all those cases where an individual reported by family members as having been killed was the same individual whose remains were tallied from the mass grave exhumations.

Documentation Center investigators subsequently concluded that the 3.3 million death toll figure reported by this Research Committee may have been overestimated by a factor of perhaps 50 percent, putting the actual death toll somewhere nearer to 2 million. Despite apparent flaws in their methodology, however, the work carried out by these earlier researchers provided many helpful leads to later investigators. For example, the interviews carried out by the Research Committee during their household survey garnered many details regarding specific events in various parts of the country, as well as identities for some lower-level officers in the Khmer Rouge command structure, who could later be tracked down and interviewed.

A NEW APPROACH

Since 1995, researchers at the Documentation Center of Cambodia have continued to study this elusive question of "the Number" using a new methodological approach: mass grave survey research. The goal is to locate, map, and determine the provenance of each and every mass grave in Cambodia. As previously noted, the Documentation Center has located mass grave sites in virtually every district visited so far by its field researchers. The results from the first five years of surveys are quite startling. Some 20,000 mass graves dating from the Khmer Rouge regime have been located. The numbers may grow before the survey work is complete, but the data collected to date suggest that the mass graves located so far contain the remains of 1,110,829 victims of execution. Table 7.1 gives a province-by-province breakdown of the data.

Let's look a little more closely at these numbers. Between 1995 and the beginning of 2000, Documentation Center mass grave mapping teams had visited nineteen out of Cambodia's twenty-one provinces. Of Cambodia's 170 districts, the teams had made at least one visit to 150 of the districts. In the process, they managed to survey approximately two-thirds of Cambodia's subdistricts. Many subdistricts in the northern and northwestern regions of the country have not yet been carefully surveyed, due to obvious security considerations, as these areas are often still controlled by "former" Khmer Rouge who are not always enthusiastic about this research. Preah Vihear province has not been surveyed at all, as yet. Some Khmer Rouge remained in armed opposition to the government in these regions until the beginning of 1999, and though the armed insurgency has since ceased, these same people still live there, and they remain armed.

Because it is likely that densely populated northwestern provinces such as Battambang and Banteay Meanchey had high rates of execution during the Khmer Rouge regime, it seems probable that the estimate of the number of victims in the mass graves may rise when the mapping surveys are finally completed. If so, the total number of victims identified in mass graves would eventually end up higher than the figures presented here.

The 20,000 or so mass graves mapped thus far are virtually all located at, or near, Khmer Rouge security centers. Witnesses at most of the mass grave sites testify that the graves contain victims brought there by Khmer Rouge security forces and that the victims were killed either in the adjacent prisons or at the mass grave sites themselves. Thus, one can conclude that virtually all of these mass graves contain victims who were executed by the Khmer Rouge or who died in custody.

Table 7.1 shows that the mapping teams had by the beginning of 2000 examined a total of 432 different "genocide sites," as the locations of prisons, mass graves, and memorials are known to Documentation Center team members. There are many types and sizes of mass graves at these sites. These include the most common type of mass grave, the simple earthen pit, as well as more unusual types, such as wells, caves, kilns, and open paddy land.

Table 7.2 shows that there is an average of 169 victims per mass grave, though if we neglect the data for one anomalous province, Kratie, this figure would be reduced to about 51. But even that is misleading, because it appears that there were several different "modes" of mass grave creation. There are very large numbers of small mass graves, each containing perhaps 5 victims or so, in many cases apparently members of the same nuclear family: husband, wife, and a few children. Mapping teams have also found a large number of medium-sized mass graves, containing perhaps from 100 to several hundred victims. Witness testimony suggests that this type of mass grave was most often created when the inmate population of a particular security center was flushed out to make room for a new batch of prisoners.

Then, there are the big ones: mass graves containing thousands of victims. These seem to be more common in certain provinces such as Kampong Chhnang, Kampong Thom, and Kampong Cham, though they do

TABLE 7.1. INTERIM SUMMARY STATISTICS ON MASS GRAVE SURVEYS, 1995–1999*

Province	Total # of Sites	Estimated # of Pits	Wells/Other Used as Graves	Prison Sites	Memorial Sites	Estimated # of Victims	**Estimated # of Complaints
Banteay Meanchey	17	567	0	4	3	40,782	***
Battambang	22	1,070	0	8	6	37,195	429,480
Kampong Cham	61	3,035	11	13	9	176,423	79,450
Kampong Chhnang	30	3,143	1	6	3	253,154	44,865
Kampong Speu	20	1,549	1	4	2	24,332	50,808
Kampong Thom	18	1,427	5	6	5	123,808	119,578
Kampot	22	2,761	0	7	3	55,625	25,632
Kandal	43	504	4	13	9	102,804	68,680
Koh Kong	1	0	0	1	0	17,349	5,670
Kratie	9	7	1	1	4	13,339	—
Mondulkiri	2	1	0	1	0	0	—
Phnom Penh	7	0	0	3	2	0	—
Preah Vihear	Not Yet Surveyed					—	—
Prey Veng	43	1,804	12	8	3	89,406	68,351
Pursat	21	2,167	10	13	3	53,050	38,576
Ratanakiri	4	33	0	1	0	2,300	—
Siem Reap	29	715	5	9	2	77,873	3,952
Krong Preah Sihanouk	15	570	0	6	0	2,600	—
Stung Treng	8	61	0	4	1	4,000	8,053
Svay Rieng	35	166	0	9	11	5,107	34,737
Takeo	25	862	0	8	5	33,682	72,244
Totals	432	20,442	50	125	71	1,112,829	1,050,076

*The data are drawn from the 1997, 1998, and 1999 Mass Grave Mapping Reports, Documentation Center of Cambodia; 1995 and 1996 data are summarized in the 1997 report.

**Estimated number of complaints from Report of Research Committee on Genocide Crime, July 25, 1983.

***Included in data for Siem Reap.

TABLE 7.2. INTERIM DESCRIPTIVE STATISTICS ON MASS GRAVE SURVEYS, 1995–1999

Province	Graves per Site	Graves per District	Graves per Prison	Prisons per District	Victims per Grave	Victims per Site	Victims per District	Victims per Prison
Banteay Meanchey	33	71	142	0.50	72	2,399	5,098	10,196
Battambang	49	134	134	1.00	35	1,691	4,649	4,649
Kampong Cham	50	190	234	0.81	58	2,892	11,026	13,571
Kampong Chhnang	105	393	524	0.75	81	8,438	31,644	42,192
Kampong Speu	78	194	388	0.50	16	1,217	3,042	6,083
Kampong Thom	80	179	239	0.75	87	6,878	15,476	20,635
Kampot	126	345	394	0.88	20	2,528	6,953	7,946
Kandal	12	46	39	1.18	204	2,391	9,346	7,908
Koh Kong	0	0	0	0.14	—	17,349	2,478	17,349
Kratie	1	2	8	0.20	1906	1,482	2,668	13,339
Mondulkiri	1	0	1	0.20	0	0	0	0
Phnom Penh	0	0	0	0.43	0	0	0	0
Preah Vihear	N/A	N/A	N/A	N/A	N/A	N/A	N/A	N/A
Prey Veng	42	151	227	0.67	50	2,079	7,451	11,176
Pursat	104	435	167	2.60	24	2,526	10,610	4,081
Ratanakiri	8	4	33	0.11	70	575	256	2,300
Siem Reap	25	51	80	0.64	109	2,685	5,562	8,653
Krong Preah Sihanouk	38	190	95	2.00	5	173	867	433
Stung Treng	8	12	15	0.80	66	500	800	1,000
Svay Rieng	5	28	18	1.50	31	146	851	567
Takeo	34	86	108	0.80	39	1,347	3,368	4,210
Averages	42	132	150	0.87	169	3,016	6,429	9,278

Average number of victims/mass grave omitting anomalous Kratie ———→ 51

Note: N/A = data currently unavailable.

occur in various other places across the country. This largest type of mass grave appears to be associated with large-scale, indiscriminate population purges, such as when it was determined that the population of an entire district was to be liquidated. The largest mass grave located to date is reported by a witness who assisted in exhuming it to have contained the remains of some 7,000 victims.

In many districts visited by Documentation Center mapping teams, additional genocide sites—some of which are reputed to be very large—are believed to exist but could not be surveyed by the team due to a variety of unfavorable factors ranging from security concerns, inclement environmental conditions, logistical difficulties, or scheduling problems. Thus, there exist more sites in districts already visited than are recorded in the data presented here. Moreover, in many cases for sites actually surveyed, for a variety of reasons the team made no attempt to estimate the actual number of mass grave pits, and therefore those sites are recorded as containing zero mass grave pits and zero victims. (We return to this question later under the topic of limitations of the data.) Thus, the raw count of some 20,000 mass graves remains a conservative estimate, even for the 150 at least partially mapped districts for which data are presented here.

BREAKING DOWN THE DATA

Tables 7.1 and 7.2 show that mass grave mapping teams had located 124 Khmer Rouge prison facilities by the beginning of 2000, an average of nearly one prison per district, which is quite a high number for a country whose officials denied the existence of any prisons at all. The data suggest that on average, each of these prisons "processed" nearly 10,000 persons each, with fatal results for every person so processed. However, as Table 7.2 demonstrates, this average varies considerably from province to province. In some provinces—Ratanakiri, Preah Sihanouk, and Svay Rieng, for example—the average is much lower, in the vicinity of 500 victims per prison, while in others—especially Kampong Chhnang and Kampong Thom—the average is significantly higher, up to more than 40,000 victims per prison in one case. An average of 150 mass graves are associated with each prison, though again, the provincial averages range widely, from a low of 8 mass graves per prison in Kratie and a high of 524 mass graves per prison in Kampong Chhnang. Table 7.2 shows an average of 42 mass graves and a little under 3,000 victims per site, which in turn reflects the finding that there were typically 3–4 mass grave sites associated with each prison.

Table 7.3 presents the data in the light of population distributions in Cambodia. Using demographic estimates of the population of each province as of June 1975, after the first major round of population relocations carried out by the Khmer Rouge, we see that there are great regional population variations, from the sparsely populated mountainous northeast where provinces such as Ratanakiri, Mondulkiri, and Stung Treng each boast less than 1 percent of the total population, to the densely populated lowland provinces such as Battambang, Kampong Cham, Kampong Thom, Kandal, and Prey Veng, which together account for more than half of Cambodia's entire population. This table attempts to address several issues. What were the regional patterns of the violence? Was the violence uniform or variable? In other words, did the Khmer Rouge kill people at the same rate everywhere?

Comparing the number of victims the Documentation Center data suggest are interred in mass graves for each province to the population of that province helps us get a better sense of the patterns of violence during the Khmer Rouge regime. Kampong Chhnang is an anomaly, with only 4 percent of the total population but more than 20 percent of the total victims. This can be accounted for due to the fact that large numbers of people were transferred to Kampong Chhnang for execution from the Eastern Zone of Democratic Kampuchea during the so-called Eastern Zone Massacres in the first half of 1978. Another factor that may account for the disproportionate execution rate in Kampong Chhnang is the fact that the Khmer Rouge, with Chinese technical assistance, were building a large military airport complex in Kampong Chhnang using slave labor, and, according to local witnesses, the slave labor brigades employed in the massive construction project were routinely executed en masse when they became too weak to perform efficiently. As a result, Kampong Chhnang earns the highest score on the "Brutality Index," which is derived by dividing the percentage of total victims into the percentage of total population for each province.

In general, provincial scores on the Brutality Index cluster around 1.0, with many provinces ranging from 0.5 to 1.5, indicating a remarkable degree of uniformity in execution rates across most parts of Cambodia. On the other end of the range from Kampong Chhnang, Svay Rieng is another anomaly with a Brutality Index score of 0.17. This may be because

TABLE 7.3. INTERIM ANALYTICAL STATISTICS ON MASS GRAVE SURVEYS, 1995–1999

Province	Population at June 1975*	% Total Population	Victims per Province	% Total Victims	Victims/ Population	Brutality Index
Banteay Meanchey**	—	—	—	—	—	—
Battambang	962	13.31%	77,977	7.01%	8.11%	0.53
Kampong Cham	1,226	16.96%	176,423	15.85%	14.39%	0.93
Kampong Chhnang	287	3.97%	253,154	22.75%	88.21%	5.73
Kampong Speu	299	4.14%	24,332	2.19%	8.14%	0.53
Kampong Thom	580	8.02%	123,808	11.13%	21.35%	1.39
Kampot	435	6.02%	55,625	5.00%	12.79%	0.83
Kandal	618	8.55%	102,804	9.24%	16.63%	1.08
Koh Kong	42	0.58%	17,349	1.56%	41.31%	2.68
Kratie	317	4.38%	13,339	1.20%	4.21%	0.27
Mondulkiri	16	0.22%	0	0.00%	0.00%	0.00
Phnom Penh	142	1.96%	0	0.00%	0.00%	0.00
Preah Vihear	39	0.54%	—	—	—	—
Prey Veng	571	7.90%	89,406	8.03%	15.66%	1.02
Pursat	444	6.14%	53,050	4.77%	11.95%	0.78
Ratanakiri	48	0.66%	2,300	0.21%	4.79%	0.31
Siem Reap***	377	5.21%	77,873	7.00%	20.66%	1.34
Krong Preah Sihanouk	0	0.00%	2,600	0.23%	0.00%	—
Stung Treng	46	0.64%	4,000	0.36%	8.70%	0.56
Svay Rieng	190	2.63%	5,107	0.46%	2.69%	0.17
Takeo	591	8.17%	33,682	3.03%	5.70%	0.37
Totals	7,230	100.00	1,112,829	100.00		
Averages					16.30%	

*Population in 1000s by province as of June 1975 from Sliwinski (1995) Table 1, p. 26.

**Banteay Meanchey was incorporated into Battambang in 1975.

***Siem Reap data include population numbers for Oddar Meanchey.

many victims from Svay Rieng—parts of which are surrounded on three sides by Vietnam—were reportedly transferred to execution sites in adjacent, more secure provinces for disposal. Another set of exceptions again is found in the provinces of the northeast, where Kratie scores just 0.27, and Ratanakiri has the lowest score of 0.04. This result is consistent with reports that Khmer Rouge leader Pol Pot developed a somewhat bizarre anthropological theory, holding that the tribal minorities populating the northeast in some sense represented pure "original" Cambodians, largely uncontaminated by Buddhism and other Khmer traditions or by urban "diseases" such as commerce. Consequently, demands from the highest levels of the party for purges of this population cohort may have been muted in comparison with the bulk of the lowland population. It should also be noted that the data on Battambang, in particular, remain incomplete, with few districts fully surveyed to date. It is therefore likely that the Brutality Index for that province will rise substantially as more data are collected.

Chapter 6 concerns the question of whether the level of Khmer Rouge violence in the Eastern Zone of Cambodia was notably less severe than in other zones of Democratic Kampuchea. In this connection, it is worth noting that the Eastern Zone was composed of Svay Rieng and Prey Veng Provinces, along with a large chunk of Kampong Cham Province and a sliver of Mondulkiri Province. The bulk of the Eastern Zone was made up of Prey Veng Province and the western part of Kampong Cham Province. Prey Veng rates a Brutality Index score of 1.02, while Kampong Cham has a score of 0.93. These data suggest that at least for most of the Eastern Zone, the levels of violence were comparable to other places in Cambodia during the Khmer Rouge regime.

ESTIMATING THE TOTAL DEATH TOLL

How can we determine the total death toll during the Khmer Rouge regime, above and beyond deaths by execution? In principle, there are several possible approaches. One method is to survey a sample of survivors about deaths in their families and then statistically extrapolate that result to the population as a whole. As noted earlier, a Cambodian government study using this method and completed in 1983 concluded that more than 3.3 million perished in the Khmer Rouge regime.[5] Ben Kiernan surveyed 500 Cambodians in 1979–1980 to extrapolate a total death toll of some 1.67 million.[6] Steve Heder surveyed more than 1,000 subjects and calculated the Khmer Rouge death toll at 1.7 million.[7] Marek Sliwinski sur-

veyed some 1,300 Cambodians in 1989–1991 and estimated the population drop during the Khmer Rouge regime at 2.16 million, of which he
concluded that 1.84 to 1.87 million were deaths due to the genocide.[8] It
is interesting that three of these investigations, all using a similar methodology, achieved similar results, in the range of 1.67 to 1.87 million. This is
particularly remarkable given the difficulties of constructing a representative sample of interview subjects.

Another approach to estimating the total death toll is through demographic analysis. A demographic study in 1980 by the U.S. Central Intelligence Agency concluded that the population of Cambodia had declined
by somewhere between 1.2 and 1.8 million during the Khmer Rouge
regime.[9] Judith Bannister and Paige Johnson calculated that the population
loss in Cambodia between 1975 and 1979 was 1.8 million, and they determined that "excess mortality" was slightly more than 1.05 million; in
other words, there were 1.05 million more deaths than would be expected
under normal circumstances.[10] Patrick Heuveline used more recent population data to conclude that excess mortality during the Khmer Rouge
regime was 2.2 million.[11] Thus, we see a wide span in the estimates derived from demographic methods, ranging from 1.05 to 2.2 million. This
uncertainty is not surprising in view of the paucity of reliable census data
in Cambodia and the lack of accurate information about trends in fertil-
ity and mortality rates.

A third approach relies on estimates of the contents of mass graves, in
combination with other information. Such an estimate is possible on the
basis of the Documentation Center mass grave data. This calculation requires determining the ratio of those who died due to mass killing to
those who perished individually from other causes such as disease, starvation, or exhaustion. Several analysts have attempted to calculate this ratio.
According to historian Ben Kiernan, data collected by Milton Osborne
indicated that executions amounted to only 31 percent of all deaths during the Khmer Rouge regime.[12] Other work carried out by a political
scientist, Steve Heder, suggested that different proportions of the total
death toll could be attributed to execution for urban versus rural dwellers,
about 33 percent among "New People" and 50 percent among "Base People."[13] The demographer Marek Sliwinski estimates that about 40 percent
of the death toll resulted from execution, 36 percent from starvation, 13
percent from disease, and the remainder from either combat or natural
causes.[14] The most methodologically sophisticated attempt to answer this
question is found in recent work by demographer Patrick Heuveline.

Heuveline's work also uses more recent data than do the other analyses. His analysis suggests that the most likely total number of deaths due to excess mortality during the four years of the Khmer Rouge regime was 2.2 million and that 50 percent of these were due to violent causes, that is, execution.[15] Because Heuveline's work takes into account the previous analyses, and because he also uses more recent population data, I conclude that his estimate of the proportion of deaths due to execution is likely to be the most reliable.

When compared with the Documentation Center mass grave data, the implications of Heuveline's analysis are striking. His estimate that 50 percent of the total death toll was the result of executions conforms precisely to the estimated number of executions found in the mass grave data, about 1.1 million. This congruence is particularly notable in view of the fact that the two methods are so different. Together, the two methods suggest that the total number of deaths is 2.2 million. If the "excess mortality" or number of people killed during the Khmer Rouge regime was 2.2 million, and if the total population was between 7.0 and 7.5 million at the outset of the mass killing, then between 29 percent and 31 percent—nearly one-third—of the Cambodian population died during the Khmer Rouge regime. It is important to note, however, that as with the survey and demographic methods discussed earlier, the mass grave method is also subject to uncertainties. We now turn to a consideration of some of these limitations in the mass grave data set.

PROBLEMS AND LIMITATIONS OF THE DATA

The Documentation Center mass grave mapping data should be considered a preliminary finding. More data need to be collected. There are numerous uncertainties in the existing mass grave data set, and resolving those uncertainties in the data requires further research. That research continues at the Documentation Center. Meanwhile, the five-year mark of this research project offered an opportunity to assess the strengths and weaknesses of the existing data and to note some problems and limitations in the methodology that should be addressed in future efforts.

Historian Michael Vickery has criticized the use of mass grave data to construct estimates of the death toll during the Khmer Rouge regime. Although his criticism predates the Documentation Center's mass grave mapping project, some of his points nonetheless apply. Referring to overall estimates of the Khmer Rouge death toll as of 1984, Vickery argued,

Given the lack of precision inherent in all the data and estimates, it is impossible to reach more accurate final totals, or to more precisely apportion the decrease [in the Cambodian population] among executions, deaths from illness and hunger, or failure to reproduce due to changed living circumstances. Some of the burial pits discovered provide the evidence that mass executions occurred, but there is as yet no way to count the number of executions separately from death due to other causes. Yathay pointed out that in Pursat in 1976–77 mass graves were for those who died of hunger and illness, while executions took place in isolation in the forest. Moreover, some of the 500,000 war victims are buried in mass graves, and without forensic tests it is probably impossible to determine whether death occurred before or after 1975. A decline of 400,000 does, I would say, indicate failure of the DK [Democratic Kampuchea] system, but some of the more extreme estimates of death from execution and hunger must be relegated to the realm of black propaganda. It is simply impossible to take the generally accepted population figure for April 1975, the population alive today, demographically acceptable birth rates, and project an extermination figure of 1–2,000,000.[16]

There are a number of points in Vickery's arguments that the Documentation Center data must address. First of all, Vickery's contention that it is demographically impossible for the "extermination" toll to have been as high as 1 million or more is not supported by the analyses of actual demographers. Marek Sliwinski's demographic analysis estimates that between 1974–1975 and 1979, the total population of Cambodia declined by somewhere between 1.9 million and 2.5 million, with his most likely estimate 2.16 million.[17] Demographers Judith Banister and Paige Johnson argue that the decline in population between 1975 and the end of 1978 was 1.8 million.[18] A study by Patrick Heuveline published in 1998 estimates that the total death toll during the Khmer Rouge regime was somewhere in the range of 1.5 to 2.5 million, with the most likely figure hovering around 2.2 million.[19] Thus, whether referring to the population decline or to the death toll, analyses by professional demographers on this demographic question do not support Vickery's conclusions.

Vickery further argues that it is impossible to distinguish between mass graves containing victims of starvation or war, as opposed to those containing victims of execution. Documentation Center mapping teams have located a number of sites where the local informants say that the mass graves were in fact not from Khmer Rouge executions but rather from the bombing, the 1970–1975 war, victims of mass starvation, and even one or two associated with the Vietnamese invasion of 1979. As Vickery suggests, however, this is difficult to prove absent forensic analysis. In some cases, starvation appears to have been a Khmer Rouge method to execute large numbers of people easily and cheaply. Even so, those instances are not recorded in the mass grave data as executions per se unless the starvation occurred in prison, since the mapping project is an effort to find out about the death of people in custody.

In two instances, Documentation Center mapping teams have discovered mass graves that were attributed to the victims of bombing during the 1970–1975 war. It appears that the vast majority of the victims of the bombing were simply vaporized, which is not surprising if one considers what happens in a B-52 "footprint." Those bombing fatalities who were not shredded to tiny bits, it would appear, were cremated according to traditional Cambodian funeral practices. The U.S. strategic bombing of Cambodia ended in August 1973, and it was just around that time that the Khmer Rouge began to institute their draconian policies in the liberated zones, which henceforth prohibited traditional religious and funerary practices, including cremation.[20]

Interviewers on the Documentation Center mass grave mapping teams have accumulated a great deal of experience in this peculiar line of work and have learned how to dig down beneath the surface claims and extract information that permits them to assess the reliability of their informants. Moreover, to call into question the information collected in subdistricts across the whole length and breadth of Cambodia, where local witnesses testify to the existence of Khmer Rouge execution centers and the location of the mass graves in which the victims' remains were discarded, presumes a nationwide conspiracy of unlikely proportions. Although it appears entirely possible that certain socially acceptable and politically shaped myths may influence the precise contours of the narratives collected by mass grave mapping teams, it seems highly improbable that these social pressures would extend so far as to the fabrication of ruins of former prison facilities, the placing of physical evidence such as shackles in those ruins, or the construction of anguished, but false, accounts of relatives killed in the Khmer Rouge extermination centers.

In any event, while interviews with eyewitnesses are an important part of the data collection procedure, they are far from the whole procedure. The first step in the mass grave mapping process is to locate the site of a former Khmer Rouge security center. The country is dotted with the ruins of these prisons, which were often destroyed by enraged locals in the immediate aftermath of the Khmer Rouge regime. In some cases, however—quite tastelessly, one has to say—Khmer Rouge execution facilities were salvaged and pressed into service as the local headquarters for the ruling party in the wake of the Pol Pot regime.

The next step in the mapping process, after finding a former Khmer Rouge prison facility, is to locate people who survived incarceration there during the Khmer Rouge regime or who were employed at the security center. This tends to be much more common than one might think. In many instances, it has been possible to find actual perpetrators—employees of the *Santebal* security organization—who worked at a particular security center. Sometimes, these people give what amount to confessions of what they and their colleagues did during the Khmer Rouge regime. From there, the mapping teams work outward to determine where inmates from a particular security center who did not survive the experience were buried. Thus, the mass grave mapping process does not simply rely on interviews with locals who happen to be randomly encountered. The mapping expeditions are carried out according to a highly structured procedure.

It bears repeating that virtually all of these mass graves sites are located at, or quite near—usually within a kilometer or so—of the Khmer Rouge security centers. In many cases, local informants recall the names of the cadre who were in charge of these Khmer Rouge prisons or killing centers. Surprisingly often, it is subsequently possible to locate these former Khmer Rouge security cadre for follow-up interviews. Moreover, the Documentation Center has a huge archive of internal documents from the Khmer Rouge secret police, and it sometimes transpires that researchers can take the names associated with a particular killing place as provided by local informants and then verify that information using the Khmer Rouge's own internal documents. Sometimes, on the other hand, this process is reversed; names are found in *Santebal* documents in the Documentation Center archive, and then Documentation Center investigators locate those individuals and, in the course of interviewing them, obtain new information about various Khmer Rouge security centers.

A key question in assessing the overall validity of the mass grave mapping data set is the reliability of estimates of the numbers of mass graves and victims. There is no doubt that the quality of the reporting by different mass grave mapping teams over the years has varied. For this reason,

some of the quantitative estimates at particular sites and some witness testimony gathered in various locales—particularly from some of the missions
carried out in the first years of work—may deserve revisiting. Still, the skill
and experience of these teams have grown year by year, mapping trip by
mapping trip, and the teams have become grimly professional at their task.
The estimates of numbers of victims in particular mass grave pits are not
based on passerby guesstimates or the lore provided by local ruling party
officials. In some cases, information about victim counts at particular sites
comes from people who participated in mass grave exhumations at those
sites. Often these verbally reported numbers can subsequently be verified
by hard skull-counts in adjacent memorials, as well as by local records kept
of the exhumations. In some cases, documents have been identified that
recorded the actual executions themselves, compiled by the perpetrators.
In other cases, investigators who have seen hundreds or thousands of mass
grave pits make the estimates themselves based on the number, type, and
size of the mass graves. In yet other cases, as previously mentioned, the victim counts are based on actual perpetrator testimony—and the perpetrators certainly do not have an obvious motive to inflate the numbers.

Fairly often, the mapping team decides that it cannot under the prevailing circumstances make a reasonable estimate of the number of victims
in a particular location where large numbers of mass graves are located.
The default procedure in such instances is to record the number of mass
graves and/or victims for that site as zero. This particular technique cre-
ates an overall conservative bias in the data. Several examples illustrate this
conservative bias in the data collection methodology.

On one mapping trip the author accompanied for auditing purposes in
1996, in Sa-ang District of Kandal Province, the team was taken to the site
of a Khmer Rouge prison and then shown the "Killing Field" mass grave
site by the district chief, who explained that many bodies had been exhumed from the pits there, most with bound wrists and still wearing blind-
folds. The chief's verbal report on the number of victims was a dubiously
accurate-sounding and improbably large number: 37,283. The mapping
team investigators did not contest this assertion but asked to see the adjacent memorial to the victims, which housed human remains. There the
team made a count of approximately 250 skulls. Given the much larger
number of femurs, it seemed likely that many skulls had been lost in the
intervening years. In view of the size and number of the excavated mass
graves, it appeared that the pits could have contained more than 250 bod-

ies, though also far fewer than the district chief's number. Due to this discrepancy and the inability of the team to construct a confident estimate, the site was ultimately recorded as containing zero victims.

In another telling example (refer to Table 7.1), the number of victims recorded for Phnom Penh is zero. This is the case despite the fact that the Documentation Center has perpetrator testimony from guards who actually executed and buried perhaps several thousand people in the formerly vacant lot adjacent to the Tuol Sleng Prison, to the west. A survivor of Tuol Sleng Prison has also confirmed this fact.[21] However, because that site has long since been built over by squatters, and because the perpetrator-informants did not seem to be very good with numbers and hence could not provide a count of either mass graves or victims on that site, consequently it is recorded in the mass grave data as zero.

A third example of this conservatism in the Documentation Center's mass grave mapping methodology comes from the 1999 data on Banteay Meanchey Province. There, local officials insisted that the total number of victims associated with a particular prison site and two adjacent mass grave sites was 8,000. However, the contemporaneous records of the mass grave exhumations showed only 700 recovered sets of remains, and so the number of victims recorded for these sites was 700, despite the fact that the mass graves appeared capable of holding a higher number of victims. Thus, the Documentation Center mass grave mapping teams tend toward circumspection. They are keenly aware of the tendency of some local informants to exaggerate the numbers, and their techniques take this factor into account.

A key element of the Documentation Center's mapping project is reproducibility, which, of course, is one of the bases of the scientific method. Each site is precisely located with Global Positioning System (GPS) technology. The information gathered via the GPS technology is then fed into a computerized Geographic Information System (GIS), allowing very precise maps of the Killing Fields to be generated. This means that investigators who come along later can actually verify the original sources of the data, in person, by finding each site and examining it themselves. This approach thus provides more scientific reproducibility than previous efforts to estimate the Khmer Rouge death toll. In the Documentation Center data, everything is recorded, and everything—including the names and addresses of all witnesses—is published in annual reports. Maps exhibiting some of this data are available on the Cambodian Genocide Program Web site at http://www.yale.edu/cgp and the Documentation Center Web site at http://welcome.to/dccam.

A significant proportion of the mass graves has been exhumed over the years by Cambodian government authorities. While they attempted to exercise care in their work, they had highly limited access to contemporary forensic sciences. A large number of the mass graves have also been opened by local grave robbers, who tended to exercise not much care at all; the Documentation Center's 1999 mapping reports actually include interviews with two such grave robbers. Both types of mass grave exhumations have been useful in assisting the Documentation Center investigators to establish benchmarks for understanding which kinds of mass graves contain what number of bodies. This has helped to improve the reliability of data in those instances where Documentation Center investigators have ventured to make an estimate of the number of victims located at a given site.

Vickery also argued that forensic investigation is necessary to confirm the time—and, one should add, the cause—of death for victims in mass graves. Forensic analysis can add a crucial element of confirmation to other sources of information about mass graves. In 1996, the Documentation Center began searching for funding to support forensic pathology and anthropology studies on a sample set of the mass graves. Initially, the prospects for such a study were discussed at some length by the Documentation Center with the officials at the U.S. military's Central Identification Lab (CIL) in Honolulu, Hawaii, which is highly experienced in the task of exhuming bodies in Southeast Asia.[22] CIL officials argued that even though the acidic content of the soil in Cambodia is generally high (consequently, bones tend to dissolve relatively quickly), nonetheless a skilled team can determine time and cause of death and in some cases even the actual identity of particular victims, even after many years have passed since the victims were interred in the graves.

The Documentation Center finally secured support early in 2002 for a preliminary forensic investigation. This pilot project involved the examination of several mass grave sites, evaluating the feasibility of a full-scale forensic mission. The forensic investigation found that a significant minority of the human skeletal remains examined revealed evidence of trauma in the form of sharp-force chopping injuries of the lower extremities, along with blunt-force trauma and gunshot wounds to the head.[23] These results suggest that the remains found at these sites were indeed victims of violent deaths—though this pilot project did not involve the substantial ad-

ditional investigation necessary to fix a time of death, nor did it attempt
to determine the identity of the victims. This forensic investigation also involved only a very small subset of the total set of sites. These additional
steps will be required to eliminate any remaining uncertainty regarding the
provenance of the mass grave sites. Further funding for forensic studies was
subsequently obtained, and in early 2004, a forensic team working under
the auspices of the Documentation Center completed site selection for a
full-scale, multidisciplinary forensic investigation. When that full-scale investigation is completed, the resulting data will add a fourth leg to the
three-legged stool of evidence compiled so far. It will complement the evidence from eyewitness testimony (both victims and perpetrators), Khmer
Rouge secret police documents that refer to the security centers, and the
hard physical evidence that the Documentation Center investigators have
touched and counted for themselves.

Besides the need for additional forensic confirmation of the mass grave
mapping work, there are other shortcomings in the Documentation Center's mass grave data set, one of which reflects the criticisms made by
Michael Vickery some twenty years ago. There remain cases where, as Vickery argued, it seems extremely difficult to precisely apportion the number
of deaths from execution versus those from illness and starvation. This difficulty continues to challenge Documentation Center mapping teams, and
they do not always manage such difficulties in scientifically defensible ways.
For example, in the 1999 mapping data for Banteay Meanchey, several mass
graves in the vicinity of the Thmar Puok District Office were said by local
witnesses to be filled with victims from two co-located Khmer Rouge security centers. However, witnesses also described a nearby Khmer Rouge
hospital facility, which was very poorly managed. "Most patients who came
to the hospital died," according to one witness who had worked in that
hospital. Given that large numbers of bodies were apparently being produced both by a Khmer Rouge hospital and by two Khmer Rouge security centers at the same general location, it is not at all clear how one can
be certain of the origin of the bodies in any mass grave in that immediate area. This type of uncertainty—even though it is the exception rather
than the rule in the overall data set—can raise questions about the validity of the data. Documentation Center mass grave mapping teams need to
exercise caution in filtering such "noise" from their data.

All in all, however, notwithstanding the limitations of the data, it is apparent that the mass grave mapping data set is the most laboriously crafted
collection of evidence yet assembled in the history of attempts to address

the question of the death toll under the Khmer Rouge regime. They are by far the most comprehensive data that have been produced so far on executions by the Khmer Rouge. This data does not consist of statistical extrapolation from nonrandom interviews in one or a few locations, as has been the case in some previous attempts to estimate the Khmer Rouge death toll, nor are they the result of demographic analysis of voter registration data and other population censuses, as in Heuveline's compelling studies. The Documentation Center mass grave data set is empirical, site-specific, nationwide, reproducible, and publicly available.

REFUTING THE DENIAL OF GENOCIDE

A great deal of work remains to be done before the mapping of Cambodia's Killing Fields is complete. To begin with, Preah Vihear Province has not yet been penetrated by mapping teams. The work is still in the early stages in the remote northeastern provinces of Ratanakiri and Mondulkiri, with Documentation Center mapping teams venturing into these jungle-clad mountainous regions for the first time in early 2000. Numerous districts in various parts of the country have not yet been surveyed. In many districts that have already been at least partially surveyed, subdistricts remain that have not yet been mapped. For many of those subdistricts, there exists preliminary information about possible mass grave sites. Many of these unsurveyed areas are in the most remote and inaccessible locations in all of Cambodia, a country known for difficulty of access in even the most forgiving regions and seasons. Some of these areas are also dangerous, due to a variety of hazards, including malarial jungles, unmarked minefields, bandits, and armed "former" Khmer Rouge, who often still exercise political control of their base areas despite the end of their insurgency. The last miles of the mass grave mapping project will be especially difficult.

In addition to the completion of the mapping studies, the Documentation Center faces another difficult and exacting phase of the work, the full-scale forensic investigations. This will be necessary for additional scientific confirmation concerning the times and causes of death of the victims in these graves, in order to augment the evidence already collected through physical inspection of the sites by the mapping teams, the testimony of local witnesses, and the wealth of information discovered in the archives of the Khmer Rouge secret police, the *Santebal*.

The dedicated personnel who have contributed to the Documentation Center's mass grave mapping project have helped to ensure that the truth about the magnitude of Khmer Rouge mass killing can be known to Cambodians and to the world. They have also helped to ensure that those who attempt to deny the truth will not prevail in civilized debate and will not find comfort in accounts written by responsible historians. We are moving from the day when the Cambodian people feared the Khmer Rouge, to a new time when the Khmer Rouge have excellent reason to fear that if they are ever brought to justice for their gigantic crimes, the evidence to secure their convictions will be plentiful. For Bun Than Eng of Lowell, Massachusetts, and all of his kind who would deny that the Khmer Rouge ruthlessly killed Cambodians on a massive scale, the evidence unearthed by the Documentation Center of Cambodia through their digging in the Killing Fields provides a devastating and incontrovertible rebuttal.

8

THE PERSISTENCE OF IMPUNITY*

Even with ample evidence of the crimes, finding justice for crimes on the scale of genocide is notoriously difficult. From a historical perspective, it is safe to say that this almost never happens. Those responsible for the crimes typically enjoy impunity for their actions. Even in a case such as the former Yugoslavia, where a well-funded international court is diligently tracking the crimes and prosecuting the criminals, only a relative handful of the perpetrators stand any chance of ever being brought to justice. There are many reasons why this kind of justice is rare and difficult to achieve.

The case of Cambodia's Khmer Rouge regime is instructive in this respect. An analysis of the challenges to accountability for *jus cogens* crimes and the persistence of impunity in Cambodia reveals many of the obstacles standing in the path of justice.[1] Repeated efforts to achieve some measure of accountability for massive violations of internationally protected human rights in Cambodia between 1975 and 1979 have foundered due to a wide range of factors. Cambodia has seen an international criminal tribunal, domestic criminal prosecutions, two proposed lawsuits before the International Court of Justice, efforts to impose financial penalties on the

*This chapter is a slightly revised version of a previous work originally published in Christopher Joyner, ed., *Reining in Impunity for International Crimes and Serious Violations of Fundamental Human Rights*, pp. 231–243. © 1998. Reprinted by permission of the International Review of Penal Law.

Khmer Rouge, an international investigative commission, a civil action prepared under the U.S. Alien Tort Claims Act, a national lustration law, efforts to set up a truth commission, renewed efforts to establish an ad hoc
international criminal tribunal, and an ongoing attempt to devise a novel
"mixed" national-international court. All of these mechanisms have been
resorted to in efforts to achieve accountability for crimes during the Khmer
Rouge regime. Despite these efforts spanning a quarter century, impunity
has continued to reign in Cambodia. Why? The range of reasons for the
failure of these efforts constitutes a rich catalog of obstacles to accountability.

A CATALOG OF ATTEMPTS TO ATTACK
IMPUNITY IN CAMBODIA

The persistence of impunity in Cambodia has been extraordinary. Cambodia's Khmer Rouge destroyed approximately one-third of Cambodia's
population during a terribly long three years, eight months, and twenty
days. Virtually every legal scholar who has examined the matter of Cambodia's Khmer Rouge has found a *prima facie* case against the leaders of
the Khmer Rouge for war crimes, genocide, and other crimes against humanity. For example, this has been found by Steven Ratner and Jason
Abrams in a book from Oxford University Press and by the UN in an official report to the secretary-general of the UN by a Group of Experts.[2]
Despite this consistent record of scholarly and legal opinion, impunity has
persisted in Cambodia in the face of repeated attempts to achieve some
form of accountability over the last twenty-five years. Several examples illustrate this persistence of impunity in Cambodia.

From August 15 to 19, 1979, an international criminal tribunal called
the People's Revolutionary Tribunal sat in Phnom Penh to judge Khmer
Rouge chief Pol Pot and his brother-in-law, Ieng Sary, on charges of genocide. The People's Revolutionary Tribunal heard evidence and then rendered *in absentia* convictions and death sentences against the two
defendants. However, the legitimacy of this proceeding and its verdicts have
been questioned, since the regime under which the proceedings were conducted was not recognized by the UN as the legal government of Cambodia. The People's Revolutionary Tribunal was also hampered by certain
procedural irregularities, such as a pair of erstwhile defense lawyers who
asserted that their own clients were guilty. In any event, the sentences were
never imposed; Ieng Sary was pardoned as part of a deal for his defection

to the government in 1996, and Pol Pot evaded capture by the government until his death in 1998.[3]

From 1979 on through the 1980s and again after 1995, there have been numerous domestic criminal prosecutions on charges relating to membership in Khmer Rouge organizations and/or the commission of criminal acts in the furtherance of Khmer Rouge aims. This little-known area of accountability for the Cambodian genocide targeted low-level perpetrators of the Cambodian genocide. However, the precise numbers of defendants targeted in these proceedings—and the exact nature of the judicial processes—remain in some doubt, as few definitive records elaborating on these cases have been discovered. Many of the earlier cases appear to have involved administrative detention rather than actual prosecution. In the prosecutions by the Royal Cambodian Government after 1995, human rights workers have shown that in numerous cases, persons charged with Khmer Rouge involvement in fact had nothing to do with the Khmer Rouge. There is substantial evidence of improper prosecutions and procedural irregularities.[4] In all these cases, no ranking perpetrator has been brought before a court in domestic prosecutions to account for his or her actions during the Khmer Rouge regime. For some of those who have been charged, there have been elements of caprice and arbitrariness in the selection of persons so prosecuted.

In the mid-1980s, the advocacy organization called the Cambodia Genocide Project sought to submit a memorandum to the International Court of Justice, outlining the case that the Khmer Rouge-dominated exile Coalition Government of Democratic Kampuchea was in violation of its obligations under the Convention on the Prevention and Punishment of the Crime of Genocide. The leading role of Pol Pot and his chief lieutenants in the Coalition Government of Democratic Kampuchea rendered that government-in-exile vulnerable to charges of harboring genocidists. The Cambodia Genocide Project dispatched human rights lawyer Gregory Stanton to work with the Commonwealth of Australia in an effort to persuade that government to challenge the Coalition Government of Democratic Kampuchea in court on these grounds. In the end, nothing came of the exercise because such an action was contrary to the agenda of ASEAN states, the People's Republic of China, and the United States, which were determined to feed, arm, and defend the legal sovereignty of the Coalition Government of Democratic Kampuchea.[5]

By September 1986, another effort to bring a case before the International Court of Justice was launched by the Cambodia Documentation

Commission. Hurst Hannum and David Hawk prepared a brief titled "The Case against the Standing Committee of the Communist Party of Kampuchea" and sought to induce a Scandinavian or other country to bring the complaint before the International Court of Justice. Again, the effort was frustrated by the exigencies of international politics, in the guise of superpower and regional power interests.[6] The requirements of the Cold War trumped the demand for justice in Cambodia.

In 1992, an attempt was made to impose immigration and travel restrictions on the Khmer Rouge under the proposed U.S. Khmer Rouge Prosecution and Exclusion Act.[7] This legislation also would have made it the policy of the United States to support efforts to establish an international tribunal to judge those accused of crimes against humanity in Cambodia. The legislation was defeated as the result of vigorous opposition by the Bush administration, on the grounds that such a measure would interfere with the Cambodian peace process. Similar legislation was introduced again in 1993 and defeated again on the same argument, this time by the Clinton administration, due to fervent opposition in the U.S. Department of State.

In 1993, there was an effort to impose financial penalties on the Khmer Rouge using Cambodian commercial law.[8] Three activists operating under the auspices of the Campaign to Oppose the Return of the Khmer Rouge suggested to King Norodom Sihanouk that he recommend to the Royal Government of Cambodia the establishment of a system of "certificates of origin" to regulate trade in tropical hardwood and gemstones. A massive, but illicit, trade in these commodities had been funding the Khmer Rouge war against the Royal Government for some time. The Cambodian government did subsequently adopt this system, aiming to rein in Khmer Rouge illegal revenues. But the Khmer Rouge were able to effectively defeat this approach by arranging to "purchase" legitimate certificates of origin for their natural resource products from corrupt officials of the Royal Government.

In the autumn of 1993, it was expected that senior Khmer Rouge leader Khieu Samphan would represent the Khmer Rouge in New York at the opening session of the UN General Assembly. Samphan had performed this function in numerous preceding years, and there was reason to believe that he might attend the 1993 session in his capacity as a member of the Supreme National Council of Cambodia, the transitional governing body established pursuant to the Paris Peace Accords of 1991. A California man named Karl Deeds decided to sue Khieu Samphan for the wrongful death of his brother, Michael Scott Deeds, who was one of four Americans known to have been tortured and executed by the Khmer Rouge at Tuol Sleng Prison.[9] Khieu Samphan was the president and head of state of Democratic Kampuchea from 1976 through the fall of the regime in January 1979, and thus he might in theory bear responsibility for such damages. Bringing such a civil action against a representative of the regime required, in the first place, that such a representative be physically present within the jurisdiction of the United States in order to be served with court papers detailing the complaint.[10] However, by the time the UN General Assembly convened in the autumn of 1993, Cambodia's Supreme National Council had been superseded by the newly established Royal Government of Cambodia—of which the Khmer Rouge were not part—and so Samphan did not appear in New York. Thus, he avoided service of the lawsuit, any proceedings, and any liability for damages that may have been awarded.

Beginning early in 1993 and continuing into 1994, there was a series of attempts to impose financial penalties on the Khmer Rouge, this time using the vehicle of the U.S. Foreign Operations Act.[11] Congress terminated some categories of U.S. military assistance to Thailand in response to continued Thai military support for the Khmer Rouge. In addition, the legislation threatened to eliminate all U.S. assistance to Thailand, if that country failed to end its role as a supplier of military equipment to the Khmer Rouge as well as to curb its highly profitable trade in gemstones and tropical hardwoods with the Khmer Rouge.[12] This pressure helped to bring an end to Thai military resupply of the Khmer Rouge. This support to the Khmer Rouge had been occuring in violation of Thailand's obligations under the terms of the Paris Accords. The Thai–Khmer Rouge trade relationship, however, continued until the final collapse of the Khmer Rouge in 1999.[13]

In May 1994, U.S. President Bill Clinton signed into law the Cambodian Genocide Justice Act.[14] This legislation directed the U.S. Department of State to contract with private individuals and organizations for an expert investigation into violations of international criminal and humanitarian law during the Democratic Kampuchea regime between April 17, 1975, and January 7, 1979. Attorneys Jason Abrams and Steven Ratner were commissioned by the State Department to prepare an analysis of the potential culpability of members of the Khmer Rouge on charges of war crimes, genocide, and other crimes against humanity. Their study concluded, in part, with respect to charges of genocide: "We find *prima facie* culpability for acts against religious and ethnic groups, such as the Cham,

Vietnamese and Chinese communities, and the Buddhist monkhood."[15] Similarly, they found *prima facie* culpability for war crimes and other crimes against humanity.

Also under the authority of the Cambodian Genocide Justice Act, the U.S. State Department concluded a cooperative agreement with Yale University's Cambodian Genocide Program (CGP), providing funds for Yale University to carry out documentation, research, and training related to the prospective establishment of an accountability mechanism to deal with Khmer Rouge crimes. As detailed in previous chapters, over the course of more than ten years of research, the CGP and its offspring, the Documentation Center of Cambodia, have assembled a remarkable collection of evidentiary materials that clearly implicates the entire top leadership of the Communist Party of Kampuchea in directing the mass terror.[16] While these efforts have greatly advanced the quality of legal opinion and the evidentiary basis upon which accountability mechanisms could be supported, these efforts alone have no force of law and hence no direct impact on impunity.

Again in 1994, there was another effort to attack Khmer Rouge impunity, this time by the Cambodians. On July 7, 1994, the Royal Government of Cambodia adopted a lustration law,[17] the "Law on the Outlawing of the Democratic Kampuchea Group." Following a spirited debate and a number of important amendments to the draft text, the "Law on the Outlawing of the Democratic Kampuchea Group" was approved by the National Assembly of the Kingdom of Cambodia.[18] Commonly known as the Anti-Khmer Rouge Law, this statute formally declares members of the Khmer Rouge political and military organizations to be criminals, placing them outside civil society and prescribing penalties for membership in the organization. The law defines persons covered under the statute and distinguishes behaviors to be treated under existing law (rape, murder, robbery, etc.) from special criminal acts to be punished under a new set of penalties (secession, destruction of the organs of state authority, incitement to take up arms, etc.). The law also provided for a six-month amnesty period, during which members of the Khmer Rouge could surrender to the government without penalty, and also reaffirmed the constitutional authority of the king to grant royal amnesty at any time. The specified six-month amnesty period did not apply to Khmer Rouge "leaders," although the law neglected to define what constitutes a leader.

In essence, the Anti-Khmer Rouge Law codified in the Cambodian legal code a policy that had been in force since 1979: rally to the government, and you will likely be forgiven for any crimes committed while having served the Khmer Rouge. Over the previous fifteen years, this policy had been successful in convincing tens of thousands of Khmer Rouge cadre and soldiers to abandon their struggle and return to the national fold. The new law not only gave this policy the force of law but also specified a date certain—January 7, 1995—after which this leniency would no longer be available. A small, but significant, rush of cadres and soldiers were thus induced to defect from the Khmer Rouge during the six-month amnesty period. At the same time, the law explicitly recognized that responsibility for genocidal acts during the Khmer Rouge regime 1975–1979 "cannot be annulled by the passage of time."[19] However, both the six-month termination date on amnesty for "members" as well as the ban on amnesty for "leaders" have been ignored in practice.

In 1996, after repeated requests from Prime Minister Hun Sen, officials of Yale University's CGP agreed to draft a law for the Cambodian government calling upon the international community to establish an international tribunal for the Khmer Rouge and specifying that if the international community did not act effectively on this request, the Cambodian government would convene a domestic criminal tribunal for senior Khmer Rouge leaders.[20] The draft was vetted by Cambodia's Council of Ministers and then presented to the National Assembly's Legislative Commission, but just as legislators were to begin debating the law, it was suddenly withdrawn by the government. It later became apparent that negotiations had begun between the government and Khmer Rouge leader Ieng Sary for the defection of a major portion of Khmer Rouge military forces to the government. Evidently, the government came to the conclusion that this development rendered the proposed legislation inopportune, and it was never reintroduced.

In 1996 and early 1997 and then again in 1999, there were several efforts to establish a truth commission to deal with issues of crimes against humanity during the Khmer Rouge regime. Prominent in these efforts was Ambassador Thomas Hammarberg, the special representative of the secretary-general of the UN for human rights in Cambodia.[21] Hammarberg successfully argued before the UN Commission on Human Rights, "In relation to the problem of impunity, it was important that there be a serious discussion in Cambodia about how to handle the cases of gross violations in the past and how to investigate them."[22] The idea of a truth commission was, however, not well received by Cambodians, in part because they generally seemed to believe that they "already know the truth"

about the Khmer Rouge genocide.[23] Nothing came of these initiatives beyond a heightened interest on the part of the UN's Hammarberg as regards the matter of impunity and accountability in Cambodia.[24] In early
1999, however, the Cambodian government approached officials of South
Africa's Truth and Reconciliation Commission, exploring the idea of seeking assistance for the establishment of a truth commission in Cambodia.[25]
This move may have been a negotiating tactic aimed at thwarting a UN
recommendation to establish an international criminal tribunal for the
Khmer Rouge, rather than reflecting any serious interest in setting up a
truth-telling body. Nothing came of the brief episode.

In 1997, the UN's Ambassador Hammarberg reenergized attempts to establish an international criminal tribunal. Hammarberg persuaded the
Cambodian co-prime ministers to formally request UN assistance in setting up a judicial mechanism to try the Khmer Rouge leaders.[26] This led
the following year to UN Secretary-General Kofi Annan's appointment of
a Group of Experts. The experts were assigned to examine the Cambodian situation with a view to determining whether or not there was probable cause to believe that the Khmer Rouge had committed serious
violations of international humanitarian law. If this were to be found, then
the Group of Experts would also recommend whether or not it would be
appropriate to establish an international criminal tribunal to hear charges
against members of the Khmer Rouge for any such violations. Following
the resolution of a political crisis precipitated by fighting between factions
of Cambodia's coalition government, in late 1998 three eminent international jurists carried out a detailed investigation of the legal and factual
bases for such a tribunal, taking due account of the social and political factors impinging on the matter.

Finally, early in 1999, the Group of Experts recommended to the
secretary-general that such a tribunal should be established.[27] However,
some weeks prior to the presentation of these recommendations, the last
of the Khmer Rouge political leaders still in armed resistance surrendered
to the Cambodian government. Feeling that they now had the upper hand
over the Khmer Rouge and that an international tribunal might complicate their plans for national reconciliation by so frightening the Khmer
Rouge that some of their fighters might return to armed resistance, the
Cambodian government rejected the recommendations of the Group of
Experts. This setback was followed by years of extended negotiations between the UN and the Cambodian government, attempting to define a

formula that would satisfy the requirements of both the international community and Cambodia's leadership. As yet there has been no concrete impact on impunity.

As a final, but not exhaustive, example of efforts to attack the impunity of the Khmer Rouge, on February 4, 1999, a group of Belgian citizens of Cambodian extraction presented a civil complaint to a Belgian examining magistrate. As a result, the magistrate launched an investigation of Khieu Samphan, Nuon Chea, and Ieng Sary, examining their potential complicity in the mass killing during the Khmer Rouge regime.[28] Belgian officials were said to be preparing a formal letter of request to the Cambodian government, which would request assistance in carrying out the legal inquiry. In early April, using a new Belgian statute that permits non-nationals to initiate criminal prosecutions and claim compensation for victims of war crimes, genocide, and crimes against humanity, a group of French Cambodians joined in the lawsuit.[29] Subsequently, however, reportedly as a result of pressure from a group of Cambodians in political opposition to the current government of Cambodia, the name of Cambodia's current prime minister, Hun Sen, was added to the list of "senior" officials from the Khmer Rouge government of the 1970s to be investigated in the action. Consequently, it became certain that no cooperation would be forthcoming from the Hun Sen's government in the case. As a result, it became unlikely that the suit would yield the results originally envisioned, and officers of the Belgian justice system subsequently determined that it would not be productive to pursue the case to its logical conclusion.

IMPUNITY PERSISTS

None of these efforts to achieve accountability for the crimes of the Democratic Kampuchea regime over the last twenty-five years have yet had an appreciable impact on the persistence of impunity for the Khmer Rouge leadership. As we have seen, the reasons for the failure of these efforts to end Khmer Rouge impunity include (though they are not limited to):

1. Disputes over the legitimacy of various Cambodian regimes;
2. Irregularities in the various legal proceedings;
3. Lack of institutionalized international accountability mechanisms;
4. Failure to obtain physical custody of the accused;

5. Failure to secure statutory jurisdiction over the accused;

6. Capricious selection of persons to be prosecuted;

7. Considerations of "national reconciliation";

8. Financial corruption;

9. Superpower politics;

10. Regional politics;

11. Domestic politics; and

12. A general lack of political will.

Thus, Cambodia provides an encyclopedia of attempts to achieve accountability and, similarly, an encyclopedia of causes for the persistence of impunity. It was possible to end the impunity of the Nazi leadership and bring them to trial after World War II because the total victory of the Allies over the Axis nations swept away most of these obstacles. The failure of Vietnam to secure total victory over the Khmer Rouge—either military or political—meant that all of these obstacles would remain in the path of imposing accountability for their crimes for years to come.

Even in the face of such daunting obstacles to accountability for war crimes, genocide, and other crimes against humanity, however, there remain sensible courses of action. A wise teacher once said that the only rational response to impossible odds is to try harder. This is one response to such obstacles: seeking more vigorously to overcome the obstacles. In this respect, it is encouraging that for several years, many of those who have been seeking to end the impunity of the Khmer Rouge and achieve accountability for the alleged perpetrators of these historic crimes—seekers including private individuals, certain nongovernmental organizations, a few leading members of the community of nations, the UN Secretariat, and the Royal Government of Cambodia itself—have been demonstrating sustained strength of political will in pursuing this result. As of this writing, however, the surviving leaders of the Khmer Rouge continue to enjoy impunity.

A second course of action prepares for the possibility that accountability will never be achieved for the crimes of the Khmer Rouge. This course of action remains an essential undertaking even in the event that some form of accountability is ultimately achieved, to one degree or another. This is to see beyond the judgment of courts of law and look to history. Even if formal accountability is never achieved for their crimes, even if some or all of the chief perpetrators of the Cambodian genocide evade their just desserts under the law, the Khmer Rouge shall not escape the judgment of history. Thanks to the work of organizations like the Documentation Center of Cambodia, future generations of Cambodians will be able to know the truth about what happened under the Khmer Rouge regime. For the present, however, the persistence of impunity continues to haunt the world and the people of Cambodia.

9

THE POLITICS OF GENOCIDE JUSTICE*

The single most sensitive issue facing Cambodia today concerns the question of accountability for the crimes of the Khmer Rouge regime. This issue touches the heart of every Cambodian. Everyone's lives are connected in some way, usually in many ways, to the Khmer Rouge. Every individual in the country had members of his or her family murdered by the Khmer Rouge. Thus, it is a tremendously emotional matter for most citizens of Cambodia—and it is a tremendously intimate question for the entire political elite. Virtually every member of the elite class has been variously a subject of, a member of, allied to, and/or at war with the Khmer Rouge for more than three decades. Consequently, the matter of genocide justice in Cambodia is not merely a legal or political question—it is personal. Public opinion surveys suggest that the overwhelming majority of the Cambodian people want the Khmer Rouge leadership to be prosecuted for their crimes,[1] but thus far the political elite has been very reluctant to grant this wish, in part because nobody is completely "clean."

That crimes were committed during the Khmer Rouge regime between 1975 and 1979 is beyond debate. Some 2.2 million people perished—al-

---

*This chapter is a slightly revised version of a previous work originally published in Cesare Romano et al., eds., *Internationalized Criminal Courts: Sierra Leone, East Timor, Kosovo and Cambodia.* © 2004. Reprinted by permission of Oxford University Press.

most one-third of the entire population—during the three years, eight months, and twenty days of Democratic Kampuchea. The network of so-called security centers established by the Khmer Rouge—actually they were extermination centers—executed an estimated 1.1 million people.[2] At least three authoritative legal studies have found a *prima facie* case that these killings constituted war crimes, genocide, and other crimes against humanity.[3] Measured in terms of percentage of the national population killed, it was the largest single episode of mass murder in the twentieth century.

Yet, a quarter century after the regime that perpetrated these crimes was driven from power, no senior leader of that regime has yet faced justice before a court of law. Their impunity has not endured because of a lack of effort on the part of justice advocates; the struggle for genocide justice in Cambodia has been ongoing for more than a quarter century.[4] Rather, the politics of achieving genocide justice in Cambodia have proven to be particularly intractable. The interests of both Cambodian domestic actors as well as actors in the many other nations that have chosen to involve themselves in Cambodia's affairs over the last three decades have intersected to create a terrible political tangle that has yet to be unraveled.

At a 1995 conference organized in Phnom Penh by Yale University's CGP in cooperation with the U.S. Department of State, then-second prime minister Hun Sen delivered a keynote address, and in reference to the notion of a tribunal for the Khmer Rouge, he declared, "This is not about politics, this is about justice."[5] In reality, of course, the problem of finding justice for perpetrators in the wake of genocidal atrocities is always intensely political. The relationship of politics to genocide justice in Cambodia is the topic of this chapter. The ensuing analysis addresses various political aspects associated with the proposed Cambodian tribunal, including both the domestic and the international political dimensions of the failure thus far to achieve justice for the crimes of the Khmer Rouge regime.

DOMESTIC POLITICS—THE RULING PARTY

Cambodia's ruling party is the Cambodian People's Party or CPP. The CPP traces its roots to the same conference in 1951 that the Khmer Rouge have cited as their founding congress. Most of the CPP's senior cadres began their careers as low- or midlevel Khmer Rouge functionaries, fled to Vietnam to escape Khmer Rouge leader Pol Pot's vicious purges, and then formed a Marxist–Leninist front that took power after a Vietnamese invasion ousted the Khmer Rouge regime in 1979.[6] In 1989, as the Vietnamese occupation forces withdrew from Cambodia, the party publicly abandoned socialism along with command-and-control economic policies and adopted the name Cambodian People's Party. The party did not, however, abandon its internal Leninist structure and procedures, which it retains to this day.

Within the ruling party, there is a complex mix of views on the Khmer Rouge tribunal. Some are strongly opposed to the idea, some are strongly supportive, and strict rules of Leninist party discipline make it difficult to discern where the balance of opinion lies. Even so, it is possible to identify various viewpoints within the party.

A group we may designate as the "Nativists" opposes any UN involvement in a tribunal, reflecting an abiding revulsion at external interference in Cambodia's internal affairs. For these people, the sovereignty issue is their lodestone. It is easy to dismiss claims of "sovereignty" as mere posturing, but to do so is to underestimate the psychological importance and emotional potency of the question after nearly a century of French colonialism, the Japanese occupation in the 1940s, the U.S. intervention in the early 1970s, the Vietnamese occupation of the 1980s, and the UN "transitional authority" in the early 1990s. The Royal Government of Cambodia is now accepted as a legitimate state among the community of nations, and Cambodia's leaders demand that their regime be given the deference accorded to sovereign entities.

Another group, the "Rejectionists," opposes the idea of any tribunal at all, on the grounds that it could be harmful to the process of national reconciliation. People holding this view see peace, security, and stability as the central issues. This is also an easy position for outsiders to dismiss out of hand, particularly in view of the total collapse of the Khmer Rouge political and military organizations in 1998 and 1999, but the public hunger for peace and stability in Cambodia in the wake of the Thirty Years War is palpable. Moreover, the Royal Government's security officials know that there are still many trained and armed Khmer Rouge cadre in the hinterlands, some of whom are still fanatically loyal to the old-line Khmer Rouge leadership. They also know that, for example, a small unit commando attack on a tourist hotel at the Kampong Som beach resort would be easy to execute and would have a devastating impact on one of the country's principal legitimate sources of hard currency—tourism.

A third grouping is what may be termed the "Protectionists." They oppose any international involvement in the tribunal on the grounds that too many core CPP cadre have too many skeletons in their closets. For those of this persuasion, maintaining the unity and solidarity of the ruling party is the primary objective. A number of core members of the party—for the most part, not the prominent names one tends to see in the press but important figures within the party nonetheless—would be potentially liable to indictment by a free and unfettered prosecutor. The party elders are supremely reluctant to sacrifice any core members over the Khmer Rouge accountability issue.

Counterpoised against these various threads of opposition to a Khmer Rouge tribunal (or at least to UN involvement in a tribunal) is another set of views within the ruling party that tends to be supportive of the idea of genocide justice in Cambodia. "Internationalists" understand that cooperation with the UN on the tribunal can bring many side benefits in the international arena, from increased bilateral and multilateral aid, to greater political credibility in regional forums such as ASEAN and global forums such as the UN General Assembly. They view a fully legitimated tribunal as a way for Cambodia to become a fully accepted member of the international community. The Internationalists also tend to think that a tribunal would constitute proof that they were right and that the UN was wrong when the world body continued to give Cambodia's UN seat to the Khmer Rouge through the 1980s and into the 1990s.

"Modernizers" look to the domestic benefits of a well-conducted tribunal, including combating the culture of impunity, weeding out undesirable elements in the party, and providing a salutary example of the value of an independent judiciary. This last element is particularly salient for the Modernizers, as many of them see that the existing weak judiciary severely limits the possibilities for foreign investment and economic development. The Modernizers can be seen as the party's "good government" faction.

The "Triumphalists" view a full-scale, fully internationally legitimated tribunal as the final act of revenge against those who destroyed Cambodia's revolution and wrought so much havoc, the final nail in the Khmer Rouge coffin. They would also see a tribunal as the final "proof" that the party's perception of its own historical role is correct. They believe it is the People's Party that represents the true and legitimate heritage of the Cambodian revolution, as opposed to the "Pol Pot group."

Where is the balance of opinion in the ruling party? This difficult to determine, but it seems likely that a solid majority of the rank-and-file members support a tribunal. Among the party leadership, however, views are decidedly more mixed, with several key members of the party's policy-making politburo clearly uneasy at the prospect of real justice for the Khmer Rouge. Consequently, the consensus-driven "democratic centralism" of the CPP's policy-making body—debate and then a vote, with all bound by the result—has resulted in a very deliberate approach to the establishment of an internationalized accountability mechanism that could bring the Khmer Rouge leadership to book. Other domestic actors, however, further complicate the political calculus of genocide justice in Cambodia, beginning with the ruling party's coalition partner in the government, the royalist party.

THE ROYALISTS

The royalist party, FUNCINPEC, was founded in the early 1980s by the former and then once-again king, Norodom Sihanouk.[7] The party began primarily as a vehicle to serve Sihanouk's interests. Sihanouk established FUNCINPEC because he wanted to play a role in expelling the Vietnamese forces occupying Cambodia after the overthrow of the Khmer Rouge regime. Not incidentally, he also wanted to regain the throne. He achieved the first goal in 1989 and the second in 1993. In the eyes of many Cambodians, however, the royal family's legacy—as well as Sihanouk's personal legitimacy—was compromised by the fact that in the 1980s they joined an exile coalition government dominated by the Khmer Rouge.

Since the royalists took the lead in forming a national government following their victory in the UN-sponsored election of 1993, FUNCINPEC's fortunes have steadily declined. They rode into power on the strength of the royalist party's association with the beloved King Sihanouk. As an elite organization largely led by members of the royal family and their partisans, FUNCINPEC has had difficulty building and maintaining a mass following. Under the leadership of Sihanouk's son, Norodom Ranariddh, the party's share of seats in parliament has fallen steadily from fifty-eight seats in the 1993 election, to forty-three in 1998, to just twenty-six in 2003. The royalist party was also badly damaged when the Hun Sen's People's Party ousted Ranariddh from his role as first prime minister in a bloody 1997 episode of dueling coups d'état, on accusations that the royalists were once again scheming with the Khmer Rouge, which was true, as far as it went.[8] A continuous stream of FUNCINPEC corruption scandals and the leadership's casual attitude about them have further damaged the royalist party's standing among the public. After the 1998 national elections, FUNCINPEC again entered a governing coalition with the People's Party, this time officially relegated to the role of junior partner, with Ranariddh installed as president of the National Assembly. Unable to articulate significant policy differences with the People's Party, many royalist supporters became further alienated. In the 2002 commune elections, for example, they won control in only ten of Cambodia's 1,621 communes.[9]

In terms of tribunal politics, all of this means that both Ranariddh and the FUNCINPEC party he leads have been Hun Sen's willing pawns in parliament. At the same time, however, the royalist party in some ways has tried to distance itself from the tribunal, hoping for political gain in the event that the tribunal process goes poorly and significant portions of the electorate are dissatisfied by the outcome. For example, Ranariddh was absent for the final vote in the National Assembly on the Khmer Rouge tribunal law, even though he is the leader of that body, asserting that he had to attend a birthday party. He has also occasionally voiced his opinion that vigorous UN participation is necessary in any trials in order to ensure due process for Khmer Rouge suspects. "I don't believe that the tribunal process will follow that required in a court of law and within the justice framework, even if there is participation of foreign judges," Ranariddh told reporters after the UN withdrew from negotiations in February 2002. "[Without the participation of the UN] there will be no guarantees about transparency and justice."[10]

THE OPPOSITION

The Sam Rainsy Party is the vehicle for the political aspirations of its namesake, Sam Rainsy, and it functions as Cambodia's opposition—though the party is not necessarily what one would term a "loyal opposition." Rainsy's party is a splinter group from the royalist party, from which he was expelled in 1995 for his outspoken criticism of corruption in the government in general and FUNCINPEC in particular. The Sam Rainsy Party has modest representation in both houses of parliament and enough members to block the formation of a quorum in the National Assembly when the party wishes to make a point. The party campaigns on a platform of good government, and its founder is notable both for his exceptional personal courage and for his seemingly irrepressible energy, as well as for his often shrill style and erratic approach.

Rainsy has been generally opposed to the Royal Government's plans for a Khmer Rouge tribunal, arguing instead for a Hague-style proceeding that would, not incidentally, also charge Prime Minister Hun Sen with war crimes. Rainsy enjoys strong backing from the Republican caucus in the U.S. House of Representatives, which in 1998 adopted a Sense of the House resolution supporting Rainsy's call for an international criminal tribunal to prosecute Hun Sen.[11] Some Republicans in the United States feel that Rainsy is Cambodia's best hope for building a more democratic system and that Hun Sen, by contrast, is the greatest obstacle to that goal.

THE KING

The position of King Norodom Sihanouk on the Khmer Rouge tribunal is most complex and, as with most other aspects of Cambodian politics, mostly opaque.[12] At one time or another, King Sihanouk has taken every conceivable position on the merits of a tribunal, pro, con, and ambiguous. He retains a visceral hatred of the Khmer Rouge for what they did to his happy little kingdom—not to mention the fact that while they held him prisoner in his palace, fourteen of his children and grandchildren were executed by the Khmer Rouge.[13] Sihanouk, however, clearly retains a sense of loyalty toward some former members of the Khmer Rouge, as they continue to play a prominent role on the palace staff.[14] These same feelings of loyalty may extend also to such individuals as former Khmer Rouge Deputy Prime Minister and Foreign Minister Ieng Sary, who was responsible for minding the deposed monarch during the civil war in the first half of the 1970s and continued to assist in that role during the Democratic Kampuchea regime in the second half of the 1970s. In 1996, Sihanouk was persuaded by the government to grant a Royal Pardon to Ieng Sary, washing away the death sentence imposed upon Sary's conviction for genocide at the 1979 People's Revolutionary Tribunal.[15]

Sihanouk's power as king has been tightly circumscribed by both the constitution and the wiles of the ruling party, though he still wields a certain amount of symbolic power and has the experience to know when to show it for maximum effect.[16] His principal interest in a tribunal may ultimately be as a forum to declaim his innocence, as some still whisper that none of this would have happened in the first place were it not for Sihanouk's vain alliance with the Khmer Rouge, seeking revenge against Lon Nol and his associates for ousting him in 1970.[17] Then, there is also the fact of Sihanouk's long-standing warm relations with the People's Republic of China; the Chinese provide a royal residence for Sihanouk in Beijing, to which he frequently retreats. Thus, China's opposition to an international tribunal for the Khmer Rouge may have some influence on him. Even so, Sihanouk has always been a master practitioner of telling people what they want to hear, and consequently different people come away from an audience with Sihanouk bearing diametrically opposed versions of what he really believes regarding the Khmer Rouge tribunal issue.

THE KHMER ROUGE

The Khmer Rouge themselves have proven to be an unexpected wild card in Cambodian tribunal politics. A "post–Khmer Rouge" political organ created in 1996 by former Khmer Rouge chieftain Ieng Sary, known as the "Democratic National United Movement," has sought to present a unified political line on the question of the tribunal on behalf of all former Khmer Rouge. The Democratic National United Movement has been lobbying the government with a mixture of threats of a return to violence, carefully targeted financial inducements, and good old-fashioned politicking to ensure maximum impunity in any judicial accountability on the genocide.

This post–Khmer Rouge political operation has issued frequent communiqués extolling the importance of national reconciliation, exhorting the people to "forgive and forget" the past. In subsequent paragraphs, these missives typically switch to a passive subjunctive voice and warn that a new war may "happen" if this sage advice is not heeded. For example, at a public meeting in Battambang in January 2000 on the topic of the Khmer Rouge and reconciliation, the group's spokesman said,

> Mechanisms toward the trial for the leaders of the Democratic Kampuchea are under way. The point is not whether or not to have a trial, but whether or not the process will affect national reconciliation. . . . Everyone knows that the war just ended a year ago, after the second national election. Despite the end of the war, nobody can affirm that the war will not happen again in our country, especially the random attacks that disturb development work. So, the peace we are enjoying today is still fragile.[18]

Similar thinly veiled threats have been repeatedly made by Khieu Samphan, one of the highest-ranking Khmer Rouge leaders. He argued at the end of 1998 that a trial would be a mistake: "If we have to say who was wrong and who was right, etc., etc., we cannot have national reconciliation. We cannot put an end to the war."[19] In other words, the bargain being demanded by these former leaders of the Khmer Rouge is that they will cease killing and return to live in normal society, unless they are held accountable under the laws of that society. The implicit threat is that a failure to accept this bargain will result in the killers returning to their previous violent behavior.[20]

Over the course of the last several years, however, it appears that the Khmer Rouge leadership has been losing control over their own rank-and-file personnel and/or former personnel. With the fragmenting of the formerly monolithic Khmer Rouge into many isolated groups scattered mostly around the western and northern border areas and the disintegration of the party's mechanisms of discipline, their erstwhile followers have begun to ask difficult questions. Many are coming to wonder, for example, Why, when I devoted my entire life to the revolution, were so many members of my family executed as enemies of the people? Such questions have led an increasing number of rank-and-file Khmer Rouge to openly call for a tribunal for their former leadership, in hopes of finding answers to this question.[21]

An interesting illustration of this trend occurred in January 2000, when a private Cambodian organization, the Center for Social Development, organized a "national reconciliation forum," with public meetings in three Cambodian cities.[22] The first of these meetings was held in Battambang City, near the heart of Khmer Rouge territory. Of the more than 100 people attending the forum, approximately 75 percent were Khmer Rouge. Only one speaker at the meeting had the courage to openly advocate a tribunal and call for accountability for the crimes of the Khmer Rouge. Most of the speakers at the forum were Khmer Rouge leaders, carefully selected to present a cohesive message. That message was the value of stability, the danger of renewed war, and the importance of letting bygones be bygones. However, at the end of the forum, the Center for Social Development distributed an anonymous questionnaire. Seventy-five percent of the respondents endorsed the concept of a tribunal for the Khmer Rouge leadership, which meant that at least half of the former Khmer Rouge in the audience agreed with that view. Events like this strike fear into the hearts of the old guard and suggest they have lost the hearts and minds of their own people.

THE PUBLIC

What about the Cambodian public in general? Several surveys in recent years have attempted to plumb the depths of public opinion on the tribunal question. The results of these surveys have been quite consistent, with strong majorities of from 75 to 85 percent of respondents favoring a tribunal for the Khmer Rouge leadership.[23] This is a slightly curious result in view of the fact that Cambodia has little recent history of formal justice in the Western sense. In Cambodia, higher legal proceedings have historically been the venue to punish offenses against the sovereign or the state, with minimal concern for the rights of individual citizens.[24] It is not for nothing that the Cambodian word that means "prisoner" or "suspect" translates literally as "the guilty one."

Of course, the Cambodian people have plenty of reason to believe that the government wishes to punish the Khmer Rouge, after two decades of government vilification of the Khmer Rouge and warfare against them. Every May 20, the official annual "Day of Hatred" against the Khmer Rouge is still observed, notwithstanding the imperatives of national reconciliation. This unusual holiday has effectively focused public opinion on the "otherness" of the Khmer Rouge, solidifying popular support for the regime. Over the years, however, people have come to recognize the explicitly political character of the official observance, and participation has gradually dwindled to include mostly the ruling party faithful, as well as those who attend the ceremonies—typically held at genocide memorial sites—in order to conduct private religious ancestor veneration rituals.

When one probes beneath the surface public attitudes in favor of a tribunal, what most often comes out is not a wish for retributive punishment, but rather a desire for answers, for an explanation to the elusive, existential question, Why? Why did Pol Pot do it? Why did we have to suffer so much? Why was our country destroyed by its own children? While the accusatorial format of criminal prosecution may not necessarily provide immediate answers to such questions, Khmer Rouge trials could have the effect of stimulating a broad national discussion of the issue—as the Eichmann trial did in Israel—and consequently generate some answers in the aftermath of the tribunal.[25] The people may somehow sense this, and they want it.

The ruling party's lack of internal cohesion on the Khmer Rouge tribunal question is reinforced by broad divisions among other members of the country's political elite on the issue. Given the widespread popular demand for genocide justice in Cambodia, Cambodia's non–Khmer Rouge political elite is virtually unanimous in loudly proclaiming the necessity and inevitability of a genocide tribunal. At the same time, however, that elite has encountered endless obstacles in actually bringing about an accountability process. With this domestic political setting as the background, the role of international political actors in the process of bringing about genocide justice in Cambodia has also been crucial—though no less problematical. The struggle for justice has been so long and hard not only because of the internal complications of the issue inside Cambodia but also because of the witheringly complex set of interests and perspectives brought to the issue from interested external actors.

INTERNATIONAL DIMENSIONS

In addition to the domestic actors, a variety of regional, global, supranational, and transnational actors have played crucial roles in the politics of genocide justice in Cambodia. First, by virtue of their geographical proximity, one must consider Cambodia's neighbors in ASEAN. Of these, Thailand and Vietnam are special cases due to their shared borders with Cambodia, and their intimate involvement with the Khmer Rouge issue. Thailand and Vietnam both have very complicated histories in Cambodia, in general, and with the Khmer Rouge, in particular. The Vietnamese communists were, in a sense, marriage partners of the Khmer Rouge during the Second Indochina War from 1954 to 1975. They soon sued for divorce, however, engaging the Khmer Rouge in the first full-scale war between socialist nations in the Third Indochina War, which began in 1975 and lasted until the Paris Peace Accords in 1991. Thailand followed a converse trajectory, beginning as an enemy of the Khmer Rouge and ending up serving as a life preserver for their apocalypse by providing sanctuary and military support when the Vietnamese overthrew the Khmer Rouge regime.

Though Vietnam has viewed the Khmer Rouge as a mortal enemy, several problems have induced them to take a low profile on the issue of the Khmer Rouge tribunal. One of the foremost is that after their recent military occupation of Cambodia from 1979 to 1989, they do not wish to expose themselves to further accusations of interfering in Cambodia's internal affairs. Fortunately for them, it is easy to avoid any such perception because Vietnam has a close relationship with Cambodia's ruling party, and hence there are many channels through which they are able to make their views known on any matter of concern. Another issue for the Vietnamese is their own rapprochement with the People's Republic of China and their sensitivity to China's opposition to the idea of a Khmer Rouge tribunal. The Vietnamese see no need to rub the Khmer Rouge tribunal issue in the face of one of the sole remaining countries with which they enjoy fraternal party-to-party communist ties.

To a certain extent, the Vietnamese may have the sense that they had their say in 1979, when they orchestrated the People's Revolutionary Tribunal, condemning Pol Pot and Ieng Sary to death. Ultimately, as hardcore realists, the Vietnamese know that the Khmer Rouge—regardless of the tribunal question—are finished as a political or military threat. As things stand, the Vietnamese seem relatively satisfied with their current relationship to the authorities in Phnom Penh. This is not to say, however, that the Vietnamese always see eye to eye with Cambodia's ruling party on the Khmer Rouge issue, because the question of genocide justice has caused bilateral strains from time to time. For example, after Prime Minister Hun Sen received surrendering Khmer Rouge leaders Nuon Chea and Khieu Samphan and suggested that the Cambodian people should "dig a hole and bury the past," Vietnam's People's Army newspaper lashed out at the Cambodian prime minister. The paper demanded a tribunal, saying that Khmer Rouge "crimes cannot be forgotten and must be punished."[26]

Thailand, likewise, finds itself in a somewhat delicate situation. For centuries, the Siamese have not been shy about their willingness to host and sponsor Cambodians who are attempting to seize state power. However, their most recent episode of such sponsorship—backing the Khmer Rouge for nearly two decades after they were driven from the seat of power—ended badly, with their clients on the losing end of the game. The Thai thus embarked on something of a campaign to make amends with Hun Sen's government, the winner of that contest. This was most concretely seen in their cooperation with the surrender of the final elements of the Khmer Rouge political leadership late in 1998 and the capture of the last Khmer Rouge military leader, Ta Mok, early in 1999. With the election of Prime Minister Thaksin Shinawatra, this Thai diplomatic initiative accelerated rapidly. For example, Kraisak Choonhaven, the chairman of the Thai Senate Foreign Relations Committee, visited Cambodia in March 2001 and publicly admitted past Thai support for the Khmer Rouge—something previously unheard of—declaring that this policy had been wrong and that Thailand owed Cambodia an apology.[27] Thai Prime Minister Thaksin paid a state visit to Cambodia in June 2001 and hailed a "new era" of bilateral cooperation between the two countries.[28] In this emerging environment, it appears likely that Thailand will ultimately support Cambodia on the tribunal.[29]

The other ASEAN states do not share a strong consensus on the tribunal issue, reflecting the general political incoherence that has emerged in ASEAN since the expansion of ASEAN's traditional six members to the present slate of ten nations. Generally speaking, Singapore and the Philippines have been supportive of the tribunal idea, while Myanmar, Indonesia, and Malaysia have tended more toward a negative perspective. Laos and Brunei have been relatively neutral, consumed with their own internal issues.

Singapore, despite the mildly authoritarian one-party rule by the People's Action Party, seeks to promote its image as the most cosmopolitan state in Southeast Asia. One element of this image is that Singapore often sides with European countries on issues of international humanitarian law. Likewise, the Philippines tends to take a modernist approach to issues of international law, a tendency that has remained consistent through several changes of national leadership. The Philippines has occasionally expressed interest in helping to deal with the tribunal issue, at one point even provisionally agreeing to seat an international Khmer Rouge tribunal in Manila, as had been suggested in the January 1999 Report of the UN Group of Experts.[30]

As the poster-boy pariah state of Southeast Asia, Myanmar's military junta does not tend to figure prominently in most regional political calculations. During Cambodian Premier Hun Sen's occasional outbursts of nationalistic rhetoric on the tribunal issue, nonetheless, Myanmar military spokesmen routinely respond with approving noises, insofar as they have developed a visceral dislike for any and all UN enforcement and human rights mechanisms.

Indonesia has so many problems of its own that it, too, has maintained a fairly low profile on many regional issues in recent years. This tendency became even more pronounced under President Megawati Sukarnoputri's troubled administration, but the tribunal issue has been an exception to this rule. Fearful of being held accountable for the genocidal carnage wrought in East Timor by the Indonesian military, Indonesia has been in a mood to reflexively oppose the application of any external accountability measures for violations of international humanitarian law. Malaysia's recently retired Prime Minister Mahathir, with his unique conception of "Asian Values," similarly has bridled against any attempt to defend international law when it could potentially threaten the interests of a regional ruling elite.

Thus, there is not a strong consensus on the Khmer Rouge tribunal issue within ASEAN. This fact, combined with ASEAN's slightly frayed principle of noninterference in the internal affairs of its members, means that neither ASEAN collectively nor any of its members individually are likely to exert a great deal of influence on the issue of the Khmer Rouge tribunal. Thus, it is all the more remarkable that at the thirty-fifth annual ASEAN Ministerial Summit meeting in Bandar Seri Begawan, Brunei, on July 30, 2002, the Southeast Asian nations acquiesced in the Cambodian government's request to issue a call for renewed engagement by the UN in the tribunal negotiations. ASEAN pledged to support the Royal Government's "continued efforts" to bring the Khmer Rouge to justice.[31] In line with that commitment, in the December 2002 UN General Assembly vote on a resolution requesting that the UN secretary-general resume negotiations with the Royal Government on the establishment of a genocide tribunal, all ten ASEAN members supported the resolution. Friends of Cambodia in the international community were thus pulling the train toward genocide justice over the objections of the UN itself.

CHINA

As befits their status, the Great Powers have had more influence on the tribunal negotiations than have regional actors. One of the most closely concerned countries has been China, and its position has been clear. The Chinese take a very dim view of international involvement in a Khmer Rouge tribunal, for several obvious reasons. For one thing, they consider the concept of prosecuting the leaders of an Asian communist revolution for the deaths of millions of people during the revolution to be a very bad precedent, indeed.[32] Moreover, as the principal ally and patron of the Khmer Rouge for several decades, they have no wish to hear the details of their state-to-state and party-to-party relations with the Khmer Rouge, much less accusations of their own culpability, argued in a genocide court. Finally, the Chinese know the value of long-term loyalty toward allies, and they are not about to betray their long-standing solidarity with the Khmer Rouge. That could potentially jeopardize their ongoing assiduous courtship of other nations in the region.

As a result, China has pursued an aggressive lobbying strategy, attempting to kill the baby tribunal before it is born. Chinese officials have made clear that they would veto any attempt by the UN Security Council to create a Cambodia tribunal using the council's powers to protect the peace.[33] They have relentlessly opposed the efforts by the UN bureaucracy to persuade the Cambodians to adopt structures for the tribunal that meet what Kofi Annan calls "international standards."[34] Chinese officials have been omnipresent in Cambodia over the last several years, including visits by President Jiang Zemin and Premier Zhu Rongji, showering Cambodia with gifts and favors. They have repeatedly feted Cambodian ruling party President Chea Sim in Beijing. They have funded the construction of a new building in the National Assembly compound and another in the Senate compound. China is funding military demobilization, military procurement, land mine removal, flood relief, energy development, agricultural irrigation, and many other projects in Cambodia. In November 2002, Chinese Premier Zhu Rongji visited Phnom Penh and forgave the Khmer Rouge state debt to China, reportedly amounting to as much as $2 billion.[35]

There are certainly other reasons for the intense Chinese interest in Cambodia, above and beyond opposing an international tribunal for the Khmer Rouge. These reasons span the spectrum of economic, political, and security interests. Particularly important motivations for Chinese foreign policy behavior in Cambodia include driving a strategic wedge into ASEAN and challenging U.S., Indian, Japanese, and other Great Power influence in the region at large. Establishing beachheads from which to exploit the region's natural resources and enhance trade and investment opportunities is another factor. Even so, one of the principal facets of Chinese diplomacy toward Cambodia over the last several years has been to make sure that any Khmer Rouge tribunal will not be harmful to the interests of the People's Republic of China.

The United States

The U.S. government has also been a consistent player in the Khmer Rouge tribunal issue, at least since the U.S. Congress forced a change of policy in the early 1990s. Since the passage of the 1994 Cambodian Genocide Justice Act, the U.S. government has faithfully implemented that law, which made it the "policy of the United States to support efforts to bring to justice those accused of crimes against humanity" in Cambodia.[36] In the early years of the Clinton administration, this support was mostly in the form of financial assistance to the investigations being carried out by Yale University's Cambodian Genocide Program.[37] In subsequent years, under the leadership of Secretary of State Madeleine Albright, with the hands-on diplomacy being conducted by Ambassador-at-Large for War Crimes David Scheffer, numerous initiatives were launched in an attempt to bring about accountability for the Khmer Rouge leadership. These included looking at the possibility of domestic U.S. prosecutions for the murder of U.S. citizens by the Khmer Rouge, an ill-fated draft statute for a UN Security Council-mandated tribunal, efforts to persuade allies such as Canada, Australia, and Israel to agree to prosecutions in their own country under the principle of universal jurisdiction, a covert attempt to purchase Khmer Rouge leader Pol Pot from his rebellious troops in barter for rice and medicine, and finally, attempting to serve as an "honest broker" in the negotiations to establish the proposed "mixed" tribunal.[38]

The policy of the George W. Bush administration on the Khmer Rouge tribunal has been notably less energetic than the Clinton team's efforts, but it has not fundamentally altered the long-standing Clinton policy. Ideological fault lines among Republican activists have resulted in an internal struggle over this issue. Some conservative activists favor a proliferation of temporary international tribunals like the International Criminal Tribunal for Yugoslavia, courts with carefully circumscribed mandates, as a way to undermine the mandate of the permanent International Criminal Court. The results of this policy tendency can be seen in continued U.S. support of a Khmer Rouge tribunal, along with other tribunals including those for Sierra Leone and Kosovo, and perhaps a new tribunal for East Timor, as well. We have also seen preparations for an Iraq Tribunal by the Bush administration.[39] This project has significantly quickened in the wake of Saddam Hussein's ouster.[40]

On the other side of the policy divide, there is a very different current of thought animated by a neoconservative political orientation. For activists of this school, there remains unfinished business from the Cold War, personified by postcommunist characters as diverse as Slobodan Milosevic of Yugoslavia, Jose Eduardo Dos Santos of Angola—and Hun Sen of Cambodia. From this perspective, the priority must be on purging the authoritarian vestiges left behind in the collapse of world socialism and attempting to reinforce such democratic trends as may emerge in these countries. In Cambodia, this means opposing Hun Sen and his Cambodian People's Party, along with opposing any distraction to the primary project. Such distractions include things like a Khmer Rouge tribunal. Thus do some Republican foreign policy activists and organizations, such as the International Republican Institute (IRI), view the Khmer Rouge tribunal proposal so dimly. It is significant that both the former president of IRI, Lorne Craner, and IRI's former Asia director, Paul Grove, moved into positions of policy influence at the U.S. Department of State and in the U.S. Senate, respectively, during the Bush administration.[41] Like Cambodia's Sam Rainsy, some activists of this persuasion argue that it is not worth establishing a Khmer Rouge tribunal unless the tribunal is configured in such a way that it can indict Cambodian Prime Minister Hun Sen.

U.S. government officials have frequently denounced the International Criminal Court as a threat to U.S. sovereignty, citing their concern over potential "politically motivated" prosecutions of U.S. officials by the court. These concerns are a mirror image of the Cambodian government's concerns about a purely UN-controlled court. Those Cambodian concerns have been made all the more acute by calls from Republicans in the U.S. Congress, echoing calls by Cambodian opposition political leader Sam Rainsy, for Prime Minister Hun Sen to be brought before a tribunal and prosecuted for war crimes. The irony of this mirror image seems to be entirely lost on those U.S. legislators who simultaneously denounce the International Criminal Court as well as Hun Sen's cautious attitude about a internationally controlled criminal tribunal for the Khmer Rouge.

The U.S. Congress has been fractious and inconsistent on these issues. The House of Representatives is divided on the Khmer Rouge tribunal, and the initiative there was held until early 2004 by antitribunal voices such as California's Dana Rohrabacher. In March 2004, Representative Rohrabacher had a change of heart, cosponsoring a resolution that called on the president to support the Khmer Rouge tribunal.[42] In the Senate, until early 2001, there was a solid bipartisan majority in favor of continued support for the tribunal. Some creative legislation on the Khmer Rouge tribunal issue was put forward by Republican Senator Mitch McConnell.[43] In 2001, however, McConnell announced his opposition to the tribunal as currently envisioned and called on the Bush administration to reverse the U.S. policy of support for genocide justice in Cambodia. McConnell has had the support of some key Democratic senators for this change of position.[44] It remains to be seen if the Bush administration's neoconservative political appointees will exhibit enough energy, and are willing to expend enough political capital, to overcome the institutional momentum of the career bureaucracy on this issue. Thus, it is presently unclear whether either of these two orientations among Republican foreign policy activists will eventually come to dominate Bush administration policy on the Khmer Rouge tribunal, or whether we will continue to see a muddled and ongoing struggle between the two. These internal U.S. struggles on the Khmer Rouge tribunal issue do little to benefit the Cambodian people's aspirations for genocide justice, primarily serving only to further complicate the matter.

OTHER WESTERN PROTRIBUNAL NATIONS

Of European countries with a lively interest in the Khmer Rouge tribunal issue, the British, Dutch, Danish, Norwegians, and Swedish have shown the most consistent level of interest in, and support for, UN involvement in a Khmer Rouge tribunal. Along with two large English-speaking nations, Canada and Australia, this group has encouraged movement in the tribunal negotiations process not only by diplomatic means, but through other measures as well. For example, all seven have provided direct funding to the Documentation Center of Cambodia. These countries have also pressed hard in seeking to improve the quality of jurisprudence at a Khmer Rouge tribunal. In this respect, it is notable that six of these seven—Australia was the sole exception—abstained in a UN General Assembly vote on December 18, 2002.[45] That vote resulted in the adoption of a resolution requesting that Secretary-General Kofi Annan resume negotiations with the Royal Government on the establishment and implementation of the tribunal. The abstainers felt that the effort was flawed by Cambodia's refusal to officially cosponsor the resolution, as well as by the flaccid negotiating mandate given to the secretary-general in the resolution. Again, this rift among even the most steadfast Western supporters of a Khmer Rouge tribunal points up the complexity of the international negotiations to establish the tribunal.

JAPAN

Japan has shown a strong and consistent interest in Cambodia for more than a decade, beginning with the appointment of a Japanese diplomat as head of the UN peacekeeping mission in Cambodia in the early 1990s and the concurrent first-ever dispatch of Japanese armed forces to participate in a UN peacekeeping operation. The Japanese also serve as cochair of the Consultative Group, which is the international aid donor's mechanism for Cambodia that arose out of the 1991–1993 UN intervention. In addition, Japan has been the single largest bilateral provider of aid to Cambodia over the last decade, pledging in excess of US$100 million at the 2001 annual Consultative Group meeting alone for such large-scale infrastructure projects as bridges, roads, ports, hydro dams, water distribution, telecommunications, and power plants. In Kampong Cham Province, for instance, Japan recently completed Cambodia's first bridge across the Mekong River. Japan's focused interest in developing close relations with

Cambodia has been reflected in their posture on the Khmer Rouge tribunal, as well.

Japan has offered to provide a jurist to serve as one of the international judges on a Khmer Rouge mixed national-international tribunal.[46] Moreover, according to some in the diplomatic community, at one point Japan was contemplating a contribution of as much as $60 million to the funding of the tribunal.[47] As a measure of relative interest in the Khmer Rouge tribunal, the contribution the Japanese were reportedly considering compares favorably with the mere $2 million that had been earmarked for the purpose of Khmer Rouge tribunal support in U.S. legislation—prior to the November 2002 U.S. election, at least, when control of the U.S. Congress shifted to Republicans, along with their policy agenda. As recently as December 2002, Japan coauthored with France the successful UN General Assembly resolution urging the UN Secretariat to reengage with the Khmer Rouge tribunal process, a move that cleared the way for the final deal between the UN and Cambodia.[48] Thus, the Japanese remain very interested in the prospects for a Khmer Rouge tribunal, and they have been showing that interest in concrete ways.

RUSSIA, INDIA, AND FRANCE

Though they have obvious differences, Russia, India, and France can be grouped together for purposes of analyzing Khmer Rouge tribunal politics. These countries have divergent interests in the region in general and Cambodia in particular, but all three share a somewhat equivocal view of UN involvement in a Khmer Rouge tribunal. All three countries would be likely to support a decision by the Cambodian government to proceed with a Khmer Rouge tribunal absent the participation of the UN. Russian and Indian lawyers, along with French journalists, attended the 1979 People's Revolutionary Tribunal in Phnom Penh, which sentenced Pol Pot and Ieng Sary to death *in absentia*. Twenty years later, lawyers from all three countries were invited to Cambodia to consult with the government as it crafted the Khmer Rouge tribunal law in 1999 and 2000.[49]

India has been the most aggressive in paving the way for an independent Cambodian tribunal. Indian Prime Minister Atal Behari Vajpayee publicly announced in Phnom Penh on April 9, 2002, that his country would provide judges and other aid for a Khmer Rouge tribunal if the UN declined to be involved.[50] India has a long-standing diplomatic interest in Cambodia, and cultural ties between the two countries go back thousands of years.

Though France has cooperated with the United States on the tribunal issue in various ways, the French have sent mixed signals on the tribunal from time to time. The French legal scholar Claude Gour was one of the principal architects of the first draft of the Cambodian tribunal law,[51] a draft that was rejected by UN legal experts on the grounds that it was seriously incompatible with international legal standards.[52] Officials at the UN Secretariat have complained privately on occasion about the French role in the tribunal negotiations. This long-standing aggravation was exacerbated by the December 2002 General Assembly resolution, coauthored by France, which forced the Secretariat back into the negotiations it had abandoned ten months previously. There often seems to be a sense in Paris that as a member of Francophonie and a former colony, Cambodia has a special relationship with France, and the interference of other countries with that relationship is not welcome.

The UN

One supranational actor quite deserves mention in Cambodian genocide tribunal politics—the UN itself. Most often in matters of high politics, the UN acts primarily as an agent for UN member states. In the Khmer Rouge tribunal saga, however, the UN role has been partially autonomous and highly complex. Action by UN officials was central in driving the whole tribunal process forward for more than five years.

In June 1997, three officials of the UN Office for Human Rights in Phnom Penh—David Hawk, Brad Adams, and Christophe Peschoux—worked with the secretary-general's special representative for human rights in Cambodia, Ambassador Thomas Hammarberg, to get the signatures of Cambodia's then-co-prime ministers on a letter requesting UN assistance in setting up a Khmer Rouge tribunal. In turn, this led to the secretary-general's appointment of the UN Group of Experts, who examined the situation in late 1998 and recommended in January 1999 that the International Criminal Tribunal for the former Yugoslavia should essentially be cloned for Cambodia.[53]

The Cambodian government flatly rejected that proposal, leading to four years of on-again, off-again negotiations by the UN Secretariat, represented by the UN's Office of Legal Affairs, attempting to find a formula acceptable to the Cambodian government.[54] This process resulted in the Khmer Rouge tribunal law that was promulgated in Phnom Penh but that the UN found to be unsatisfactory.[55] The UN General Assembly then forced the UN Secretariat's hand in accepting a tribunal deal based on the Cambodian law.

Why has the UN pushed so hard? Partly this is a result of the combination of pressures from the five permanent members of the UN Security Council. The Chinese have resisted the tribunal with all their might, but the United States has pushed back even harder, with support from Britain and France, while the Russians have been mostly passive, but in any case have never posed a serious obstacle. The result of this correlation of forces was steady political support for the UN Secretariat's initiatives on the tribunal, up to, but not including, the Secretariat's attempt to withdraw from the negotiating process.

Perhaps the most significant factor has been an idiosyncratic one, in the person of the secretary-general himself. Over the resistance of his own legal advisers, Hans Corell and Ralph Zacklin, Kofi Annan personally kept the tribunal project alive long after his Office of Legal Affairs began advocating a UN withdrawal. One factor seems to be that Annan felt he and the UN had something to prove after the UN's debacles in Rwanda and the Balkans. The secretary-general has publicly commented many times about the UN's failure to protect the people of Rwanda in 1994 and has vowed that the UN will improve its performance on issues pertaining to genocide for the remainder of his tenure.[56] Whatever Annan's motivation, there is no question about the fact that he has led the UN to play a key role in seeking accountability for the crimes of the Khmer Rouge.

NonGovernmental Actors

Some transnational nonstate actors have had a notable impact on the course of tribunal negotiations, including Amnesty International and Human Rights Watch. Both of these venerable human rights organizations generally supported the proposal put forward by the UN Group of Experts for a cloning of the Yugoslavia tribunal. Both organizations, however, have been fiercely critical of the tribunal law ultimately adopted by the Royal Government.[57] They argue that Cambodia's Khmer Rouge tribunal law constitutes "second-class justice" for Cambodia and that it sets an unfortunate precedent for the enforcement of international humanitarian law in view of the newly established International Criminal Court. UN officials have been remarkably sensitive to criticism from these human rights groups and privately noted their pleasure at the support they received from both Human Rights Watch and Amnesty International for the decision to withdraw from the tribunal negotiations in February 2002.

Another important transnational actor is the Documentation Center of

Cambodia. The Documentation Center has played, and continues to play, a significant advocacy role not only within Cambodia but also on the international stage. On the Cambodian domestic political scene, in some respects, the Documentation Center is an 800-pound guerilla. Among Cambodian politicians—virtually all of whom have had some sort of connection to the Khmer Rouge—no one knows exactly what is contained in the 1 million pages of primary documents held by the center. This fact contributes materially to the high level of deference accorded to the Documentation Center in almost all quarters. One thing is for certain, however: among the enormous archive of documents and other materials gathered by the Documentation Center, there is evidence aplenty to trouble the defense attorneys of the surviving Khmer Rouge leadership, should they ever be brought to justice. On the international scene, the Documentation Center has worked closely with the UN in preparing for a Khmer Rouge tribunal and has carried out sustained advocacy in support of the tribunal among the community of interested governments across the globe.

In general, then, it can be said that there is strong support across all categories of actors in the international community for the principle of genocide justice in Cambodia. Those few that have taken an opposing view—primarily the People's Republic of China—have been able to block certain potential mechanisms, such as a Security Council-mandated organ, but have not been able to stem the rising tide of international support for a tribunal. Even so, the interplay of overlapping interests among those members of the international community who do support the idea of a Khmer Rouge genocide tribunal has ensured that the negotiating process would be long and Byzantine. When one combines this welter of contending international interests with the complexities of the views on the tribunal among Cambodia's political elite, the issue becomes mind-numbingly complex. We now conclude our analysis of the politics of genocide justice in Cambodia with a brief consideration of how the domestic and international aspects of the issue interact in practice.

INTERACTION OF DOMESTIC AND INTERNATIONAL POLITICAL DIMENSIONS

Cambodian Prime Minister Hun Sen faces the challenge of balancing these competing domestic and international viewpoints. It is difficult to assess how the prime minister intends to accomplish this balancing act. His recorded statements on the tribunal issue are all over the map. Looking at how the premier has managed the issue thus far in terms of concrete action, however, one can register slow—very slow—forward progress toward some sort of tribunal, but the pace of that progress has been so glacial that it has given rise to reasonable doubts about whether or not it will ever arrive at its destination.

That Cambodia may never achieve real genocide justice is one distinct possibility. At a ruling party Central Committee meeting in February 2000, Hun Sen addressed the gathered core members of the party, reassuring an antitribunal cadre that there was no need to worry about the tribunal, because he had successfully stalled progress on the negotiations for the previous three years, and he would continue to stall the international community until all of the key suspects had died natural deaths, thus rendering the entire question moot.[58] Did Hun Sen say this simply as a tactic to cut off debate among Central Committee members opposed to a tribunal, or did it reflect his real policy intentions? The available evidence is consistent with either interpretation.

In July 2001, however, members of the ruling party who are in favor of a Khmer Rouge tribunal privately asserted that the party's politburo had forged an internal consensus to go ahead with the tribunal. Exactly when and under exactly what circumstances such a tribunal would go ahead remained ambiguous. Again, then, the available evidence as to the real intentions of the ruling party leadership on the Khmer Rouge tribunal appeared to be inconclusive. It may well be that this was precisely the impression the ruling party leadership wished to give, because there have been significant incentives for the ruling party to leave the international community guessing about where this issue will finally come to rest.

The Royal Government often insists that it desires international assistance for a Khmer Rouge tribunal, and it continues to seek further negotiations with the UN and interested states for the establishment of such a tribunal. Some countries, such as the United States, say that Cambodian cooperation with the international community on establishing Khmer Rouge trials is a requirement for continued foreign aid. The Royal Government has consistently told these countries that it is doing its best to cooperate with the international community and the UN on the Khmer Rouge trials. In part as a reward for this cooperative attitude on the tribunal issue, the international community has provided billions of dollars in aid to Cambodia over the last several years.

Other countries—the People's Republic of China in particular—have made clear that they oppose an international tribunal for the Khmer Rouge. The Royal Government has consistently told the Chinese that it is following the "Two Victories Policy." One of those "victories" is to "forget the past."[59] Avoiding a Khmer Rouge tribunal is one way to forget the past. To help encourage this friendly attitude from the Royal Government, China has provided huge amounts of financial assistance to Cambodia, by some estimates as much as billions of dollars in just the last few years.

In these circumstances, the Royal Government has had a strong economic incentive to delay a Khmer Rouge trial indefinitely. As long as no trial has been convened, but a trial is still possible, China will continue to shower gifts on the government, hoping to influence that decision. As long as the Royal Government continues to negotiate with the rest of the international community about a Khmer Rouge trial, Europe, Japan, the United States, and other countries may well continue to provide foreign aid as an incentive to encourage Cambodia to "continue to move in the right direction."

Thus, the mere prospect of Khmer Rouge trials has produced a financial windfall for the Royal Government. The possibility that a Khmer Rouge tribunal might be established has kept billions of dollars of assistance flowing into Cambodia, both from those who oppose as well as from those who support the idea of a trial for the Khmer Rouge. A final decision to convene such a tribunal—or to conclusively reject the idea of a genocide trial—would eliminate this ambiguity and result in the alienation of one or the other of two crucial international constituencies the Royal Government has been courting. This logic is why some find it reasonable to suspect that the Royal Government may never come to a final decision about whether, when, or how to bring justice to the victims of the Khmer Rouge.

In this respect, Hun Sen's management of the tribunal issue illustrates an important technique of weak power diplomacy. Hun Sen has a tendency to tell everyone what he or she wants to hear, and then he wobbles a bit to keep everyone off-balance and continuing to beat a path to his door with additional inducements. It is a technique he learned from his greatest teacher, Norodom Sihanouk.[60] To Chinese audiences, Hun Sen repeats the same mantra: Cambodia is following the "Two Victories" policy, which is to forget the past and concentrate only on the future—forgetting the past being the key phrase the Chinese want to hear. To American audiences, Hun Sen demands that the tribunal be convened before the end of this year—no matter what year one might be talking about—arguing that the Cambodian people deserve justice for the crimes of the Khmer Rouge regime. To French, Russian, and Indian audiences, he complains about the bullying of the sole superpower and the dangers of UN interference in one's internal affairs, while lauding the importance of national sovereignty. To Australian, Canadian, and Dutch audiences, he speaks of the need for Cambodia to move beyond its communist past and put to rest the ghosts of the Cambodian genocide. To Japanese audiences, he talks of the importance of developing Cambodia's economy and the crucial role a prosperous, modern, leading Asian nation like Japan can play in the growth and strategic stability of the entire region. Hun Sen is a superb tactician and is reputed to be a master-level chess player. It shows in the way he manages both his domestic and foreign policy challenges.

With the extended political deadlock following the national elections of July 2003, the Royal Government was not in a position to make genocide justice a policy priority during the second half of 2003 and the first half of 2004. The pace of the prior negotiations had been very leisurely, indeed, with long delays attributed to a range of causes. There was a delay due to termites infesting the roof of the National Assembly. There were long delays laid to governmental preoccupation with the annual flooding. There was the inexplicable five-month struggle to fashion an unnecessary one-sentence amendment to the Khmer Rouge tribunal law pointing out that Cambodia's Constitution prohibits the death penalty. There was a delay in providing an English translation of the promulgated law to the UN. The Royal Government has appeared to be in no big hurry to resolve the Khmer Rouge tribunal issue, notwithstanding regular statements by senior Royal Government officials calling for the prompt convening of the tribunal.[61] Additional delays from the UN side—for virtually the entire year of 2002—only exacerbated the problem of the ticking clock. It remains to be seen if the casual attitude by the Royal Government toward satisfying Cambodian popular demands for genocide justice will continue into the future, or, now that the UN has agreed to the tribunal on terms amenable to the Cambodian government, if it will finally move forward with dispatch.

In the meanwhile, there are reports that the health of several of the principal surviving suspects—particularly Nuon Chea, Ieng Sary, and Ta Mok—continues to deteriorate. Within Cambodia's domestic political sphere, a range of competing and sometimes contradictory interests continues to raise the threat of additional delays to the process of establishing a tribunal. International and intraorganizational disagreements on how to handle the Khmer Rouge tribunal issue within the UN system continue to threaten additional delays. Political and bureaucratic struggles within the U.S. government and in other key governments over the issue also pose a danger of further complicating the matter. One might also anticipate that inducements to the Royal Government from those in the international community with interests in the outcome of the question will continue to accumulate. So it is that Cambodia's culture of impunity remains intact, and that an entire people's hopes to achieve accountability for one of the worst episodes of mass murder in modern history have for so long been held hostage to the politics of genocide justice in Cambodia.

10

CHALLENGING THE CULTURE
OF IMPUNITY

The "culture of impunity" has strong roots in Cambodia, plunging deep into the past and widely spread in the present. It represents one of the most fundamental obstacles to the development of social unity and to the flowering of peace and democracy in the future. By a culture of impunity, I mean a set of social expectations—structured by supporting laws, customs, and behaviors—that the strong can do what they will and the weak will suffer what they must. In essence, the term describes an anarchical society in which the principal forces of anarchy wield social, economic, political, and/or military power and are unconstrained by any effective sanctions against predatory behavior.

It has been acknowledged at the highest levels of the Royal Government that Cambodia has a serious problem in the culture of impunity. In September 1999, Prime Minister Hun Sen told UN Secretary-General Kofi Annan that the Royal Government would reject the UN's second proposal to establish an international criminal tribunal, expressly designed to address the problem of impunity for violations of international humanitarian law during the Democratic Kampuchea regime of the 1970s. Instead, the prime minister declared, Cambodia would deal with this problem by forming a national tribunal to bring Khmer Rouge perpetrators to justice. Such a policy, the prime minister asserted, would strike an effective blow against the "culture of impunity."[1]

This final chapter analyzes Prime Minister Hun Sen's proposal to address the problem of impunity in Cambodia using a national criminal tribunal with international elements, to mete out retributive justice for the crimes of the Khmer Rouge regime. We begin by briefly examining the historical origins of the culture of impunity in Cambodia. We then outline the consequences of a culture of impunity for the present and future of social development in Cambodia. Finally, we consider the prospects for transforming Cambodia's culture of impunity into a culture governed through the Rule of Law by attacking impunity using judicial measures. This analysis includes an examination of how impunity has and has not been changed through the application of retributive justice measures in other countries. The analysis concludes with an examination of how varying approaches to the problems of justice and reconciliation in Cambodia might have an impact on the culture of impunity.

THE ROOTS OF IMPUNITY

The roots of impunity in Cambodia run deep and have been conditioned by both domestic and international influences over the millennia. For centuries, the Cambodian God-King's word was law, and there was no appeal save by violent overthrow of the sovereign. When the God-King appointed a governor to rule a region of the country, that governor was given a warrant to "consume" the people and the land under his control.[2] This system represented institutionalized impunity, and that ancient practice has many echoes in the way Cambodia is governed today. More recently, in the current Kingdom of Cambodia, provincial governors and military commanders exercise a great deal of autonomy from the central government, sometimes operating with the sanction of Phnom Penh and in other cases operating entirely outside the control of national authorities. Whether acting with or without permission from the government, they operate with impunity in extracting human and natural resources from the areas over which they hold sway.[3] Though the times may have changed, the pattern of impunity has remained the same. The rule of law has never been an important factor at any stage in Cambodian history.

Impunity has been a consistent characteristic of Cambodian political life. Under the government of Prince Norodom Sihanouk in the 1950s and 1960s, as Steve Heder has observed, impunity was also the order of the day. In 1959, Sihanouk promulgated a law that reconstituted a French colonial institution, the "Special Military Court." This legal mechanism was used to repress domestic political opposition of all stripes, including Sam Sary, the father of current opposition leader Sam Rainsy.[4] Again, there was no appeal. This pattern of institutionalized impunity for the ruling class did not change appreciably under any of the subsequent regimes, through the Khmer Republic, Democratic Kampuchea, the People's Republic of Kampuchea, and the State of Cambodia; nor, as noted earlier, did it change even under the ostensibly liberal democratic constitution of the present Kingdom of Cambodia.

We can see the pattern of impunity in present-day Cambodia through incidents of violence both large and small. During the fighting between troops loyal to the Cambodian People's Party and units loyal to the royalist FUNCINPEC party in July 1997, for example, perhaps 100 or more people were killed, some of them through extrajudicial execution; no one has ever been charged with a crime in those murders.[5] The "Easter Massacre" of March 1997 against opposition politician Sam Rainsy and his supporters claimed perhaps a score or more lives, yet no one has been prosecuted for those killings, even though the atrocity was committed directly in front of the National Assembly and in plain view of hundreds of witnesses, including numerous journalists.[6] More than a dozen people were brutally murdered during the street demonstrations following the 1998 elections, and no perpetrator of those crimes has been seen in a court of law,[7] nor has anyone ever been charged with the savage public assassination of Cambodia's favorite actress in 1999.[8] So many murders, and not a suspect to be found anywhere. Sadly, it is the norm in Cambodia that a poor person might be brought before the court to answer for a murder committed in passion, in greed, or in desperation, but it is rare that a rich or powerful person will suffer consequences for a similar crime, whether it is motivated by passion or greed or by politics.

When one thinks of impunity in Cambodia, the first thing that comes to mind for most people is the Khmer Rouge. In terms of impunity, however, the difference between the Khmer Rouge regime and succeeding, as well as previous, regimes is a difference of degree rather than difference of kind. Even so, this pattern of official impunity clearly attained its most extreme expression in the context of the Khmer Rouge. No senior perpetrator has been brought to account before a court of law for the 2 million or more untimely deaths, many of them brutal executions, that occurred during the Khmer Rouge regime of 1975–1979. The pervasive impunity in Cambodian society is most ostentatiously exemplified by the crimes of the Khmer Rouge.

THE PERNICIOUS INFLUENCE
OF IMPUNITY

Thus, impunity suffuses contemporary Cambodian cultural and political life, but the pernicious effects of impunity reach far deeper than a failure to find justice for 2 million victims of a genocide, or 100 victims of a massacre, or even for a single life evidently taken by order of a jealous spouse. The disease of impunity impacts the way Cambodians look at everyday life and their relationship to society and has an especially corrosive effect on the socialization of the young. When, despite their noble, but patently false, rhetoric to the contrary, the leadership of the country does not respect the law, then how can young people learn respect for the Rule of Law? The young will not fail to notice that the key variable governing the success of society's elite is not law, but rather power. In such a society, there will be a natural tendency for the young to focus not on living their lives as good citizens under the law, but rather on finding people who are more vulnerable than they, so that they, too, may advance their own interests at the expense of others.

Thus, when the ethical underpinnings of Cambodian society were ruthlessly torn asunder by the Khmer Rouge, the impunity traditionally practiced by the elite henceforth came to infect the outlook of the common person. This is why the rehabilitation of Cambodia necessarily entails not only rebuilding the economic base of society but also reviving a sense of moral integrity in Cambodian society. The most crucial place to begin is with the problem of impunity.

Some wonder, Why bother? Why bother to trouble ourselves with the Khmer Rouge, who now amount to little more than a few discredited old men who have been stripped of their ability to kill? The answer is clear. Crimes against humanity are the worst crimes, worse than crimes against an individual, worse than crimes against the state. These are crimes against all of humanity. When the most monstrous crimes humans have ever conceived go unpunished, why should Cambodians worry about lesser crimes?

What is wrong with insulting my elders and ignoring their words? The Khmer Rouge insulted elders in my village and then killed them, but no punishment was ever meted out for that. What is wrong with threatening to kill a taxi driver in order to possess his motorcycle? The Khmer Rouge stole every motorcycle and everything else in the entire country, and no one was ever punished for that. What is wrong with intimidating political opponents, even killing some of them? The Khmer Rouge killed all of their opponents and a goodly number of their supporters; they were never punished. Any crimes I could commit will be less than those committed by the Khmer Rouge. They got away with it, so why should I also not do as I wish? This goes to the root of the problem of impunity.

A brief glance at the police blotter page in the biweekly *Phnom Penh Post* confirms the anarchy that prevails on Phnom Penh's streets. Until the worst crimes are punished, lesser crimes will be relativized. Until the matter of Khmer Rouge impunity is formally addressed, there will always be a ready excuse for the anarchy in Cambodian society: the Khmer Rouge were worse. Until the worst perpetrators are brought before the law, there can be no Rule of Law in Cambodia. This is why genocide justice is an essential measure for reconciliation and national reconstruction in Cambodia.

TRIBUNALS AND IMPUNITY

We now briefly consider the prospects for transforming Cambodia's culture of impunity into a culture governed through the Rule of Law by attacking impunity using new judicial measures. Bringing a number of Khmer Rouge leaders before a tribunal to answer for their crimes would certainly bring an end to their long-standing personal impunity as individuals. Whether or not it would also have a significant impact on the deeply entrenched culture of impunity in Cambodia is a much more complicated question. The answer to that question depends entirely on the details of how such a tribunal is structured and how its operations unfold in practice.

Cambodia's judicial system remains undertrained, underfunded, and underdeveloped. Cambodia's legal code is an anarchic mishmash of laws from the 1950s French-derived legal system, socialist decree laws from the 1980s, a UN-imposed legal code from the early 1990s, and additional laws promulgated since the Royal Government was formed in 1993. Only a small percentage of Cambodia's judges have had any formal academic legal training, and as a result, many of them are unaware of the basic procedures and practices common to their profession in most other countries of the world. The salaries of judges are very low, well below the minimum level required to sustain their own livelihoods, much less to support their families. This fact, as a practical matter, almost necessitates the corruption that is endemic throughout the Cambodian judicial system.[9] The state budget for the operation of the legal system is also woefully inadequate, and consequently judges and other court personnel often lack the basic tools they need to administer justice, including such fundamental materials as the legal texts delineating the laws they are supposed to be upholding.

Efforts at reforming Cambodia's legal system since the formation of the coalition government in 1993 have failed miserably. In January 2003, the UN's Cambodian Office of the High Commissioner for Human Rights released an analysis of a decade of attempts to reform Cambodia's legal and judicial system. After noting that the government had missed all targets for the reform of various aspects of the judiciary, the analysis concluded, "The reform measures envisaged in 1994 and 1995 failed to produce any concrete results."[10] The challenges in this regard remain immense.

The most serious problems with the judicial system in Cambodia go deeper than mere issues of professional incompetence and inadequate resources. The very structure of Cambodia's legal system ensures that judicial independence and legal professionalism cannot obtain in practice. Since 1979, Cambodian judges have been appointed, and their tenure ensured, on the basis of loyalty to the ruling party, rather than on fealty to the standards of the legal profession.[11] In the parlance popularized during the UN intervention of the early 1990s, there is no "neutral political environment" in the administration of justice. The structures of the state and the ruling party are intimately intertwined. Consequently, cases that bear on political matters tend to be decided on political rather than legal criteria; ordinary cases often go to the highest bidder, or the party with the most powerful connections.

Proponents of a tribunal for the Khmer Rouge have long held that one of the principal benefits of such an undertaking, above and beyond the inherent value of bringing to justice some of the world's most ruthless and prolific violators of human rights, would be the "demonstration effect" that a well-conducted tribunal would have on Cambodia's judicial system.[12] An international tribunal on the model of the International Criminal Tribunal for Yugoslavia, as suggested in the Report of the UN Group of Experts, for example, could be expected to operate according to the highest standards of legal integrity and professionalism. The contrast between such a modern judicial proceeding and the summary execution so rife during the Khmer Rouge regime might be startling to some Cambodians. Indeed, the contrasts that would be apparent between a court that operates according to international legal standards, on the one hand, and the current operations of the Cambodian judicial system, on the other hand, would be so strong that they might well inspire Cambodians to become more serious about the reform of their own system. Once people have experienced a better way, they tend to want it and generate political pressure to get it, even if their leaders might resist. That is the theory, at least.

If a properly conducted tribunal has the potential to buttress the Rule of Law, what might be the effect of a Khmer Rouge tribunal conducted according to standards less strict than what is often termed "international standards"? Let us hypothetically consider the extreme example of a blatant political "show trial." In the show trial, the political leadership determines beforehand who will be prosecuted, of what crimes they will be accused, what the verdict of the court shall be, and what punishments shall be meted out to those "found" guilty in court. A script is then devised to realize this scenario, and such evidence as is deemed necessary to inform the desired result is obtained or, if necessary, fabricated. Personnel are then recruited to enact the roles laid out in the script, and the morality play is then set in motion, moving inevitably toward the foreordained result. It is theoretically possible that such a proceeding could be "just," in the highly limited sense that the defendants might actually be guilty of having committed the crimes with which they were charged, and be deserving under the law of the penalties that were politically selected for them.

Even if it were just in this limited sense, such a scenario would not have a beneficial impact in combating the culture of impunity. Indeed, such a trial would be a prime example of the culture of impunity in action, despite the fact that an individual perpetrator might see his personal impunity come to an end. Power and political interests, rather than law and principle, would determine the outcome. The proceedings, though nominally cloaked in the Rule of Law, would in fact be only a masquerade thinly concealing the political will of the ruling elite. If a Khmer Rouge tribunal were to unfold according to this scenario, the entire process would ultimately have the effect of simply reinforcing the culture of impunity.

What, then, might one expect of a tribunal that fell somewhere in between the two extremes of "international legal standards" and political "show trial"? That would depend on the particulars of the actual conduct of the tribunal, because there are so many gradations between these two extremes. Near one end of this range of gradations, for instance, one can imagine a case in which one potential suspect, say Ieng Sary, were to be shielded from prosecution by political influence from powerful elites. At the same time, the remainder of the suspects might be subjected to a judicial accountability process in a relatively orderly and lawful fashion. In this scenario, although the particular case of Ieng Sary might represent a travesty of justice and a victory for the impunity of an individual, the sum total of the result could still constitute a significant blow against the culture of impunity. At the other end of the range of gradations, one can imagine a situation in which continual attempts to exercise political influence on judges, prosecutors, lawyers, defendants, and witnesses plague the proceedings of the tribunal from start to finish, but in the end, the responsible officers of the court rise to the challenge and carry out their duties strictly in accord with the law. Under this scenario, justice would ultimately have been served in the specific cases at issue, but at the same time, the atmosphere would be so clouded by suspicion and doubt that any possible "demonstration effect" could be lost in the fog, and the culture of impunity might well emerge intact.

These hypothetical scenarios are suggested simply to underline the fact that the connection between impunity and a tribunal is not a direct, simple relationship. The proof is not in the pudding, as is sometimes said, but rather in the eating. The extent to which a Khmer Rouge tribunal might have a beneficial impact on the culture of impunity depends intimately on how that tribunal is conducted. Unless the trials are conducted strictly under the Rule of Law, and unless this Rule of Law eventually becomes institutionalized in the structures of the government and internalized in the hearts and minds of the leaders and the people, then it is entirely possible that the tribunal will ultimately have no appreciable long-term impact on Cambodia's culture of impunity. Contrariwise, an improperly conducted tribunal may actually have the potential to reinforce the culture of impunity. To further explore this question, we now move beyond speculation on hypotheticals into an examination of some actual instances where criminal tribunals have been used in an attempt to attack impunity for gross violations of international humanitarian law.

COMPARATIVE APPROACHES TO IMPUNITY

Let us now briefly review some approaches to the problem of impunity that have recently been or may soon be applied in various countries. The cases of Yugoslavia, Rwanda, Ethiopia, Sierra Leone, and the newly established International Criminal Court provide some background by which we may be better able to assess Prime Minister Hun Sen's proposed plan for addressing impunity in Cambodia.

The International Criminal Tribunal for the Former Yugoslavia

The Federal Republic of Yugoslavia began to disintegrate in a series of wars among its constituent republics in the early 1990s. The conflict reached an acute phase with serious fighting among various elements of Bosnia and Herzegovina's multiethnic population in April 1992, violence supported in significant measure by two neighboring republics, Croatia and Serbia. The war riveted the world as the international community helplessly floundered amid the escalating violence. In the process, the term "ethnic cleansing" entered everyday language as a way to describe the process of forcibly expelling ethnic groups from territories in order to achieve a "pure" ethnic composition of the population. Thousands were slaughtered in the worst violence Europe had experienced since World War II.[13]

Finally, on May 25, 1993, with Resolution 827, the UN Security Council took the unprecedented step of establishing the International Criminal Tribunal for the Former Yugoslavia (ICTY), aiming to prosecute "persons responsible for serious violations of international humanitarian law committed in the territory of the former Yugoslavia since 1991."[14] The ICTY is based in The Hague, the Netherlands. Ten years after the establishment of the court, more than 100 persons had been indicted on charges of serious offenses against international criminal and humanitarian law. Of those indicted, approximately half were in custody, either with trials in progress or serving sentences after conviction.[15] Yugoslavian President Slobodan Milosevic—who is considered by many to have been the mastermind of the carnage in Bosnia—was extradited to the ICTY in June 2001 on charges of war crimes, genocide, and crimes against humanity.[16] His trial is expected to require many years to complete. While Milosevic has been brought to justice, numerous other key indictees remain at large, and the vast majority of those who perpetrated atrocities during the Yugoslav wars will never face charges from The Hague.

Thus, this form of international justice is a slow, laborious process and ultimately involves trial and punishment for only a very tiny minority of the individuals who were involved in atrocities. Under this approach to justice, most of the actual perpetrators will continue to enjoy impunity. Moreover, because the court is seated in the Netherlands, far from the scene of the crime and the survivors, it is not clear to what extent the sur-

viving victims of these crimes can see that justice is being done, even for
those few who have been prosecuted. Many of Milosevic's fellow Serbs appear to believe that his trial has nothing to do with justice.[17] It is also an
exceedingly expensive approach to achieving justice, costing on the order
of $100 million per year. Even though ad hoc tribunals such as the ICTY
are seen by many as the "gold standard" of international justice, then, there
are some disadvantages to this approach. Perhaps chief among these defects
are the facts that most perpetrators will never be brought to justice and
that both victims and perpetrators may be left with the impression that
justice in fact has not been done.

THE INTERNATIONAL CRIMINAL TRIBUNAL
FOR RWANDA

On April 6, 1994, a radical faction of the dominant Hutu ethnic group
in Rwanda seized state power and began killing members of the minority Tutsi ethnic group at the rate of more than 5,000 per day. The mind-
boggling frenzy of hacking, slashing, and burning went on for more than
100 days. By the time it was over, somewhere between 500,000 and
800,000 Tutsi and moderate Hutu had been murdered in one of the most
intense outbursts of violence in modern times.[18] In response to the killing,
the UN decided that rather than intervene to put a stop to the mayhem,
it would withdraw an international peacekeeping force already in place in
the small African country. It was a shameful decision and was largely orchestrated by the government of U.S. President Bill Clinton.[19]

In a belated and wholly inadequate response to the Rwandan debacle,
on November 8, 1994, the UN Security Council passed Resolution 955.[20]
This resolution established the ad hoc International Criminal Tribunal for
Rwanda (ICTR), effectively cloning a new chamber for the ICTY. The
ICTR's mandate is to prosecute leaders responsible for violations of international humanitarian law and international criminal law during the
Rwandan genocide. Like the ICTY, setting up the ICTR required a full
two years of preparatory work before the court was able to begin deliberations. Much time was required to write the court's legal statutes, recruit
judges and other personnel, set up the physical infrastructure for the tribunal, and complete other necessary preparations. Eventually, however, the
court was seated in Arusha, Tanzania—nearly 500 miles from Rwanda—
and began to hear cases. Soon the court began to set new precedents in
international criminal law.

A decade after the Security Council ordered the establishment of this court, fewer than ten persons had been convicted by the ICTR. Several dozen more were in custody and either awaiting or undergoing trial. Among those convicted or being tried were many of the top leaders of the regime responsible for the genocide. Despite the relatively small number of indictments, the court has set some important precedents. On September 2, 1998, in its first case, the ICTR found Jean Paul Akayesu guilty of genocide. This was the first time an international court had ever convicted someone on that charge. Moreover, the judges also found that systematic rape can constitute genocide, and Akayesu was also found guilty on this charge.[21]

Despite these successes, the court has been troubled from the outset by insufficient funding, procedural and personnel issues, and other difficulties. Perhaps most troubling is the fact that the ICTR has never enjoyed the confidence of the Rwandan government or, apparently, of the Rwandan people.[22] The lack of knowledge among the Rwandan people about the ICTR, along with their lack of faith in that tribunal's deliberations, raises serious questions about the utility of this entire, extremely expensive enterprise.

The ICTR has been a phenomenally expensive undertaking. It has been estimated that as of the end of 2002, with eight convictions and one acquittal, it cost $61 million to reach each of these nine judgments.[23] If the ICTR were the only opportunity to achieve justice for the Rwandan genocide, then just as is the case with the ICTY, the overwhelming majority of those who carried out the Rwandan genocide would escape justice and continue to enjoy impunity. Also as with the ICTY, as noted earlier, because the ICTR is seated in a foreign country, many Rwandans are not well informed about the meting out of justice to those who have been convicted. In this respect, one cannot avoid the conclusion that the impact of the ICTR on impunity in Rwanda has been limited.

Rwandan Domestic Genocide Prosecutions

In part due to the lack of confidence in the ICTR by the Rwandan government, as well as the fact that it was clear the ICTR would prosecute only the most senior leaders of the genocide, the Rwandan government that replaced the Hutu genocidal regime decided to initiate domestic genocide prosecutions. The regime set about arresting suspects and preparing criminal cases against the thousands of perpetrators who would never rise to the attention of the international court and who would otherwise enjoy impunity for their crimes. Eventually, more than 130,000 accused persons were arrested. Seven years later, more than 100,000 suspects were still languishing in detention, accused of complicity in the genocide but not brought to trial.[24] The number of accused was far beyond the capacity of the relatively primitive Rwandan justice system to process in any form of orderly trials. The truly horrific conditions under which these suspects were being held led to the death of many detainees from diseases and other preventable causes. Thus, the new regime faced the dilemma of being accused of violating the human rights of the genocide suspects, while being unwilling to release the suspected *genocidaires*. It is virtually certain that some of those being held have been falsely accused, as it is also certain that most of them are indeed guilty of participating in the genocide.

Despite these difficulties, growing numbers of the Rwandan genocide perpetrators have been convicted and sentenced—some to death—in these domestic prosecutions. Between 1997 and the end of 2002, some 7,000 domestic Rwandan genocide cases were concluded, with only a minority resulting in the death penalty.[25] In 1999, for example, 116 convicted *genocidaires* were sentenced to death.[26] In addition to the convictions at trial, more than 30,000 suspects have pleaded guilty to the charges against them.[27]

The Rwandan government has introduced a unique innovation in an attempt to cope with the overwhelming caseload faced by the decimated Rwandan criminal justice system. Rwanda has implemented a modified version of a traditional, community-based form of justice called *gacaca*.[28] Under this system, a significant number of the suspects being detained on suspicion of involvement in the genocide will be judged in the local communities where the crimes allegedly occurred.[29] This experiment attempts to combine aspects of restorative justice with retributive justice, and thus it has the potential to address the problem of impunity at a more fundamental level than ordinary criminal prosecutions. In the *gacaca*, perpetrators come face-to-face with their victims and, under certain circumstances, might find themselves negotiating the terms under which they can be accepted once again into the good graces of the community. Should it succeed, the *gacaca* experiment could potentially provide a model for other afflicted countries, such as Cambodia.

Thus, a wide range of measures has been taken to combat impunity in the wake of the Rwandan genocide. There have been international prosecutions for the top leaders of the genocide, thousands of prosecutions of rank-and-file genocide perpetrators in domestic Rwandan trials, tens of thousands of additional perpetrators confessing their guilt, and tens of thousands more cases that will be dealt with in the context of a community-based restorative justice process. Combined, then, it is clear these measures have dealt a serious blow to impunity in Rwanda.

ETHIOPIAN DOMESTIC GENOCIDE PROSECUTIONS

In 1974, a coup in Ethiopia overthrew Emperor Haile Selassie, along with the country's 3,000-year-old monarchy.[30] The Armed Forces Co-ordinating Committee, also known as the "Derg" (which means "shadow" in the Amharic language), established a military junta and set a course of Soviet-style reforms. After a period of internal turmoil within the Derg, a senior figure in the junta named Mengistu Haile Mariam managed to purge his rivals, emerging as the head of state and chairman of the junta. Mengistu then launched a period of intense repression that came to be known as the "Red Terror." Estimates of the death toll under the rule of the Derg range from 150,000 to 500,000, many of whom perished in summary executions.[31] The Derg regime finally collapsed in 1991 under the pressure generated by multiple rebellions.

The successor regime established an Office of the Special Prosecutor (OSP) to address impunity for crimes against humanity, genocide, and other serious violations of the law.[32] The OSP has indicted 5,198 suspects on charges of killing 8,752 particular victims, "disappearing" 2,611 people, and torturing 1,837 others. The suspects have been divided into three distinct categories, defined by degree of responsibility: policymakers and decision makers; officials who passed on orders or reached decisions on their own; and those directly responsible for committing the alleged crimes. Of those indicted, 2,246 suspects were in custody as of 1998, and the remainder were being prosecuted *in absentia*. When the trials commenced in September 1997, some of the accused had been in custody for more than six years.

There are several unique things about the Ethiopian genocide trials. When Ethiopia adopted its domestic implementing legislation after signing the Genocide Convention in 1957, the government elected to include political groups as protected groups for the purposes of the convention. Consequently, genocide defendants of the Derg regime cannot simply claim political motives in an attempt to avoid culpability. Ethiopia has also decided to use the Derg trials as a "truth-telling" forum, a variant on the truth commission, in which people are encouraged to air their grievances against the Derg regime as part of the evidentiary presentation in court. This has resulted in a large number of witnesses—by some accounts, more than 20,000 individuals so far—coming forward to lodge complaints in connection with various defendants, adding substantially to the length of time involved in the trials. Again, in a manner similar to Rwanda's *gacaca* system, the fact that perpetrators in Ethiopia must face their victims and hear their individual stories of suffering gives the process a deeper impact on impunity than in the case of ordinary criminal prosecutions.

The Ethiopian genocide prosecutions have been in progress for more than a decade. Derg leader Mengistu, though he is being prosecuted *in absentia*, enjoys continuing personal impunity in Zimbabwe. In November 1999, Mengistu traveled to South Africa for medical treatment; South Africa commenced investigating an Ethiopian extradition request, but the accused returned to his sanctuary in Zimbabwe before the legal process reached its conclusion.[33] As for the other 2,951 fugitives from genocide justice in Ethiopia, Ethiopian officials assert that Kenya and the United States have the highest number of accused Ethiopian war criminals residing on their territories. The international dimensions of impunity, as Cambodians know only too well, can pose significant obstacles to prosecuting suspected perpetrators of crimes against humanity and combating the culture of impunity.

THE SIERRA LEONE SPECIAL COURT

The West African nation of Sierra Leone suffered a particularly violent war lasting more than a decade.[34] Shifting coalitions of rebel groups ravaged the country, and the responses of government and government-sponsored militias only made matters worse. The most heinous of the actors in the conflict was the insurgent Revolutionary United Front (RUF), which engaged in widespread atrocities highlighted by its signature action, hacking off the limbs of civilians with machetes. The general tenor of RUF activities is suggested by the name of one campaign the organization launched, "Operation No Living Thing."[35] But the RUF was far from the only perpetrator of violence during the conflict. The war was so complex that Sierra Leone's attorney general and Ministry of Justice established a "Documentation and Conflict Mapping Program." This project is being implemented by an independent international nongovernmental organization, with the mission of determining the precise contours of the conflict.[36]

On August 14, 2000, the UN Security Council requested that Secretary-

General Kofi Annan negotiate an agreement between the world body and the government of Sierra Leone to establish a mixed national–international tribunal to judge crimes committed in the course of this war.[37] On October 4 of that year, scarcely more than six weeks after the Security Council had requested that the Secretariat intervene in the conflict, the secretary-general announced that a draft agreement for the Sierra Leone tribunal had been concluded between the UN and government of Sierra Leone.[38] It required more than a year to finalize the arrangements and to attract adequate funding to support its operations, but on January 16, 2002, the UN and the government signed an agreement establishing a precedent-setting Special Court.[39] The Special Court has worked in concert with a Truth and Reconciliation Commission, which is responsible among other things for cases of child soldiers who committed atrocities, but who were judged to be too young for formal prosecution by the Special Court.

In March 2003, the Special Court issued its first indictments.[40] The Special Court's will to attack impunity is suggested by the fact that among the initial indictees were not only RUF leader Foday Saybana Sankoh but also Sierra Leone's incumbent minister of interior, Sam Hinga Norman. However, in an eerie echo of the Cambodian cases of Son Sen and Yun Yat, two key indictees of the Special Court, Sam "Mosquito" Bockarie and Johnny Paul Koroma, appear to have been murdered by their colleagues, perhaps in an effort to avoid being implicated by their testimony. In another similarity to the Cambodian case, RUF leader Foday Saybana Sankoh died before he could be tried.[41] A fourth major suspect wanted by the Special Court, Liberian warlord Charles Taylor, was awarded sanctuary in Nigeria as part of a peace deal, thus at least temporarily managing to elude the long arm of the law; this, too, echoes events in Cambodia, where Ieng Sary was awarded amnesty as part of a peace deal. Impunity has an unfortunate way of enduring even after the establishment of an international criminal court.

One ironic aspect of the Sierra Leone tribunal is that it is modeled on the July 1999 UN proposal for a Khmer Rouge tribunal. Sierra Leone reached agreement in principle on the tribunal with the UN in a mere six weeks. In contrast, it was nearly six years from Cambodia's request for UN assistance on a tribunal until the two parties were able to reach an agreement in principle in March 2003, a contrast that suggests the relatively intractable nature of the Cambodian situation. Moreover, it is instructive that the final implementation of the Sierra Leone Special Court was delayed by more than a year due in large part to the difficulties of attracting funding to finance the court. If the international community approaches the question of genocide justice in Cambodia with this same lack of financial commitment, there may be a significant extension of Khmer Rouge impunity before justice is done.

THE INTERNATIONAL CRIMINAL COURT

On July 17, 1998, 149 nations meeting in Rome voted to establish an International Criminal Court (ICC).[42] Four years later, on July 1, 2002, having secured the necessary sixty national ratifications—of which the Royal Government of Cambodia was one—the ICC came into existence. The mandate of the ICC is to enforce international criminal law and international humanitarian law, punishing serious violations by holding perpetrators accountable for their actions. It is the first permanent international criminal court authorized to impose individual criminal accountability. Other international judicial institutions, such as the International Court of Justice, hear only cases involving state-to-state disputes. The ICC will combat impunity for gross violations of international law, including war crimes, genocide, and other crimes against humanity.[43]

The ICC has prospective temporal jurisdiction, meaning that it cannot hear cases involving crimes that occurred prior to the establishment of the court. Consequently, the court will not be able to address any matters relating to the crimes of the Khmer Rouge during the 1970s. It is nonetheless hoped that the court will bring about a new era of accountability for the authors of atrocities around the world, notwithstanding the opposition of the United States to its activities. In March 2003, judges were appointed to the court, and the following month a prosecutor was selected.[44] The ICC prosecutor began examining the more than 200 potential case files that had already accumulated in his offices and in February 2004 announced that his first case would involve the Lord's Resistance Army in Uganda.[45] Because it is a newly created institution, however, the practical impact of the ICC on the problem of impunity remains to be seen, not least because of the tenacious opposition the United States has brought to bear against the new court.

THE IMPACT OF A KHMER ROUGE TRIBUNAL ON IMPUNITY

What conclusions can we draw from the foregoing brief, comparative review of efforts to address the problem of impunity with criminal tribunals? One conclusion is that civilization has thus far not yet managed to devise anything approaching "perfect" justice when dealing with crimes of the magnitude of genocide. So it is, and so it shall be in Cambodia.

In early 1999, the UN proposed to address Khmer Rouge impunity with an international tribunal based on the Yugoslavia and Rwanda precedents; that solution would not have completely resolved Cambodia's culture of impunity. Similarly, the "mixed" model for Cambodia that was proposed by the UN in August 1999 and later implemented in Sierra Leone would not and could not comprehensively address the problem of impunity. Likewise, it should be clear that the strictly national model proposed by the Cambodian government in December 1999 would not completely satisfy Cambodians' aspirations to combat the culture of impunity. By the same token, the tribunal outlined in the "Law on Extraordinary Chambers in the Courts of Cambodia" in August 2001, agreed on in principle by the UN in March 2003, will also fail to deliver anything remotely approaching a complete solution to the problem of impunity in Cambodia.

When one examines the details of how tribunals are structured, it becomes clear that no solution can yield a completely satisfactory outcome on all the competing values at stake. We see, for example, a range of approaches to the question of personal jurisdiction, that is, who should be prosecuted in a genocide tribunal. Though the approaches vary widely, each of them has both advantages and disadvantages with respect to the question of impunity. Cambodia's 1979 People's Revolutionary Tribunal prosecuted only two people, leaving many other culpable senior leaders untouched, along with the thousands of people who carried out the actual killing. The ICTR has indicted and/or prosecuted more than seventy people, but this is totally unsatisfactory to many Rwandans, who find tens of thousands of genocide perpetrators living among them.[46] The ICTY has indicted some 150 individuals, creating a large and time-consuming caseload but still leaving many perpetrators harmless in the former Yugoslavia.[47] The Ethiopian courts are prosecuting more than 5,000 suspects, though that process has been criticized for violating the rights of the accused, and in any case it still leaves low-level perpetrators beyond the reach of the law. In Rwanda, more than 100,000 persons suspected of involvement in the genocide have languished in detention for years with no prospect that they will ever receive fair trials in a court of law, solely due to the fact that the sheer numbers of accused overwhelm the capacity of the Rwandan justice system. As a practical matter, then, there may be no ideal solution to the problem of personal jurisdiction for the crime of genocide.

How many Khmer Rouge will ultimately have their impunity challenged in court? Cambodia's Khmer Rouge tribunal law specifies that the tribunal will aim to prosecute "senior leaders of Democratic Kampuchea and those who were most responsible for the crimes." Though this formulation is somewhat ambiguous, during the negotiations both UN officials and the Cambodian government were in agreement that the total number of indictments should remain small. The number to be prosecuted most likely will be no more than a dozen, and perhaps only half that many, leaving thousands of perpetrators free to roam among their former victims. The Cambodian government wishes to keep the number small in order to avoid what it sees as potential threats to political stability and national reconciliation, while the international community wishes to keep the number small because it does not care to create yet another UN-funded judicial institution that will cost hundreds of millions of dollars. Thus, in the end, personal jurisdiction is inevitably a function of political and financial constraints, rendering a comprehensive internationalized solution to the problem of Khmer Rouge impunity beyond reach.

Another challenge in achieving justice for the Cambodian genocide has to do with the question of temporal jurisdiction, or the span of time during which applicable crimes may be prosecuted. The proposed Khmer Rouge tribunal would limit its temporal jurisdiction to the period between April 17, 1975, and January 7, 1979. Thus, only criminal acts that were committed in that time frame could be prosecuted by the Khmer Rouge tribunal. This makes sense, insofar as that was the period during which the Khmer Rouge controlled Cambodia's capital and also the period of the most intense killing by the Khmer Rouge, but it is also true that the Khmer Rouge executed and otherwise abused many innocent people prior to April 17, 1975, and they also continued to carry out atrocities long after they were driven from power on January 7, 1979. By limiting temporal jurisdiction to this period, people who were victimized by the Khmer Rouge at any time outside of that tightly constricted time frame might feel as if they have been denied justice for the crimes committed against them and therefore that impunity continues to reign.

Another reason this restrictive time period was selected is that if one goes outside that limited range, other issues might arise that could be objectionable to certain parties whose cooperation is important for the conduct of a mixed national-international Khmer Rouge tribunal. For example, if temporal jurisdiction were expanded back in time to encompass crimes committed during the early 1970s, it is possible that some former U.S. government officials might find themselves indicted for war crimes because of large-scale civilian casualties from the area bombing carried out by the U.S. Air Force in Cambodia. If temporal jurisdiction were pushed further back in time, to the late 1960s, King Norodom Sihanouk could conceivably find himself in peril of being charged with crimes against humanity for the brutal repression of the Samlaut peasant uprising, a repression that led directly to the Khmer Rouge declaration of armed struggle. If temporal jurisdiction were to be expanded forward in time beyond the end date of January 7, 1979, officials who served the People's Republic of Kampuchea and the Socialist Republic of Vietnam might find themselves answering questions about excesses associated with the K-5 Plan, in which many civilians died working in "defense of the fatherland."[48] Former foreign chief executives such as Britain's Margaret Thatcher and U.S. presidents Jimmy Carter and Ronald Reagan might be accused of complicity in genocide after the fact for aiding the revival of the Khmer Rouge after they were driven from power. The prospect of current or former top leaders of many nations simultaneously finding themselves implicated in various peripheral aspects of the Khmer Rouge genocide would ensure that the international community would never support such a tribunal, and thus, to a certain extent, tightly delimited temporal jurisdiction is simply a matter of practicality. If only for raw political reasons, then, the architects of the Khmer Rouge genocide tribunal find it wise to maintain a focus on the period of time during which the chief perpetrators of the genocide acted more or less alone, but this also means that those who were victims of the Khmer Rouge prior to or after the limits of temporal jurisdiction might be justified in concluding that the tribunal will not find justice for them and that impunity continues.

A similar set of questions could be raised with respect to the subject matter jurisdiction, or what crimes will be prosecuted. For example, a growing body of evidence suggests that rape was common at the lower levels of the Khmer Rouge security organization, particularly the rape of female prisoners who were slated for execution.[49] Recent precedents established by the ad hoc international criminal tribunals mean that when rape is assessed as having been systematic or widespread, this could constitute a war crime or a crime against humanity.[50] Rape in war is always a war crime, but what is new under these recent precedents, where widespread or systematic, is that it can now trigger the doctrine of "command responsibility," putting senior leaders at risk for the crimes of their subordinates. In the Cambodian case, however, the available evidence suggests that whenever the top leadership of the Khmer Rouge uncovered such "moral" infractions by their cadre, those accused of such acts faced summary execution. Consequently, the top Khmer Rouge leaders can argue that they did everything possible to suppress such crimes, and therefore they cannot be held responsible. If, due to the limited definition of personal jurisdiction, only top leaders are prosecuted, but they are absolved of responsibility for rapes, then any woman who was raped by a lower-level Khmer Rouge cadre or soldier may feel that she has not received justice and that impunity continues. Again, it would seem that there is no universally satisfactory way to address the problem of impunity for crimes on the scale of those carried out under the Khmer Rouge.

Another set of questions has to do with the extent of international involvement in a tribunal. The ICTY, the ICTR, and the ICC are in the nature of international experiments in combating impunity. As such, these judicial institutions have been fraught with start-up difficulties. They are also enormously expensive undertakings—which is one reason that several members of the UN Security Council were reluctant to see a similar model implemented in the case of Cambodia's Khmer Rouge. A major advantage of the ad hoc international tribunals is that they tend to provide the highest legal standards of international justice, but in so doing, they also require a great deal of time and money in order to render justice to only a small minority of the perpetrators. Moreover, with the ICTY seated in the Netherlands, and the ICTR in Arusha, Tanzania—both at some distance from the territories where the crimes were actually committed—the surviving victims who have the greatest right and need to see justice done in most cases are simply too far from the court to see any justice being done at all. On the other hand, in the Rwandan domestic prosecutions, in a country where the legal profession and the courts were totally destroyed during the genocide, the relative lack of international involvement can be seen as a factor contributing to the procedural shortcomings of the process and the long delays in rendering justice for the victims and the accused alike. The same might be said of the Ethiopian prosecutions.

Thus, there seems to be no optimum level of international involvement in tribunals designed to combat impunity. If the tribunal is entirely internationalized and seated outside the territory where the crimes were committed, there is a danger that those most in need of seeing justice done will not perceive any effective impact on impunity. Those few perpetrators who find themselves before the court will be prosecuted under alien laws and in an unfamiliar language, all far away from the scene of the crime. On the other hand, when tribunals are conducted strictly as a national affair in the immediate aftermath of terrible devastation, local judicial and political conditions may not be strong enough to deliver fair and impartial justice, as we saw with the People's Revolutionary Tribunal in 1979. However, it may turn out that the proposed mixed model for Cambodia— with internationals on the court and with the proceedings conducted where the crimes occurred—could be a good compromise to balance these competing values.

On balance, then, when we look under the hood of international tribunals at their internal workings, it is clear that there is no ideal, one-size-fits-all solution. When weighed against the enormity of the crimes at issue, questions of personal, temporal, and subject matter jurisdiction, along with the degree of international involvement, generally tip the scales of justice toward an unsatisfying outcome.

CHALLENGING THE CULTURE OF IMPUNITY

Cambodian Prime Minister Hun Sen has asserted that a Khmer Rouge tribunal will help to "end the culture of impunity."[51] He is not alone in making such assertions. For example, the British government has expressed similar hopes for what a Khmer Rouge tribunal might accomplish. An official of the British Foreign Office, Mike O'Brien, expressed this view of the proposed Khmer Rouge tribunal: "The Tribunal will be an important development in promoting the rule of law in Cambodia and will bring an end to the climate of impunity."[52] As we have seen, however, impunity was the order of the day in Cambodia long before the Khmer Rouge arrived on the scene. The phenomenon of impunity is deeply embedded in Cambodian political culture and deeply ingrained in the habits of the ruling elite. A trial of just a few Khmer Rouge perpetrators goes only so far in combating the underlying social and political structures that sustain impunity. Moreover, as envisioned in the Khmer Rouge tribunal law, Khmer Rouge impunity itself will in large measure be sustained, because only a handful of perpetrators are likely to face any consequences for their actions.

Thus, it seems clear that more will have to be done, above and beyond a tribunal for the Khmer Rouge leadership, if Cambodia is to be successful in combating the culture of impunity. Cambodians have not yet adequately grappled with this question, though some have begun to ask the right questions. For example, Ok Serei Sopheak of the Cambodian Development Resources Institute has argued that the problem of Khmer Rouge impunity is subsumed as one element of a much larger question of multifaceted reconciliation, going well beyond the Khmer Rouge in and of itself:

> For the last few years, about two years, I believed in the approach, a comprehensive approach, to the genocide of the Khmer Rouge, you know. It does not only consist of the tribunal itself. . . . The question is, how to build upon this life experience, not only for this generation, but for generations to come, so it will not happen again. . . . You know, you build roads so they can be connected with the others . . . you bring clean water, you bring electricity, you bring television, you bring this and that and so on, and in different places open the path along the border, and you call it reconciliation. But . . . it brings only one part of reconciliation, not in-depth reconciliation, because reconciliation needs a lot of confidence, it needs peacebuilding confidence, it needs intellectual confidence, it needs also feeling confident, it needs social, economical, and needs also religious [or] spiritual confidence.[53]

The kinds of measures Ok Serei Sopheak calls for could take many different forms. Cambodia could decide to organize a truth commission, as has been done in Sierra Leone. The government could elect to proceed with domestic prosecutions of low-level perpetrators, as in Rwanda, or even encourage civil suits by individual victims, as is permitted under Cambodian law. Or, in responding to continuing impunity by the Khmer Rouge, Cambodia could resort to some form of restorative justice, such as Rwanda's *gacaca* process. In Cambodia, something along those lines might be facilitated by Buddhist monks, who still carry enormous moral authority throughout much of the country and whose precepts call for all individuals to look within their own hearts in order to purge their sins.

In the final analysis, the long struggle to challenge Cambodia's culture of impunity will not be definitively resolved solely by a Khmer Rouge tribunal, though such a tribunal is an essential element in the process of at least beginning a serious challenge to the impunity plaguing Cambodian society—assuming those trials are properly conducted. Cambodia, however, must also transform its political culture, so that the elite class will no longer assume that power brings with it unlimited privileges over the weaker members of society. The Cambodian people themselves must gain experience with, and confidence in, a system of democratic accountability, so that they can play the major role in enforcing and sustaining these changes, to transform the culture of impunity that Cambodian elites have grown to consider their birthright. Such changes will take a long time.

In the meanwhile, even if the Khmer Rouge tribunal is carried out according to the highest "standards of international justice," the result can never be anything more than some minimal form of justice. The issues of personal, temporal, and subject matter jurisdiction are too vexing. The damage done in genocidal crimes is grotesque beyond earthly recompense. The scale of the crimes in question here is so huge that no conceivable compensation is adequate to restore to the surviving victims their sense of being whole, and no punishment is truly adequate to give the perpetrators what they are due.

Cambodian social development is hampered on many levels by the culture of impunity and by the lack of a firm basis for the Rule of Law. Punishing some of the perpetrators of the worst crimes ever committed in Cambodia can be the beginning of a challenge to impunity. As Cambodian villager Chhin Sovann of Kandal province expressed it, "You don't just let them go free after they have killed millions."[54] After it is established in a court of law that society finds the murder of 2 million people unacceptable and that there are personal consequences for the authors of such actions, Cambodian society may begin to challenge the notion that it is reasonable to expect to get away with murdering hundreds of people or scores of people and, eventually, even one person. "I think when we have a trial," says Um Oeurn, a farmer in Kampong Chhnang Province, "it will tell the young generation, the next generation, not to kill the people."[55]

When that point is reached, Cambodian society will be well on the road to recovery from the genocide and headed toward success in the battle against the culture of impunity. Though it will not solve the problem of impunity in its entirety, bringing the leadership of the Khmer Rouge regime to justice before a fair and impartial court of law is the most reasonable way to begin putting the demons of Cambodia's tortured modern history to rest and to teach Cambodia's children that there is a better way.

Uon Sokhan was a Khmer Rouge regimental commander, and she is typical of the overwhelming majority of Cambodians who demand genocide justice. "I think that there must be a tribunal for those leaders, the Khmer Rouge leaders," Sokhan says, "so they can learn that they will not do the bad things, to repeat doing the bad things again in the future."[56] Most of all, she insists, the tribunal is a necessary lesson "for the children." A genocide tribunal is a necessary first step for Cambodians and their children to begin to move beyond the culture of impunity and to build a new life for Cambodia after the Killing Fields.

NOTES

CHAPTER 1: THE THIRTY YEARS WAR

1. Marwaan Macan-Markar, "Cambodia Turns Its Back on Its Past," *Asia Times Online*, March 4, 2003.
2. Craig Etcheson, "The Khmer Way of Exile: Lessons from Three Indochinese Wars," in Yossi Shain, ed., *Governments in Exile in Contemporary World Politics* (New York: Routledge, 1991), 92–116.
3. Ben Kiernan, "Resisting the French, 1946–1954: The Khmer Issarak," in Ben Kiernan and Chanthou Boua, eds., *Peasants and Politics in Kampuchea, 1942–1981* (New York: M. E. Sharpe, 1982), 127–133.
4. Cambodia's role in the Second Indochina War has been the subject of many treatments. For a range of views, see Craig Etcheson, *The Rise and Demise of Democratic Kampuchea* (Boulder, CO, and London: Westview Press and Pinter Publishers, 1984); Malcolm Caldwell and Lek Tan, *Cambodia in the Southeast Asian War* (New York: Monthly Review Books, 1973); and William Shawcross, *Sideshow: Nixon, Kissinger and the Destruction of Cambodia* (New York: Simon and Schuster, 1979).
5. See, for example, Craig Etcheson, "Civil War and the Coalition Government of Democratic Kampuchea," *Third World Quarterly* 9:1 (January 1987): 187–202; David Elliott, ed., *The Third Indochina Conflict* (Boulder, CO: Westview Press, 1981); William Turley and Jeffrey Race, "The Third Indochina War," *Foreign Policy* 38 (Spring 1980): 92–116; and Bernard Gordon, "The Third Indochina Conflict," *Foreign Affairs* 65:1 (Fall 1986): 66–85.
6. For more on the origins of the Cambodian communist movement, see Etch-

eson, *Rise and Demise of Democratic Kampuchea*; see also Ben Kiernan, *How Pol Pot Came to Power* (London: Verso, 1985).

7. Sara Colm, *The Khmer Rouge and the Tribal Minorities in Northeastern Cambodia* (Phnom Penh: Documentation Center of Cambodia, 1996), 56.

8. Ibid., p. 60.

9. Timothy Carney, *Communist Party Power in Kampuchea: Documents and Discussion*, Cornell University Southeast Asia Program, Data Paper # 106 (Ithaca, NY, 1977), 32.

10. Norodom Sihanouk, *War and Hope: The Case for Cambodia* (New York: Random House, 1980), 29. A penetrating biography of Cambodia's longtime king is Milton Osborne, *Sihanouk: Prince of Light, Prince of Darkness* (Chiang Mai, Thailand: Silkworm Books, 1994).

11. Useful accounts of the Khmer Rouge years in power include Etcheson, *Rise and Demise of Democratic Kampuchea*; Elizabeth Becker, *When the War Was Over* (New York: Simon and Schuster, 1986); Nayan Chanda, *Brother Enemy: The War after the War* (New York: Macmillan, 1988); Karl Jackson, ed., *Cambodia 1975–1978: Rendezvous with Death* (Princeton, NJ: Princeton University Press, 1989); Ben Kiernan, *The Pol Pot Regime: Race, Power, and Genocide in Cambodia under the Khmer Rouge, 1975–79* (New Haven, CT: Yale University Press, 1996); and David P. Chandler, *Voices from S-21: Terror and History in Pol Pot's Secret Prison* (Berkeley: University of California Press, 1999).

12. Raymund Johansen, "The Khmer Rouge Communications Documents and the 'Nexus to Armed Conflict' Requirement for Crimes against Humanity" (Documentation Center of Cambodia, Phnom Penh, Cambodia, 1999).

13. See Stephen J. Morris, *Why Vietnam Invaded Cambodia: Political Culture and the Causes of War* (Stanford, CA: Stanford University Press, 1999), especially Chapter 4, "The Public Disintegration of Militant Solidarity," for details of Khmer Rouge attacks on Vietnam. For the Vietnamese version of these attacks, see *Kampuchea Dossier*, 3 vols. (Hanoi: Le Courier du Vietnam, 1978).

14. Asia Watch, "Violations of the Laws of War by the Khmer Rouge" (April 1990): 1.

15. Christophe Peschoux, *Les "Nouveaux" Khmers Rouges (1979–1990)* (Paris: L'Harmattan, 1992).

16. UN, Secretariat, Department of Public Information, *Agreements on a Comprehensive Political Settlement of the Cambodian Conflict*, DPI/1180 92077, January 1992.

17. See, for example, Steve Heder, "The Resumption of Armed Struggle by the Party of Democratic Kampuchea: Evidence from National Army of Democratic Kampuchea 'Self-Demobilizers,' " in Steve Heder and Judy Ledgerwood, eds., *Propaganda, Politics and Violence in Cambodia: Democratic Transition under United Nations Peace-keeping* (Armonk, NY: M. E. Sharpe, 1996), 50–72; and Jay Jordens, "Persecution of Cambodia's Ethnic Vietnamese Communities during and

since the UNTAC Period," also in Heder and Ledgerwood, *Propaganda, Politics and Violence in Cambodia*, 134–158.

18. For example, see UN, Secretariat, Secretary-General, *Fourth Progress Report of the Secretary-General on the United Nations Transitional Authority in Cambodia*, S/25719, May 3, 1993; see especially the section titled "Attacks on UNTAC personnel," para. 39–41.

19. For an account of a 1993 Khmer Rouge massacre in Siem Reap Province's Chhong Kneas village, see Craig Etcheson, "Genocide Continues as UN Watches," *Vietnam Today* (Spring 1993): 3, 4.

20. Peter Maguire, "The Cambodia Quagmire" (unpublished typescript, March 10, 2003). The UN did ultimately impose some halfhearted and ineffective economic sanctions against the Khmer Rouge, but the UN's military commanders determined that they did not have the appropriate force structure to confront the Khmer Rouge, and in any event, the UN's political officials vetoed any notion of adopting a more muscular approach to resisting these Khmer Rouge crimes. For more critical views of the UN mission, see Ben Kiernan, "The Inclusion of the Khmer Rouge in the Cambodian Peace Process: Causes and Consequences," in Ben Kiernan, ed., *Genocide and Democracy in Cambodia: The Khmer Rouge, the United Nations and the International Community* (New Haven, CT: Yale University Southeast Asia Studies, 1993), 191–272; and David W. Roberts, *Political Transition in Cambodia 1991–99: Power, Elitism and Democracy* (Richmond, Surrey: Curzon Press, 2001).

21. One example was the kidnapping and murder of British demining expert Christopher Howes by the Khmer Rouge in March 1996. See "British End Howes Murder Inquiry," *Phnom Penh Post*, August 6–19, 1999.

22. Bou Saroeun and Peter Sainsbury, "The Infamous Tiger Cages," *Phnom Penh Post*, May 22–June 4, 1998.

23. Author's interview with Chhin Sovann, Prek Tatoch village, Boeung Kchang commune, Kandal Stung District, Kandal Province, July 24, 2002.

CHAPTER 2: A DESPERATE TIME

1. The information in this paragraph is drawn from the CGP's Biographical Database, available online at http://www.yale.edu/cgp.

2. An English-language translation of Decree Law No. 1 is reproduced in Howard J. DeNike, John Quigley, and Kenneth J. Robinson, eds., *Genocide in Cambodia: Documents from the Trial of Pol Pot and Ieng Sary* (Philadelphia: University of Pennsylvania Press, 2000), 45–47. Khmer-language originals of most People's Revolutionary Tribunal documents, as well as English and French translations of some documents, can be accessed on the CGP Web site at http://www.yale.edu/cgp.

3. DeNike et al., *Genocide in Cambodia*, 504.

4. Ibid., 507.

5. Ibid., 511.

6. Ibid., 98.

7. Ibid., 396.

8. Ibid., 168.

9. Cited in Steve Heder, "Hen Sen and Genocide Trials in Cambodia: International Impacts, Impunity and Justice," in Judy Ledgerwood, ed., *Cambodia Emerges from the Past: Eight Essays* (DeKalb: Northern Illinois University Southeast Asia Publications, 2002), 189 n. 20.

10. Ibid., 221. According to Heder, "Hun Sen's reliance on past French and Vietnamese models reflected not only interest, but also familiarity . . . [they were] part of the Cambodian justice system that Hun Sen grew up with."

11. Ibid., 187 n. 15, citing the Khmer version of the "Communiqué of the Solidarity Front for the Salvation of the Kampuchea Nation," December 2, 1978.

12. Ibid., 187.

13. Patrick Raszelenberg and Peter Schier, *The Cambodia Conflict: Search for a Settlement, 1979–1991* (Hamburg: Institute of Asian Affairs, 1995), 21.

14. Steve Heder, "Cultures of Genocide, Impunity, and Victors' Justice in Cambodia, 1945–1999: Colonial, Communist and Other International Sources" (unpublished typescript, 2000), 36; a later version of this paper was published as Heder, "Hun Sen and Genocide Trials," but the published version does not contain this quoted passage.

15. Heder, "Hun Sen and Genocide Trials," 188f.

16. Author's interview with You Huy, alias Him, Koh Thom District, Kandal Province, February 29, 1996.

17. People's Republic of Kampuchea, Ministry of Interior, *Directive: Instructions on the Implementation and Reviewing for Amnesty and Acquittal in Favor of the Culprit*, Doc. No. 221 M.Ch., February 21, 1984; original in Khmer, copy on file with the author.

18. From a Report to the People's Republic of Kampuchea Council of Ministers, cited in Evan Gottesman, *Cambodia after the Khmer Rouge: Inside the Politics of Nation Building* (New Haven, CT: Yale University Press, 2003), 239f.

19. "Will Change Tactics, Cambodian Rebel Says," *Los Angeles Times*, January 12, 1985.

20. Nick B. Williams, "Cambodian Resistance Goes on Offensive: Despite Differences, 3 Factions Operate as 'More of a Guerrilla Force,'" *Los Angeles Times*, August 8, 1985.

21. Jacques Bekaert, *Cambodian Diary: Tales of a Divided Nation, 1983–1986* (Bangkok: White Lotus Press, 1997), 274f.

22. People's Republic of Kampuchea, Council of Ministers and Ministry of Interior, *Mastery Plan to Destroy the Enemy Continuously*, Doc. No. 148 S.J.N., March 25, 1986; original in Khmer, copy on file with the author.

23. This effect was pervasive and enduring, especially in the cities. The author recalls that more than five years later, during the UN intervention of the early 1990s, many attempted interviews never got off the ground, rebuffed with a furtive comment to the effect that they could not talk because, the would-be subjects insisted, "the government has spies everywhere."

24. Margaret Slocomb, "The K5 Gamble: National Defense and Nation Building under the People's Republic of Kampuchea," *Journal of Southeast Asian Studies* 32:2 (June 2002): 196. See also Margaret Slocomb, *The People's Republic of Kampuchea, 1979–1989: The Revolution after Pol Pot* (Chiang Mai: Silkworm Books, 2003), 229–251.

25. Personal communication from Carlyle Thayer, May 9, 2001.

26. Slocomb, "The K5 Gamble," 198.

27. Nick B. Williams Jr., "Vietnam Moves to Crush an Elusive Foe: Cambodian Rebels, Disrupted and Exiled to Thailand, Able to Fight On," *Los Angeles Times*, March 2, 1985.

28. Sam Rainsy interview with Pen Sovann, "Revelations by Pen Sovann about Hun Sen," April 25, 1998.

29. After his ouster, Sovann was held in solitary confinement in Vietnam for several years without trial and finally was permitted to return to Cambodia in the mid-1990s. Michael Vickery believes the reason for Sovann's ouster from these posts was based on domestic politics rather than foreign pressure, but a key issue in Cambodian domestic politics at this time was defense policy, a policy arena where Vietnam exerted significant influence; see Michael Vickery, *Kampuchea: Politics, Economics and Society* (London and Boulder, CO: Frances Pinter Publishers and Lynne Rienner Publishers, 1986), 45–46 and 123. See also an analysis by Kristina Chhim, "The Reconstitution of the Cambodian People's Party 1979–1989" (Paper delivered to the 5th Socio-Cultural Research Conference on Cambodia, Phnom Penh, November 6–8, 2002). Chhim's analysis lends support to Vickery's contention that internal regime politics was the major factor in Sovann's ouster.

30. For one analyst's explanation of the K-5 plan, see Carlyle Thayer, "The Vietnam People's Army Today," *Indochina Issues*, Center for International Policy No. 72 (Washington, DC, January 1987), 1–7. Canadian journalist Robert Karniol argued that the five phases of the K-5 plan were (1) destruction of the Khmer Rouge and allied bases on the Thai border; (2) the sealing of the border; (3) clearing resistance in the interior; (4) consolidation of the Cambodian regime; and (5) withdrawal of Vietnamese troops from Cambodia by 1990. See Slocomb, "The K5 Gamble," 196. Slocomb herself argues that K-5 refers only to the plan for sealing the Thai border.

31. Esmeralda Luciolli, *Le Mur de Bambou—Le Cambodge après Pol Pot* (Régine Deforges Edition, 1988). Excerpts of *Le Mur de Bambou* were translated and distributed by the Sam Rainsy Party (SRP) under the title "Pol Pot Number

Two Still Alive," as a document for the Consultative Group Meeting, Paris, May 25–26, 2000. These and subsequent English excerpts of the Luciolli book are taken from the Sam Rainsy Party translation. See also similar excerpts in Sam Rainsy Party, "Hun Sen Must Be Prosecuted for Crimes against Humanity," December 25, 1998, at http://www.garella.com/rich/camelect/srpdocs9.htm.

32. Slocomb, "The K5 Gamble," 201.
33. In July 1985, Dr. Saren So, the deputy director of the Kampuchean–Soviet Friendship hospital in Phnom Penh, defected to Thailand and told journalists in Bangkok that workers on the K-5 project were suffering a high incidence of malaria; see *Indochina Chronology* IV:3 (July–September 1985), 9. According to Evan Gottesman, officials in the PRK (People's Republic of Kampuchea) Ministry of Health estimated that 80 percent of the K-5 workforce had malaria; personal communication, November 2, 2000. See also the account in Luciolli, *Le Mur de Bambou*, as well as Evan Gottesman, *Cambodia after the Khmer Rouge: Inside the Politics of Nation Building* (New Haven, CT: Yale University Press, 2003), 234–236.
34. "Cambodia Faces Severe Food Shortage in 1985," *Los Angeles Times*, November 16, 1984.
35. Personal communication with Evan Gottesman, November 2, 2000.
36. Luciolli, *Le Mur de Bambou*, Sam Rainsy Party excerpts.
37. Carlyle Thayer, personal communication, May 9, 2001.
38. Luciolli, *Le Mur de Bambou*, Sam Rainsy Party excerpts. The land mines laid by the Khmer Rouge and their allies and by the Vietnamese and their allies, along with all the mines left over from the Second Indochina War, continue to kill and maim Cambodians on a virtually daily basis today, long after the end of the wars in which they were deployed. See, for example, *Land Mines in Cambodia: The Coward's War* (New York: Asia Watch and Physicians for Human Rights, 1991).
39. Luciolli, *Le Mur de Bambou*, Sam Rainsy Party excerpts.
40. Indeed, the K-5 plan has remained a potent point of political propaganda among Cambodian political actors opposed to the Cambodian People's Party through the 1990s and into the present decade. See, for example, a Web site erected by a partisan of the Sam Rainsy Party, who argued in favor of a resolution in the U.S. House of Representatives calling for the establishment of an international tribunal to investigate Cambodian Prime Minister Hun Sen on charges of "serious violations of international human rights laws." The K-5 plan is 'Exhibit A' among many such partisans. See http://members.aol.com/munysara/cambodge/MurDeBambou.htm.
41. People's Republic of Kampuchea, Council of Ministers and Ministry of Interior, *Mastery Plan to Destroy the Enemy Continuously*, Doc. No. 148 S.J.N., March 25, 1986; original in Khmer, copy on file with the author.

42. People's Revolutionary Party of Kampuchea, Central Committee, Monitoring Committee, *Instruction: Increase the Work of Monitoring and Discipline in the Party in Keeping with the New Situation*, Doc. No. 250 S.P.N.M.Ch., November 8, 1989, signed by Sim Ka; original in Khmer, copy on file with author.

43. Luciolli, *Le Mur de Bambou*, Sam Rainsy Party excerpts.

44. Jacques Bekaert, *Cambodian Diary: A Long Road to Peace, 1987–1993* (Bangkok: White Lotus Press, 1998), 20.

45. Ibid.

46. Williams, "Vietnam Moves to Crush an Elusive Foe."

47. Carlyle Thayer, personal communication, May 9, 2001.

48. Raszelenberg and Schier, *The Cambodia Conflict*, 261.

49. Michael Haas, *Genocide by Proxy: Cambodian Pawn on a Superpower Chessboard* (New York: Praeger, 1991), 213.

50. Raszelenberg and Schier, *The Cambodia Conflict*, 262.

51. Ibid., 266.

52. Ibid.; see also Haas, *Genocide by Proxy*, 214.

53. State of Cambodia, Ministry of Interior, *Directive: Implementing the Sub-Decree on Registration for Military Service for National Defense*, Doc. No. 003 S.R.N.N., May 3, 1991, signed by Interior Minister Sin Song; original in Khmer, copy on file with author.

54. See, for example, Raszelenberg and Schier, *The Cambodia Conflict*; Haas, *Genocide by Proxy*; Bekaert, *Cambodian Diary: Tales of a Nation Divided, 1983–1986*, and also his *Cambodian Diary: A Long Road to Peace, 1987–1993*; MacAlister Brown and Joseph J. Zasloff, *Cambodia Confounds the Peacemakers, 1979–1998* (Ithaca, NY: Cornell University Press, 1998); Raoul M. Jennar, *Cambodian Chronicles: Bungling a Peace Plan, 1989–1991* (Bangkok: White Lotus Press, 1998); and Amitav Acharya et al., eds., *Cambodia—The 1989 Paris Peace Conference: Background Analysis and Documents* (Toronto: Center for International and Strategic Studies, 1991). Also of special interest are Chapters 8 and 16 of Peter W. Rodman, *More Precious Than Peace: The Cold War and the Struggle for the Third World* (New York: Scribner's, 1994); and Chapters I and II of Roberts, *Political Transition in Cambodia*.

55. See Harish C. Mehta and Julie B. Mehta, *Hun Sen: Strongman of Cambodia* (Singapore: Graham Brash, 1999), 47.

56. This document is reproduced in Raszelenberg and Schier, *The Cambodia Conflict*, 370–377.

57. Ibid., see "Joint Statement of the Jakarta Informal Meeting on Cambodia," 393–395.

58. State of Cambodia, Ministry of Interior, *Resolution: Organizational Assignment, Role, Task and Rights of the Secret Messenger Network*, Doc. No. 079 L.S.R., February 4, 1991, signed by Sin Song; original in Khmer, copy on file with author.

59. David Ashley, "The Nature and Causes of Human Rights Violations in Bat-

tambang Province," in Steve Heder and Judy Ledgerwood, eds., *Propaganda, Politics, and Violence in Cambodia: Democratic Transition under United Nations Peace-keeping* (Armonk, NY: M. E. Sharpe, 1996), 167.

60. Ministry of Interior, *Resolution: Organizational Assignment, Role, Task and Rights of the Secret Messenger Network.*

61. Steve Heder and Judy Ledgerwood, "Politics of Violence: An Introduction," in Heder and Ledgerwood, eds., *Propaganda, Politics, and Violence in Cambodia*, 39.

62. "Reaction Forces and 'A' Groups," undated and unattributed document from UNTAC, probably originating from the Analysis/Assessment Unit of UNTAC's Information/Education Division.

63. Ibid.

64. Though we have no direct evidence that would confirm it, I believe that covert networks such as the Z-91 messenger unit were used to provide positive command and control for these operational units in the field.

65. Ashley, "The Nature and Causes of Human Rights Violations," 174.

66. See, for example, Figures 4.1 and 6.1 in Craig Etcheson, *The Rise and Demise of Democratic Kampuchea* (London and Boulder, CO: Pinter Publishers and Westview Press, 1984), 46–47 and 78–79.

67. For more details on the economic changes introduced after the Vietnamese military withdrew from Cambodia, see Gottesman, *Cambodia after the Khmer Rouge*, especially Chapter 12, "The Politics of Economic Reform."

68. Author's interview with Ta Thom, March 28, 2002, Pean Meas village, Samrong commune, Tram Kok District, Takeo Province.

69. For example, Cambodia was a state-party to the 1930 Convention on Forced Labor and the 1956 Supplementary Convention on the Abolition of Slavery, the Slave Trade and Institutions and Practices Similar to Slavery. See Steven R. Ratner and Jason S. Abrams, *Accountability for Human Rights Atrocities in International Law: Beyond the Nuremberg Legacy* (Oxford: Oxford University Press, 1997), 254–255.

70. The author is grateful to Ben Ferencz, Francisco Forrest Martin, Anthony D'Amato, Catherine Fitzpatrick, George Lombard, Ewen Allison, Victor Conde, R. John Pritchard, and Jason Abrams for discussions on this question.

71. 58 Stat. 1544, E.A.S. No. 472, 82 U.N.T.S. 280. See also Frank Newman and David Weissbrodt, *International Human Rights: Law, Policy and Process*, 2nd ed. (Cincinnati, OH: Anderson Publishing Co., 1996), 276.

72. *International Military Tribunal Charter*, art. 6(b).

73. Helen Jarvis Interview with Hun Sen, Phnom Penh, January 27, 1999.

CHAPTER 3: AFTER THE PEACE

1. Interview with Warren Christopher on the MacNeil/Lehrer News Hour, Public Broadcasting System, June 1, 1993.

2. *Indochina Digest*, May 28, 1993.

3. U.S. Congress, House Committee on Foreign Affairs, Subcommittee on Asia and the Pacific, *Statement of Peter Tomsen, Deputy Assistant Secretary of State, Bureau of East Asian and Pacific Affairs*, 103rd Cong., 2nd sess., May 11, 1994, 2.

4. Quoted in the "CPR Info Packet," distributed by the Coalition for Peace and Reconciliation, Wat Sam Peo Meas, Phnom Penh, Cambodia, May 31, 1994.

5. For accounts of the Paris Agreements, see Craig Etcheson, "The 'Peace' in Cambodia," *Current History* (December 1992): 413–417; Ben Kiernan, "The Inclusion of the Khmer Rouge in the Peace Process: Causes and Consequences," in Ben Kiernan, ed., *Genocide and Democracy in Cambodia* (New Haven, CT: Yale University Southeast Asia Studies, 1993), 191–271; and MacAlister Brown and Joseph J. Zasloff, *Cambodia Confounds the Peacemakers, 1979–1998* (Ithaca, NY: Cornell University Press, 1998). The UN intervention in the Congo (1960–1964) rivaled the Cambodian operation in size and scope; for details on the Congo, see *The Blue Helmets: A Review of United Nations Peace-keeping* (New York: UNDPI, 1990).

6. UN, Department of Public Information, *Agreements on a Comprehensive Political Settlement of the Cambodian Conflict*, DPI/1180 92077, Paris, January 1992.

7. For example, journalist Elizabeth Becker suggested that the UN's Cambodian intervention provided a model for collective security in the post–Cold War world order; interview with Elizabeth Becker on National Public Radio, "Talk of the Nation," May 27, 1993. See also Etcheson, "The 'Peace' in Cambodia," 416f.

8. Particularly instructive in this regard is Peter W. Rodman, *More Precious Than Peace: The Cold War and the Struggle for the Third World* (New York: Scribner's, 1994).

9. The pernicious effects of the U.S.-led trade and aid embargo against Cambodia are documented in Eva Mysliwiec, *Punishing the Poor: The International Isolation of Kampuchea* (Oxford: Oxfam, 1988).

10. For example, see *Something like Home Again: The Repatriation of Cambodian Refugees* (Washington, DC: U.S. Committee for Refugees, May 1994).

11. See Harish C. Mehta, *Cambodia Silenced: The Press under Six Regimes* (Bangkok: White Lotus Press, 1997).

12. UN, Security Council, *Report of the Secretary-General on the Conduct and Results of the Elections in Cambodia*, S/25913, June 10, 1993.

13. The overall costs of the Agreements on a Comprehensive Political Settlement of the Cambodia Conflict include an estimated $1.9 billion for the UN peacekeeping operation, more than $100 million for the refugee repatriation, and some $880 million for the reconstruction of Cambodia's economy. See U.S. Congress, House Committee on Appropriations, *Foreign Operations, Export Financing, and Related Programs Appropriations for 1994. Hearings before a Subcommittee of the Committee on Appropriations*, "Avoiding a New War in Cambodia," Testimony of Craig Etcheson, March 1, 1993, 103rd Cong., 1st sess., 1993.

14. See also Asia Watch, "Political Control, Human Rights, and the UN Mission in Cambodia" (September 1992).

15. Interview with Warren Christopher on the MacNeil/Lehrer News Hour, June 1, 1993.

16. As one analyst observed, "Military activity has increased throughout the country since the beginning of 1993, including in formerly 'peaceful' areas. Increased territory has also come under the effective control of the National Army of Democratic Kampuchea [NADK—the Khmer Rouge army]." Grant Curtis, "Transition to What? Cambodia, UNTAC and the Peace Process," UN Research Institute for Social Development, Workshop on the Social Consequences of the Peace, Geneva, April 29–30, 1993.

17. Alexander Krylovich and Vaidimir Supruns, "Russia Calls to Help Cambodia Solve Domestic Problems," ITAR-TASS, July 14, 1994. According to Phnom Penh government radio, in August 1994 Russian President Boris Yeltsin offered "his readiness to discuss the cooperation and development of Cambodia in the political and economic spheres." "Yeltsin Affirms Support for Government Policy," FBIS-EAS-94-162, August 22, 1994, 69.

18. Data from the U.S. Agency for International Development, "USAID Assistance Strategy for Cambodia, FY 1994–97" (draft), May 1994. See Table C.1, p. 66.

19. For background on the Cambodian Genocide Justice Act, see Craig Etcheson, "Congress and Administration Negotiate on Khmer Rouge Genocide Investigation," Indochina Interchange 4:2 (June 1994): 13; and Chapter 4 in the present volume.

20. "Commission to Review 'US War of Aggression,'" FBIS-EAS-94-191, October 3, 1994, 69.

21. For example, see "Commentary Views Prosecution of Khmer Rouge," FBIS-EAS-95-157, August 15, 1995, 67; the author was one of the miscreants "convicted" by the Khmer Rouge.

22. See, for example, Craig Etcheson, "Sanctions Needed to Curb Thai Military Support of Khmer Rouge," Indochina Interchange 4:3 (September 1994): 8f. See also Craig Etcheson, "Punish Thai Military over Khmer Rouge Aid," Asian Wall Street Journal Weekly, June 27, 1994.

23. See, for example, "U.S. Military Delegation to Visit Phnom Penh," Reuters, September 10, 1994.

24. "Li Peng Letter Denies PRC Aid to Khmer Rouge," FBIS-EAP-94-157, August 15, 1994, 51.

25. For the negotiations to build an industrial city, see Nate Thayer, "City of Dreams," Far Eastern Economic Review, August 11, 1994, 20.

26. See, for example, Raoul Jennar, "Before It Becomes Too Late," Cambodia Chronicles VII, European Far Eastern Research Center, February 15, 1993, 17–19. Jennar accurately noted that "Thai governments change, but their ac-

tive sympathy for the Khmer Rouge remains." See also Jennar's "18 Years Later," *Cambodia Chronicles VIII*, European Far Eastern Research Center, April 17, 1993, 12f, for additional documentation on Thai disregard for Cambodian sovereignty and violations of the Comprehensive Settlement.

27. For an analysis of Thailand's military alliance with the Khmer Rouge after the new Cambodian government was formed, see *Cambodia Still Waiting for Peace: A Report on Thai–Khmer Rouge Collaboration since the Signing of the Cambodia Peace Accords* (Boston: Oxfam America, February 1995).

28. Quoted in "Thailand to Abide by U.N. Ban on Cambodia Logs," Reuters, January 8, 1993; see also *Cambodia Peace Watch* 2:1 (January 1993).

29. See "Prasong Says Thailand No Longer Supports KR," *Bangkok Post*, October 12, 1993.

30. See "Time for Phnom Penh to Prove Its Point or Keep Silent," *Sunday Post* (Bangkok), July 10, 1994, 22; reprinted in FBIS-EAS-94-134, July 13, 1994, 65.

31. For maps of Khmer Rouge areas of operation, see Kiernan, "The Inclusion of the Khmer Rouge in the Peace Process," 214–215.

32. UN secretary-general Boutros Boutros-Ghali's special representative for Cambodia, Yasushi Akashi, warned on May 19, 1993, that the Khmer Rouge had recently "increased their military strength by at least 50 per cent" and had obtained new weapons. See Reuters News Agency report dated May 19, 1993. Other reports on Thai military and economic support for the Khmer Rouge include "Thai Military Role," *Indochina Digest*, November 6, 1992; "Doing Business with Pol Pot," *The Economist*, November 7, 1992; Ken Stier, "Log Rolling," *Far Eastern Economic Review*, January 21, 1993; "Thai's Supply Khmer Rouge Army," *Cambodia Peace Watch* 2:1 (January 1993); and "Thailand Rearms Khmer Rouge Army," *Cambodia Peace Watch* 2:5 (May 1993).

33. Author's interviews with confidential UN sources in Phnom Penh, Cambodia, March 7, 1993. Also see Craig Etcheson, "Without Any Pretensions, Dump the Khmer Rouge," *Bangkok Nation*, September 28, 1993; and Craig Etcheson, "Khmer Rouge Issues Hurt Thai–Cambodian Relations," *Indochina Interchange* 3:4 (December 1993): 10f.

34. Craig Etcheson, "The Calm before the Storm" (Campaign to Oppose the Return of the Khmer Rouge, Washington, DC, April 1993).

35. Ibid. For an analysis of the Chenla-II operation, see Craig Etcheson, *The Rise and Demise of Democratic Kampuchea* (Boulder, CO, and London: Westview Press and Pinter Publishers, 1984), 110–115. See also Sak Sutsakhan, *The Khmer Republic at War* (Washington, DC: U.S. Army Center for Military History, 1980), 13.

36. For example, see John C. Brown and Ker Munthit, "KR Close to Recapturing Pailin," *Phnom Penh Post*, April 22–May 5, 1994.

37. Mark Dodd, "Sihanouk Warns of Khmer Rouge Return to Power," Reuters,

May 12, 1994. Sihanouk went on to say, "The only way to save Cambodia is by helping the royal government and the royal army and by training the soldiers and by giving them lessons in behavior."

38. See the discussion of the "K-990" operations in Chapter 2.

39. Quoted in "PDK Team Affirms Desire for Peace," from Khmer Rouge clandestine radio, printed in *Foreign Broadcast Information Service*, EAS-94-120, June 22, 1994, 43.

40. The text of the "Law on the Outlawing of the Democratic Kampuchea Group" can be found in the *Phnom Penh Post*, July 15–28, 1994.

41. For background on the so-called Provisional Government for National Solidarity and National Salvation of Kampuchea, see "Khmer Rouge Form Provisional Government," Associated Press, July 11, 1994; "Khmer Rouge Proclaim New 'Capital,'" United Press International, July 13, 1994; and "Khmer Rouge Pick Remote Province as Seat of Provisional Government," Deutsche Presse Agentur, July 13, 1994.

42. For example, a May 5, 1994, Khmer Rouge communiqué stated with respect to Norodom Ranariddh and Hun Sen, "We are obliged to push more on the battlefield to convince them that they will not get anything more by military means." Quoted in William Shawcross, *Cambodia's New Deal* (Washington, DC: Carnegie Endowment for International Peace, 1994), 97.

43. The author observed an April 1994 Khmer Rouge demonstration in Washington, D.C., at the White House, the object of which was to protest proposals for U.S. lethal assistance to the Royal Government in support of its military struggle with the rebels. Another example of this propaganda offensive is found in a newspaper called the *Cambodian Press*, published in Lowell, Massachusetts, a town well known among Cambodian-Americans as a stronghold of Khmer Rouge activism in North America. In the June 1, 1994, edition, the *Cambodian Press* published a front-page story titled, "Stop US Military Aid—Why?" This article recounts the demonstration at the White House and includes such comments as, "the Khmer Rouge under the leaderships [*sic*] of Mr. Khieu Samphan is doing right for the country and the people."

44. According to a Khmer Rouge defector, Pol Pot instructed Khmer Rouge military officers in 1988, "The fruit remains the same; only the skin has changed." See David P. Chandler, "The Red Khmer and the UN Agreement on Cambodia," *Conference Report on the Challenge of Indochina*, Aspen Institute 7:3 (May 8–10, 1992): 14.

45. An excellent study that amply demonstrates the extent to which Khmer Rouge goals had remained unchanged since the 1970s is Christophe Peschoux, *Les "Nouveaux" Khmers Rouges 1979–1990* (Paris: L'Harmattan, 1992).

46. A revealing look at Khmer Rouge warfare methods is *Violations of the Laws of War by the Khmer Rouge*, Asia Watch, April 1990.

47. A captured Khmer Rouge document dated January 10, 1992 emphasized, "We must concentrate first on accelerating the infiltration of category one forces in order gradually to establish in advance the pre-requisites" for the takeover of his hapless allies. Nayan Chanda, "Cambodia: In Search of an Elusive Peace," *Conference Report on the American–Vietnamese Dialogue*, Aspen Institute 8:2 (February 8–11, 1993), 26f, n4.

48. Norodom Sihanouk, "Forging Cambodian Nationhood," *Far Eastern Economic Review*, January 13, 1994, 26.

CHAPTER 4: DOCUMENTING MASS MURDER

1. For some background on early days of the Campaign to Oppose the Return of the Khmer Rouge, see Michael Haas, *Cambodia, Pol Pot and the United States: A Faustian Pact* (New York: Praeger, 1991), especially Chapter 6, "A Campaign to Oppose the Return of the Khmer Rouge." An example of the advocacy work carried out by the Campaign to Oppose the Return of the Khmer Rouge is U.S. Congress, House Committee on Appropriations, *Foreign Operations, Export Financing, and Related Programs Appropriations for 1994. Hearings before a Subcommittee of the Committee on Appropriations*, "Avoiding a New War in Cambodia," Testimony of Craig Etcheson, March 1, 1993, 103rd Cong., 1st sess., 1993.

2. PL 103–236, 108 Stat. 486; 22 USC 2656 (1994), *The Cambodian Genocide Justice Act.*

3. Jason Abrams and Stephen Ratner, "Striving for Justice: Accountability and the Crimes of the Khmer Rouge" (A study for the U.S. Department of State under the Cambodian Genocide Justice Act, 1995), 275. A revised version of this study was published as Steven R. Ratner and Jason S. Abrams, *Accounting for Human Rights Atrocities in International Law: Beyond the Nuremburg Legacy* (Oxford: Oxford University Press, 1997).

4. The Cambodian Genocide Program released periodic progress reports, including "The Cambodian Genocide Program: First Progress Report," Yale Center for International and Area Studies, New Haven, CT, September 15, 1995; "The Cambodian Genocide Program, 1994–1997," Yale Center for International and Area Studies, New Haven, CT, February 1998; and "The Cambodian Genocide Program, 1997–1999," Yale Center for International and Area Studies, New Haven, CT, April 1999.

5. Dr. Ben Kiernan was the director of the CGP from December 1994 through April 1999. Dr. Craig Etcheson was the program manager from December 1994 through December 1997, served as acting director in 1997, and was the director of the Documentation Center of Cambodia in 1995 and 1996; since January 1998, he has served as an adviser to the Documentation Center. Youk Chhang was the program officer in 1995 and 1996 and has continued as di-

rector of the Documentation Center since 1997. Dr. Susan Cook was director from May 1999 through 2001. Dr. Helen Jarvis served as documentation consultant from 1994 through 2001. According to Dr. Gustav Ranis, the director of the Yale Center for International and Area Studies (which has housed the program at Yale), the program was to be phased out before the end of 2001. See *Yale Daily News*, "Kiernan Leaves Post as Director of Cambodian Genocide Project," March 31, 1999. After 2001, however, Kiernan resumed his role as director and has continued to maintain the CGP Web site. The Documentation Center of Cambodia remains as a permanent institution.

6. An early summary of the efforts of the CGP can be found in Craig Etcheson, "From Theory to Facts in the Cambodian Genocide," *International Network on Holocaust and Genocide* 12:1–2 (1997): 4–7. See also Helen Jarvis and Robert Loomans, "The Cambodian Genocide Program (CGP)," *Proceedings of the Second New South Wales Symposium on Information Technology and Information Systems*, Sydney: School of Information Systems, University of New South Wales, 1997; and Helen Jarvis, "Cambodian Genocide Program," *Newsletter* of the Centre for Comparative Genocide Studies, Macquarie University, 2:2 (December 1995–January 1996).

7. The Documentation Center is funded primarily through contributions from various governments, including the United States, the Netherlands, Britain, Norway, Sweden, Canada, Australia, New Zealand, and Japan.

8. Recent reports on the activities of the Documentation Center include *Annual Report* (Phnom Penh: Documentation Center of Cambodia, 2000); and *Annual Report: DC-Cam's Achievements and Progress, 2001* (Phnom Penh: Documentation Center of Cambodia, 2002).

9. These developments were the occasion of some friction within the CGP management team. The director, based at Yale University, believed work should concentrate on known sources of primary documents, such as the records of Democratic Kampuchea's Ministry of Commerce, held in Cambodia's National Archives. The program officer, based in Phnom Penh, believed it would be fruitful to conduct a search for new sources of primary documentation relevant to the genocide. The program manager resolved the conflict by instructing the field staff to carry out a thorough search for new materials. The search resulted in the discovery and acquisition of numerous previously unknown caches of primary documents, including a large collection of sensitive records generated by the Khmer Rouge secret police organization, the *Santebal*.

10. For example, the Documentation Center concluded an agreement to acquire the archives of the Cambodia Documentation Commission (CDC), a nongovernmental organization founded in the mid-1980s to advocate accountability for the Khmer Rouge. The extensive archives accumulated by the CDC were transferred from the United States to the Documentation Center in

Phnom Penh. These archives include a wealth of information related to Khmer Rouge extermination of Cham Muslims, Sino-Cambodians, and Buddhist monks, as well as on purges within the Communist Party of Kampuchea and on mass graves in Cambodia. Personal communication from David Hawk, April 29, 2000.

11. For more on the selection of the project software, see Helen Jarvis, "Cataloguing the Killing Fields: The Cambodian Genocide Program," *National Library of Australia News—International Relations Quarterly Supplement* (January 1998): 10–12.

12. For details on the structure of the databases, see a monograph by Helen Jarvis and Nereida Cross, "CGDB: Cambodian Genocide Data Bases Input Manual" (Sydney and Phnom Penh: SISTM, University of New South Wales and the Documentation Center of Cambodia, 1999).

13. Intellectual property rights to the Cambodian Genocide Data Bases subsequently became an issue. Yale University asserted ownership of the databases, evidently wishing to preserve them as a legacy of the program after the anticipated termination of CGP activities in the year 2001, as well as to ensure preservation and access. However, the Documentation Center of Cambodia has continued the process of assembling information for the databases and therefore has engaged in ongoing negotiations with Yale University for the right to enhance the databases in the future and perhaps even to migrate the data to a more sophisticated multimedia platform.

14. The results of this early Cambodian research project on the Khmer Rouge regime were published in 1983, though these findings never became widely known inside Cambodia and were completely unknown outside Cambodia until the work was uncovered by the CGP and the Documentation Center in 1995. See People's Republic of Kampuchea, Research Committee on Pol Pot's Genocide Regime, "Report of the Research Committee on Pol Pot's Genocidal Regime," Phnom Penh, Cambodia, July 25, 1983. The original is in the Khmer language; excerpts have been translated by the Documentation Center of Cambodia for the CGP.

15. An example of an analysis carried out using the Cambodian Genocide Biographic and Bibliographic Databases is Craig Etcheson, "Terror in the East: Phases of Repression in Region 23 of Democratic Kampuchea" (Paper presented to the Annual Meeting of the Society for Historians of American Foreign Relations, Washington, DC, June 19–22, 1997). A revised version of this paper appears as Chapter 6 in the present volume.

16. Craig Etcheson, "Centralized Terror in Democratic Kampuchea: Scope and Span of Control" (Paper presented to the Annual Meeting of the Association of Asian Studies, Chicago, March 14–16, 1997); a revised version of this paper appears as Chapter 5 in the present volume.

17. An account of one such mass grave mapping expedition has been published

as Craig Etcheson, "The Day I Saw a Monster," *Suitcase: A Journal of Transcultural Traffic* 3:1/2 (1998): 104–116.

18. The Documentation Center's Trimble Geo-Explorer™ GPS equipment reads the precise coordinates of a given location by triangulating on signals from satellites in orbit above the earth. This equipment, when differentially corrected for magnetic distortion, locates specific places to an accuracy of within a few meters.

19. The Documentation Center uses the ArcInfo software package to compile the geographic data and the ArcView package to generate maps.

20. Some of the satellite images of Cambodia used in this aspect of the work can be accessed through the maps link on the CGP Web site at http://www.yale.edu/cgp. It is recommended that these images be accessed with high-end workstations and broadband Internet connections, as some of the images are extremely high-resolution.

21. Since 1997, the raw data compiled by the Documentation Center's Mass Grave Mapping Project have been assembled in annual reports. For example, see *Mapping the Killing Fields of Cambodia, 1997* (Phnom Penh: Documentation Center of Cambodia, 1997); *Mapping the Killing Fields of Cambodia, 1998* (Phnom Penh: Documentation Center of Cambodia, 1999); and *Mapping the Killing Fields of Cambodia, 1999* (Phnom Penh: Documentation Center of Cambodia, 2000). The Documentation Center is preparing to consolidate these mapping reports and publish them in a single volume.

22. A more complete analysis of the mass grave mapping data can be found in Chapter 7 of the present volume. The data reported in the current chapter are drawn from "Master Site Data List," Phnom Penh: Documentation Center of Cambodia, October 9, 2001, and are supplemented by additional data in "DC-Cam Quarterly Report: January–March 2004" (Documentation Center of Cambodia, April 8, 2004).

23. The most comprehensive previous work on the death toll in the Cambodian genocide is Marek Sliwinski, *Le Génocide Khmer Rouge: un analyse démographique* (Paris: Editions L'Harmattan, 1995).

24. The Web sites can be accessed at http://www.yale.edu/cgp and http://welcome.to/dccam.

25. Michael S. Pollanen, "Forensic Survey of Three Memorial Sites Containing Human Skeletal Remains in the Kingdom of Cambodia" (Mission Report to the Coalition for International Justice, Washington, DC, July 2002).

26. The Documentation Center Web site is at http://welcome.to/dccam. This site provides links to the existing databases and offers additional content as well. Included on the site is the Khmer-language version of the Documentation Center's monthly magazine, *Searching for the Truth*. Preparations are under way to add an English-language edition of the magazine to the site.

27. The Documentation Center of Cambodia can be contacted via e-mail at

dccam@online.com.kh. It is interesting to note that when the premier CD version of these databases was published by the CGP in 1997, one of the very first organizations to request a copy was the U.S. Immigration and Naturalization Service.

28. See, for example, Helen Jarvis and Nereida Cross, "New Information Technology Applied to Genocide Research: The Cambodian Genocide Program," in C. Chen, ed., *NIT (New Information Technology) '98: 10th International Conference on New Information Technology* (West Newton, MA: MicroUse Information, 1998), 19–26; see also, by the same authors, "Documenting the Cambodian Genocide on Multimedia," New Haven, CT: Yale Center for International and Area Studies, October 1998.

29. See "The Cambodian Genocide Program, 1994–1997," New Haven, CT: Yale Center for International and Area Studies, February 1998, 9.

30. See Helen Jarvis and Nereida Cross, "The Cambodian Genocide Program: Australian, Cambodian and U.S. Cooperation in Research and Documentation," Mekong Perspectives: 1st Annual Conference (forthcoming).

31. It appears, however, that in these two incidents, the destruction of the document caches was not intentional but rather was coincidental to military action. In one case, the fire that destroyed the documents was a consequence of a military assault, rather than specific targeting of the records. In the other case, the troops were engaging in a spree of punitive arson after overrunning government positions and simply happened to torch the building where the records were stored.

32. A legal training manual was produced by the CGP in both the English and Khmer languages and published as Beth Van Schaack and Noah Novogrodsky, eds., *Truth and Justice in Cambodia: A Teaching Manual for the Cambodian Genocide Justice Project* (Phnom Penh: Documentation Center of Cambodia, 1997).

33. The results of this project are reported in Jaya Ramji and Christine Barton, "Accounting for the Crimes of the Khmer Rouge, 1975–1979: Interviews with Cambodians," Phnom Penh: Documentation Center of Cambodia, 1997.

34. This project is initially being carried out by an ad hoc group of lawyers on a pro bono basis, including U.S. attorneys Beth Van Schaack, Ray Johansen, and John Ciorciari, along with Dutch attorney Jan Van Den Grinten.

35. An early result of this undertaking is Stephen Heder with Brian D. Tittemore, *Seven Candidates for Prosecution: Accountability for the Crimes of the Khmer Rouge* (Washington, DC: American University War Crimes Research Office, June 2001).

36. Of these, one is now approaching publication as an individual book. See Sara Colm, *The Khmer Rouge and Tribal Minorities in Northeastern Cambodia* (Bangkok: White Lotus Press, forthcoming).

37. Three such studies already published as books by the Documentation Cen-

ter include Meng-Try Ea and Sorya Sim, *Victims and Perpetrators? Testimony of Young Khmer Rouge Comrades* (Phnom Penh: Documentation Center of Cambodia, 2001); Ysa Osman, *Oukoubah: Justice for the Cham Muslims under the Democratic Kampuchea Regime* (Phnom Penh: Documentation Center of Cambodia, 2002); and Huy Vannak, *The Khmer Rouge Division 703: From Victory to Self-Destruction* (Phnom Penh: Documentation Center of Cambodia, 2003).

38. In 2002, the Documentation Center translated into the Khmer language and published an authorized edition of *The Diary of a Young Girl: Anne Frank* (Phnom Penh: Documentation Center of Cambodia, 2002). The center has several other projects under way aiming to translate English-language history texts into Khmer.

39. Several such volumes have recently appeared. See David Chandler, *Voices from S-21: Terror and History in Pol Pot's Secret Prison* (Berkeley: University of California Press, 1999). A second such volume is the present effort. In 2004, the Documentation Center also published an updated second edition of Heder and Tittemore's *Seven Candidates for Prosecution*.

40. The official report of the Group of Experts cited the Documentation Center and some of the work it has accomplished, calling it "the most impressive and organized effort" to build a historical record of human rights abuses under the Khmer Rouge. See UN, General Assembly, Security Council, A/53/850, S/1999/231, March 16, 1999, Annex, *Report of the Group of Experts for Cambodia Established Pursuant to General Assembly Resolution 52/135*, 16.

41. See, for example, Haas, *Cambodia, Pol Pot and the United States*, and Etcheson, "Avoiding a New War in Cambodia."

42. Sustained efforts to obtain the declassification and release of records from the U.S. Central Intelligence Agency yielded nothing of value, despite valiant assistance from allies in the U.S. Department of State and a Freedom of Information Act request, denied on grounds of national security exclusion. Similarly, requests for other records that the CGP sought from an agency of the U.S. Department of Justice were denied on grounds of the Privacy Act.

43. It was lost on some that this strident defender of American honor was in fact a citizen of Australia and, moreover, that Kiernan and Morris were bitter rivals from their Australian student days in the 1970s. See Stephen J. Morris, "The Wrong Man to Investigate Cambodia," *Wall Street Journal*, April 17, 1995, and Morris, "The Worst Possible Judge of Cambodian Crimes," *Asian Wall Street Journal*, April 17, 1995. See also "A Killing Field: The Probe of Pol Pot's Crimes Sparks a Bitter Dispute," *Asiaweek*, May 26, 1995.

44. See, for example, "The Cambodian Holocaust," *Wall Street Journal*, April 28, 1995, which includes letters to the editor from Ben Kiernan, Bob Lowy, Katherine Knight, Gaddis Smith, Paul Bushkovitch, James Scott, and Eileen Bloomenthal; "The Cambodian Holocaust II," *Wall Street Journal*, May 15,

1995, with letters from Stephen Morris, Gerard Henderson, and John Mc-Beth; and "The Cambodian Holocaust III," *Wall Street Journal*, May 30, 1995, with letters from Ben Kiernan and Charles F. Keyes, Daniel Lev, Hillel Kieval, Laurie Sears, and Judeth Henchy. Still later, the *Wall Street Journal* continued the assault with masthead editorials and other attacks on the program.

45. The letter from Congressman Hoke is on file with the author. It refers to Yale University's distinguished professor Ben Kiernan as "the notorious pro-Khmer Rouge 'journalist.'" Things like this did provide some moments of levity amid the controversy and questions as to whether or not the project could continue.

46. The letter to the secretary of state was signed by Senators Bob Dole, Jesse Helms, John McCain, Craig Thomas, Don Nickles, and Trent Lott. See, for example, Barton Biggs, "US Political Heavyweights Swing at Kiernan," *Cambodia Daily*, August 15, 1995.

47. Letter from Wendy R. Sherman, assistant secretary of state for legislative affairs, to Senator Bob Dole, September 13, 1995. The letter is on file with the author.

48. Ben Kiernan, "Bringing the Khmer Rouge to Justice," *Human Rights Review* 1:3 (April–June 2000): 102.

49. See Susan Cook, "Documenting Genocide: Cambodia's Lessons for Rwanda," *Africa Today* 44:2 (April–June 1997): 223–228. A modified version of this paper appeared as "Documenting Genocide: Lessons from Cambodia for Rwanda," in Judy Ledgerwood, ed., *Cambodia Emerges from the Past: Eight Essays* (DeKalb: Northern Illinois University Southeast Asia Publications, 2002), 224–237. Yale University subsequently launched the Rwanda Genocide Project and attempted to apply some of the same techniques used by the CGP to documenting genocide in Rwanda; see http://www.yale.edu/gsp/rwanda/index.html.

50. Personal communication from Helen Jarvis, April 4, 2000.

51. Personal communication from Youk Chhang, August 3, 2000.

52. In 1999, Yale University launched the "Yale East Timor Project: Health, Human Rights, Training and Development," aiming "to promote an appropriate Yale contribution to the international assistance needs of the people of East Timor." This project eventually sought to apply some of the techniques developed by CGP to the East Timor case; see http://www.yale.edu/gsp/east_timor/yale_east_timor_project.doc.

53. Personal communication from Youk Chhang, October 13, 2000.

54. Personal communication from Youk Chhang, October 30, 2003.

CHAPTER 5: CENTRALIZED TERROR

1. Craig Etcheson, *The Rise and Demise of Democratic Kampuchea* (London and Boulder, CO: Westview Press and Pinter Publishers, 1984).

2. Ibid., 146.

3. Ibid., 147.

4. A key source on the *Historikerstreit* is Charles S. Maier, *The Unmasterable Past: History, Holocaust, and German National Identity* (Cambridge: Harvard University Press, 1988).

5. Daniel J. Goldhagen, *Hitler's Willing Executioners: Ordinary Germans and the Holocaust* (New York: Knopf, 1996). In contrast, see Alexander Hinton, "A Head for an Eye: Revenge in the Cambodian Genocide," in Alexander Hinton, ed., *Genocide: An Anthropological Reader* (Oxford: Blackwell Publishers, 2002), 254–285.

6. See Ron Rosenbaum, *Explaining Hitler* (New York: Harper Perennial, 1999), for example, at pp. 70–71, where he discusses similar issues that constituted the *Historikerskreit*.

7. Michael Vickery, *Cambodia 1975–1982* (Boston: South End Press, 1984).

8. For example, see Kenneth Quinn's two chapters, "The Pattern and Scope of Violence" and "Explaining the Terror," in Karl Jackson, ed., *Cambodia 1975–1978: Rendezvous with Death* (Princeton, NJ: Princeton University Press, 1989), 179–208 and 215–240.

9. To date, the Documentation Center has collected some 600,000 pages of this type of material from the Khmer Rouge internal security services.

10. Prasit Sangrungrueng, "Was Ieng Sary Really 'Brother No. 2' and 'Pol Pot's Right Hand?'" Faxed typescript, August 25, 1996.

11. The Documentation Center of Cambodia has been an independent, nongovernmental research institute in Phnom Penh since 1997. For details on the origin and mission of the Documentation Center, see Chapter 4.

12. Although Ieng Sary neglected to mention it, some of the confession cover sheets also indicated that these incriminating documents had been sent to him, as well. For example, see Documentation Center Catalogue Number BBKKH412.

13. Documentation Center Catalog Number D00073, Note from Duch to "Brother," January 16, 1977.

14. Documentation Center Catalog Number J00883, Note from Duch to "Khieu" (Son Sen), March 24, 1978.

15. Documentation Center Catalog Number J00439, Cover Sheet from Son Sen to "At" (Yun Yat), July 6, 1977.

16. Documentation Center Catalog Number J00074, Note from Son Sen to Nuon Chea, November 10, 1977; and Catalog Number D00433, Note from Son Sen to Nuon Chea, November 11, 1977.

17. Uncataloged Documentation Center item, Note from "Khieu" (Son Sen) to Duch, October 5, 1977.

18. Documentation Center Catalog Number D00081, Note from (Son Sen?) to "Angkar" (Pol Pot?), October 9, 1977.

19. Documentation Center Catalog Number D01091, Note from "870" (Pol Pot?) to "Khieu" (Son Sen), n.d.

20. Documentation Center Catalog Number J00117, Letter to "870" (Pol Pot?), annotated with response from "Angkar" (Pol Pot?); the date of this document is unclear but could be September 19, 1976.

21. This organization chart is reproduced at http://www.yale.edu/cgp/tsorgchart.html.

22. Documentation Center Catalog Number D00186; Region 13 to Office 105, July 8, 1977.

23. Uncataloged item from Cambodia Documentation Commission archive, currently being processed for incorporation into the Documentation Center archives; Letter from Prison 105, April 15, 1978.

24. Documentation Center Catalog Number D01067, Letter from Battalion 502 to Duch, with notation from Duch to Chan, June 1, 1977. According to the S-21 personnel files, "Chan" (aka Mam Nay) was Duch's chief interrogator at Tuol Sleng; a confidential source reports filming "Chan" at a Khmer Rouge camp on the Thai border in the early 1990s, still interrogating prisoners. In the late 1990s, after the defection of the Pailin-based Khmer Rouge to the Royal Government in 1996, Chan became a civil servant, working as a policeman in Battambang Province. He went underground after Duch's arrest in 1999, resurfacing again in Battambang a few years later.

25. Documentation Center Catalog Number D01065, Execution Log signed by Huy and Hor, 23 July 1977.

26. Nate Thayer, " 'I Am in Danger,' " *Far Eastern Economic Review,* May 13, 1999.

27. Nate Thayer, "Death in Detail," *Far Eastern Economic Review*, May 13, 1999.

28. Documentation Center Catalog Number D01175; it is clear that the note is in Huy's handwriting, not only because he signed this document but also because Documentation Center investigators interviewed Huy and obtained a handwriting sample from him, discovering that his script and signature had changed little over the intervening years.

29. See, for example, Stephen Heder with Brian D. Tittemore, *Seven Candidates for Prosecution: Accountability for the Crimes of the Khmer Rouge* (Washington, DC: American University War Crimes Research Office, June 2001).

30. For details on the phenomenon of locally initiated killing during the Khmer Rouge regime, see Steve Heder, "Cambodia, Nazi Germany and the Stalinist Soviet Union: Intentionality, Totalitarianism, Functionalism and the Politics of Accountability" (Paper presented to the German Historical Institute Conference, Washington, DC, March 29, 2003).

CHAPTER 6: TERROR IN THE EAST

1. Opposition politician Sam Rainsy has frequently asserted that Prime Minister Hun Sen is "another Pol Pot." An instance of this political tactic is a doc-

ument prepared by the Sam Rainsy Party, "Pol Pot Number Two Still Alive," distributed at the Consultative Group Meeting, Paris, May 25–26, 2000.

2. The remnants of the Eastern Zone forces soon gained vengeance for this defeat by joining with invading Vietnamese forces in December 1978 to overthrow Pol Pot.

3. Ben Kiernan, *The Pol Pot Regime* (New Haven, CT: Yale University Press, 1996), 209.

4. Ibid., 209f.

5. Ibid., 208; there is some difficulty with this example citing "Meanchey Thmey district prison." I am unable to locate any entity in Region 23 or Svay Rieng Province named "Meanchey Thmey" or Meanchey Thmei. According to the *Geographical Gazetteer* issued by the Geography Department of the Royal Government's Council of Ministers, no district, commune, or village in Svay Rieng includes "Meanchey" (or Mean Chey or Mean Cheay) as part of its name. Similarly, there are no districts or communes named "Thmey," although there are thirteen villages in Svay Rieng Province named Thmey (Thmei is the transliteration used by the official gazetteer, and it simply means "new"). Perhaps there was a name change after the Democratic Kampuchea regime. In any case, it is difficult to evaluate the validity of this claim.

6. Henri Locard, "The Khmer Rouge Gulag: 17 April 1975–7 January 1979," Paris, June 16, 1995, sec. I-2-3, p. 6.

7. Ibid., Section II-2; Locard refers to "thirty zones under the KR." The standard nomenclature used by the Khmer Rouge divided the country into seven "zones" and, within those zones, some thirty "regions" or "sectors." For a delineation of the Khmer Rouge zones and regions, see the official Khmer Rouge map of Democratic Kampuchea in the Geographical Database of the Cambodian Genocide Data Bases on the World Wide Web at http://www.yale.edu/cgp.

8. See the Biographical Database of the Cambodian Genocide Data Bases (CGDB) at http://www.yale.edu/cgp.

9. One exception to the three-person committee structure is found at the very apex of the party, where the Standing Committee of the Central Committee constituted the highest political authority of the party and consisted of more than three persons. Even so, important subcommittees of the Standing Committee—such as the internal security committee—were organized according to the three-member cell structure principle.

10. CGDB Biographical Database Record Y00090.

11. CGDB Biographical Database Record Y03069; alias Uk Savan, alias Sau.

12. Kiernan, *The Pol Pot Regime*, 209.

13. Meas Chhuon was also known as "Vek" and "Chhean." I am grateful to David Hawk for bringing this document to my attention; the translation of this confession was done by Steve Heder for the Cambodia Documentation Com-

mission. The confession, dated June 21, 1978, is titled "The Responses of the Contemptible Chhean, Party Secretary of Sector 22, Eastern Region." It is now an uncataloged item in the Documentation Center of Cambodia archives. A copy is on file with the author.

14. See CGDB Bibliographic Database Record Number Y03052; it cites interviews by Kiernan with three different sources (BKI 131, BKI 159, and BKI 202), who suggest that Seng Hong did not take up the Region 23 secretary post until 1978. See also Steve Heder, "Racism, Marxism, Labelling, and Genocide in Ben Kiernan's *The Pol Pot Regime*," *South East Asia Research* 5:2 (1997): 101–153, especially pp. 120 and 121 and n41, where Heder discusses four different S-21 forced confessions that put the date of Sin So's (alias Uk Savan, alias Sau) dismissal as Region 23 Secretary in February 1978 and his arrest in March 1978.

15. CGDB Bibliographic Database Record Number Y03052.

16. Ibid.; several of Kiernan's informants also indicate that Seng Hong remained loyal to orders from Pol Pot well into the Eastern Zone crisis and perhaps through the end of the regime (see BKI 131, BKI 159, and BKI 202).

17. Deputy secretary of the Region 23 Committee, Maung Vuth, and the member of the Region 23 Committee, Neth Yun; CGDB Biographical Database Records B11833 and B11928, respectively.

18. CGDB Bibliographical Database Record D00006.

19. Kiernan, *Pol Pot Regime*, 208f, citing David Chandler, *The Tragedy of Cambodian History: Politics, War and Revolution since 1945* (New Haven, CT: Yale University Press, 1991), 282.

20. Documentation Center of Cambodia, Mapping Reports, "Svay Rieng Province," June 4, 1997.

21. Ibid.

22. This site was investigated and confirmed by a Documentation Center Mapping survey team. However, there is some possible confusion here, as documentary sources from the People's Republic of Kampuchea (PRK) period refer to a Wat Beoung Rai Prison in both Svay Rieng provincial town and in adjacent Svay Chrum District. Possibly there are two pagodas named Wat Beoung Rai in Svay Rieng Province, and both were converted into Khmer Rouge prisons; or, perhaps there was an error in one of the PRK reports from this period. See Documentation Center Mapping Reports. See also Renakse Document Number 364 in the Documentation Center archives and CGDB Bibliographical Database Record D00366.

23. 1997 Documentation Center Mapping Reports, "Svay Rieng Province."

24. Ibid.

25. 1996 Documentation Center Mapping Reports, "Svay Rieng Province."

26. CGDB Bibliographic Database Records D00363 and D00371. If this report from the People's Republic of Kampuchea is accurate, then the prisons of

Kompong Ro conform to Locard's hypothesis regarding the overall structure of the Khmer Rouge security system.

27. 1996 Documentation Center Mapping Reports, "Svay Rieng Province," October 14, 1996.

28. Ibid.

29. Ibid.

30. Ibid.

31. Documentation Center of Cambodia Renakse Archive Document #364.

32. See the personnel listing for Tuol Sleng's "hot group" on the S-21 organization chart shown on the CGP Web site at http://www.yale.edu/cgp.

33. 1996 Documentation Center Mapping Reports.

34. Ros Visal, "My Family during the 3-Year 8-Month and 20-Day Period," Phnom Penh: Documentation Center of Cambodia, Archive Document #604.

35. Testimony taken on March 24, 1997, in Romeas Hek District, from 56-year-old male. 1997 Documentation Center Mapping Reports, Svay Rieng Province.

36. Ibid.

37. Ibid.

38. Ibid.

39. Ibid.

40. Ibid.

41. Biography of prisoner Sa Son, uncataloged item in the Documentation Center of Cambodia archives.

42. Biography of prisoner Kul Thai, uncataloged item in the Documentation Center of Cambodia archives.

43. See, for example, Ben Kiernan, "Cambodia: the Eastern Zone Massacres," Columbia University, Center for the Study of Human Rights, Documentation Series No. 1 (New York, 1986).

44. From August 17, 1979, People's Revolutionary Tribunal, "Confession of Siv Samon." Documentation Center of Cambodia Catalog Number D441.

45. These studies are currently under way at the Documentation Center of Cambodia.

CHAPTER 7: DIGGING IN THE KILLING FIELDS

1. For additional thoughts on why genocide deniers deny, see Colin Tatz, "Why Denialists Deny," in Colin Tatz, Peter Arnold, and Sandra Tatz, eds., *Genocide Perspectives II: Essays on Holocaust and Genocide* (Blackheath, NSW: Brandl & Schlesinger, 2003), 267–284.

2. The 3 million death toll estimate appears to have been first put forward by Pen Sovann in April 1979, which was in fact long prior to the completion of any serious research on the death toll by the Cambodian government. See

Evan Gottesman, *Cambodia after the Khmer Rouge: Inside the Politics of Nation Building* (New Haven, CT: Yale University Press, 2003), 61.

3. People's Republic of Kampuchea, Research Committee on Pol Pot's Genocidal Regime, "Report of the Research Committee on Pol Pot's Genocidal Regime," Phnom Penh, July 25, 1983. The original is in the Khmer language; excerpts have been translated by the Documentation Center of Cambodia for the CGP. The quality of the data in this report appears to be uneven, at best, and should be approached with care by scholars.

4. This work by the Research Committee raises a number of complex issues, one of which is that it may have played a central role, along with the annual May 20 "Day of Hatred" ceremonies, in creating a trope for the socially and politically acceptable Cambodian genocide survivor story. The creation of this trope was, at least in part, a deliberate act aimed at creating national solidarity and political consciousness or, in other words, a national myth. The existence of this trope could present evidentiary problems at a Khmer Rouge tribunal.

5. "Report of the Research Committee."

6. Ben Kiernan, *The Pol Pot Regime: Race, Power, and Genocide in Cambodia under the Khmer Rouge, 1975–79* (New Haven, CT: Yale University Press, 1996), 458, Table 4.

7. Personal communication from Steve Heder, May 9, 2003.

8. Marek Sliwinski, *Le Génocide Khmer Rouge: une analyse démographique* (Paris: Editions L'Harmattan, 1995), 40.

9. "Kampuchea: A Demographic Catastrophe," Washington, DC: Central Intelligence Agency, January 17, 1980.

10. Judith Banister and Paige Johnson, "After the Nightmare: The Population of Cambodia," in Ben Kiernan, ed., *Genocide and Democracy in Cambodia: The Khmer Rouge, the United Nations and the International Community* (New Haven, CT: Yale University Southeast Asia Studies, 1993), 90.

11. Patrick Heuveline, "L'insoutenable incertitude du nombre: estimations des décès de la périod Khmer rouge," *Population* 3 (May–June 1998): 1103–1118; see also his "Approaches to Measuring Genocide: Excess Morality during the Khmer Rouge Period," in Daniel Chirot and Martin Seligman, eds., *Ethnopolitical Warfare: Causes, Consequences and Possible Solutions* (Washington, DC: American Psychological Association, 2001), 93–108.

12. Kiernan, *The Pol Pot Regime*, 456.

13. Personal communication from Steve Heder, April 5, 2000.

14. Sliwinski, *Le Génocide Khmer Rouge*, 82, Table 11.

15. Heuveline, "L'insoutenable incertitude du nombre," and also his "Approaches to Measuring Genocide."

16. Michael Vickery, *Cambodia: 1975–1982* (Boston: South End Press, 1984), 187f.

17. Sliwinski, *Le Génocide Khmer Rouge*, 40, Figure 5.

18. Banister and Johnson, "After the Nightmare," 90; these authors argue that "excess deaths" in this period amounted to 1.05 million, with the remainder of the decline from expected population levels under normal growth scenarios attributed to net emigration and a suppressed birthrate.

19. Heuveline, "L'insoutenable incertitude du nombre."

20. See Kenneth M. Quinn, "The Pattern and Scope of Violence," in Karl Jackson, ed., *Cambodia 1975–1978: Rendezvous with Death* (Princeton, NJ: Princeton University Press, 1989), 179–208. Personal communication from Kenneth Quinn, August 21, 1996.

21. Personal communication from Vann Nath, March 7, 1996.

22. The author traveled to the Central Identification Laboratory in Honolulu in 1996 in his capacity at that time as director of the Documentation Center to discuss the possibilities for forensic work in connection with the mass grave mapping project.

23. Michael S. Pollanen, "Forensic Survey of Three Memorial Sites Containing Human Skeletal Remains in the Kingdom of Cambodia" (Mission Report to the Coalition for International Justice, Washington, DC, July 2002).

CHAPTER 8: THE PERSISTENCE OF IMPUNITY

1. *Jus cogens* is a term of art in international law that refers to norms and rules generally accepted as universal and obligatory on all states. For example, it is obligatory to punish perpetrators of genocide.

2. Steven R. Ratner and Jason S. Abrams, *Accountability for Human Rights Atrocities in International Law: Beyond the Nuremberg Legacy* (Oxford: Oxford University Press, 1997); and the *Report of the Group of Experts for Cambodia Pursuant to General Assembly Resolution 52/135*, by Ninian Stephen, Chairman, Rajsoomer Lallah, and Steven R. Ratner, dated February 18, 1999, presented as an annex to UN, General Assembly, Security Council, *Identical letters Dated 15 March 1999 from the Secretary-General to the President of the General Assembly and the President of the Security Council*, A/53/850 and S/1999/231, March 16, 1999. For a dissenting view on whether or not the crimes committed in Cambodia constitute genocide, see William Schabas, *Genocide in International Law* (Cambridge: Cambridge University Press, 2000).

3. A more detailed description of the People's Revolutionary Tribunal can be found in Chapter 2 of the present volume.

4. See, for example, Amnesty International [AI] Report 1997 (POL 10/001/1997), June 18, 1997, where in the section on Cambodia, AI notes, "Eight people who were arrested in December 1995 on suspicion of having links with the outlawed NADK . . . were brought to trial in August. Their trial, which appeared to be politically motivated, fell short of international standards for fair trial."

5. See Greg Stanton, "The Khmer Rouge Genocide and International Law," in Ben Kiernan, ed., *Genocide and Democracy in Cambodia: The Khmer Rouge, the United Nations and the International Community* (New Haven, CT: Yale University Southeast Asia Studies, 1993), 141–162. Stanton's Cambodia Genocide Project should not be confused with the CGP at Yale University.

6. See Hurst Hannum, "International Law and the Cambodian Genocide: The Sounds of Silence," *Human Rights Quarterly* 11 (1989): 82–138.

7. See U.S. Congress, Senate, *The Khmer Rouge Prosecution and Exclusion Act*, S.2622, 102nd Cong., 2nd sess., 1992 (April 10). Compare with U.S. Congress, House, *The Khmer Rouge Prosecution Act*, H.R.5708, 102nd Cong. 2nd sess., 1992 (July 28).

8. The author was involved in this effort. Some of the results of this effort are described in Global Witness, *Forests, Famine and War: The Key to Cambodia's Future* (London: Global Witness, 1995), 7.

9. Personal communication from Karl Deeds, November 4, 1997.

10. A U.S. law known as the Alien Tort Claims Act allows plaintiffs to bring civil actions to seek remedy for damages suffered by Americans or by foreigners in jurisdictions other than the United States.

11. See, for example, U.S. Congress, House, *Foreign Operations, Export Financing, and Related Programs Appropriations Act, 1995*, Pub. L. 103–306, 103rd Cong. 2nd sess., 1994, H.R. 4426; especially Title III—Military Assistance, p. 34, ll. 9–18, describing restrictions on the International Military Education and Training program for Thailand.

12. See testimony of Craig Etcheson in U.S. Congress, House, Committee on Appropriations, Foreign Operations, Export Financing, and Related Programs Appropriations for 1994. Hearings before a Subcommittee of the Committee on Appropriations, "Avoiding a New War in Cambodia," March 1, 1993, 103rd Cong., 1st sess., 1993, 575–587.

13. Craig Etcheson, "Punish Thai Military over Khmer Rouge Aid," *Asian Wall Street Journal Weekly*, June 27, 1994.

14. PL 103-236, 108 Stat. 486; 22 USC 2656 (1994), *The Cambodian Genocide Justice Act*.

15. Jason Abrams and Stephen Ratner, "Striving for Justice: Accountability and the Crimes of the Khmer Rouge" (A study for the U.S. Department of State under the Cambodian Genocide Justice Act), 275.

16. For an early overview of the CGP's work, see Craig Etcheson, "From Theory to Facts in the Cambodian Genocide," *International Network on Holocaust and Genocide* 12:1–2 (1997): 4–7; for more detail, see Chapter 4 in this volume.

17. Lustration is the practice of barring officials of a previous regime from holding positions of responsibility in a successor regime. Cambodia's law was an atypical instance of this practice.

18. The full text of the law is reprinted in the *Phnom Penh Post*, July 15–28, 1994.
19. Ibid.
20. The author was the principal drafter of this law.
21. UN, Commission on Human Rights, 53rd session, Item 18 of the provisional agenda, *Situation of Human Rights in Cambodia: Report of the Special Representative of the Secretary-General for Human Rights in Cambodia, Mr. Thomas Hammarberg, Submitted in Accordance with Commission Resolution 1996/54*, UN Economic and Social Council, E/CN.4/1997/85, January 31, 1997.
22. Summary of Thomas Hammarberg's remarks upon presentation of the Report, E/CN.4/1997/85.
23. In a series of structured interviews carried out in a collaboration of the CGP, the Orville H. Schell, Jr., Center for International Human Rights at Yale Law School, and the Documentation Center of Cambodia, twenty-two Cambodian political leaders representing all major Cambodian parties except the Khmer Rouge were questioned. The investigators found these leaders virtually unanimous in favoring an international criminal tribunal for the Khmer Rouge over the options of a domestic tribunal or a truth commission. See Jaya Ramji and Christine Barton, "Accounting for the Crimes of the Khmer Rouge: Interviews with Cambodians," Phnom Penh: Documentation Center of Cambodia, 1997.
24. See Tricia Fitzgerald, "Truth Body Urged for Khmer Rouge Genocide," *South China Morning Post*, February 3, 1997; and Leo Dobbs, "U.N. Official Calls for Cambodian Truth Commission," Reuters, February 6, 1997.
25. "Cambodia May Consult Tutu on Khmer Trials," Agence France Press, January 17, 1999.
26. Letter from Cambodian Co-Prime Ministers to Secretary-General Kofi Annan, June 21, 1997.
27. Stephen et al., *Report of the Group of Experts*.
28. "La Belgique devient pionnière dans la lutte contre les tortionnaires," *Le Soir*, April 16, 1999.
29. "Une Action Judiciaire Pour Barrer La Route a L'impunite," *La Libre Belgique*, April 16, 1999.

CHAPTER 9: THE POLITICS OF
GENOCIDE JUSTICE

1. See, for example, "Doit-on poursuivre les chefs des Khmers Rouges?" *IFRASSORC Revue Trimestrielle* 5 (April 1999): 2–7. See also "Poll Results," Washington, DC: International Republican Institute, March 12, 2004.
2. See Chapter 7 in this volume, and Henri Locard, "The Khmer Rouge Gulag: 17 April 1975–7 January 1979," Paris, June 16, 1995.

3. See, for example, Steven R. Ratner and Jason S. Abrams, *Accountability for Human Rights Atrocities in International Law: Beyond the Nuremberg Legacy* (Oxford: Oxford University Press, 1997); and UN, General Assembly, Security Council, *Identical Letters*, A/53/850, S/1999/231, March 16, 1999, Annex, *Report of the Group of Experts for Cambodia Established Pursuant to General Assembly Resolution 52/135*; the full text of the *Report of the Group of Experts* is online at http://www.khmerinstitute.org/docs/UNKRreport.htm. See also Stephen Heder with Brian D. Tittemore, *Seven Candidates for Prosecution: Accountability for the Crimes of the Khmer Rouge* (Washington, DC: American University War Crimes Research Office, June 2001).

4. For a review of this long struggle for justice, see "The Persistence of Impunity," Chapter 8 in this volume.

5. Author's notes on Second Prime Minister Hun Sen's address to the "International Conference on Striving for Justice: International Law in the Cambodian Context," Phnom Penh, August 22, 1995.

6. An excellent recent history of the formative days of Cambodia's ruling party is Evan Gottesman, *Cambodia after the Khmer Rouge: Inside the Politics of Nation Building* (New Haven, CT: Yale University Press, 2003). See also Margaret Slocomb, *The People's Republic of Kampuchea, 1979–1989: The Revolution after Pol Pot* (Chiang Mai: Silkworm Books, 2003), and Kristina Chhim, *Die Revolutionäre Volkspartei Kampuchea 1979 bis 1989. Eine Analyse der politischen Herrschaft einer nach der vietnamesischen Intervention reorganisierten Kommunistischen Partei* (Frankfurt am Main: Peter Lang Verlag, 2000).

7. FUNCINPEC is the French acronym for National United Front for a Cooperative, Independent, Neutral and Peaceful Cambodia.

8. It is also true that the CPP was scheming with elements of the Khmer Rouge, as well. There is little consensus among Cambodians about how to describe the tumultuous events of 1997.

9. See, for example, "Cambodia Ruling Party Wins Big in Local Voting," *International Herald Tribune*, February 27, 2002.

10. Vong Sokheng, "Ranariddh Prefers UN Trial Role," *Phnom Penh Post*, April 12–25, 2002.

11. U.S. Congress, House of Representatives, *Expressing Sense of House of Representatives regarding Culpability of Hun Sen for War Crimes, Crimes against Humanity, and Genocide in Cambodia*, 105th Cong., 2nd Sess., 1998, H.Res. 533.

12. A penetrating biography of Sihanouk, long banned in Cambodia, is Milton Osborne, *Sihanouk: Prince of Light, Prince of Darkness* (Chiang Mai, Thailand: Silkworm Books, 1994).

13. Sihanouk's house arrest and other abuses suffered at the hands of the Khmer Rouge are recounted in his memoir, Norodom Sihanouk, *Prisonnier des Khmers Rouges* (Paris: Hachette, 1986).

14. For Sihanouk's defense of his practice of retaining Khmer Rouge on his staff,

see "Question de l'Equipe du BMD (Chhorn Hay, Ke Kimsè, Srey Nory) et Réponse de Sa Majesté Norodom Sihanouk," Beijing, May 12, 2003.

15. For more information on the 1979 genocide trial, see Howard J. DeNike, John Quigley, and Kenneth J. Robinson, eds., *Genocide in Cambodia: Documents from the Trial of Pol Pot and Ieng Sary* (Philadelphia: University of Pennsylvania Press, 2000). For a discussion of Ieng Sary's pardon, see "Approaches to Reconciliation," in Craig Etcheson, *Retribution and Reconciliation: Healing What Ails Cambodia* (Washington, DC: Project Report to the U.S. Institute of Peace, October 2002).

16. Cambodia's present and past constitutions can be found in Raoul M. Jennar, *The Cambodian Constitutions 1953–1993* (Bangkok: White Lotus Co., 1995), although the book does not reflect a number of post-1993 amendments to the current constitution.

17. For example, see "King Says He's Willing to Stand Trial alongside Khmer Rouge," Associated Press, January 4, 1999. More recently, the king has said that he will be willing to give testimony at the Khmer Rouge tribunal. See "King Wants to Testify at KR Tribunal," *Cambodia Daily*, April 19, 2004.

18. Excerpted from "Forgive and Forget," by Suong Sikoeun, unofficial translation of a speech made in Khmer at the Center for Social Development Public Forum, "Khmer Rouge and National Reconciliation," in Battambang, Cambodia, January 27, 2000; reproduced in *On the Record*, 13:8 (August 7, 2000).

19. Chris Fontaine, "Khmer Rouge Leaders Apologize," Associated Press, December 29, 1998.

20. More recently, see former Khmer Rouge president Khieu Samphan's statement suggesting that there would be "retaliation" for any attempt to bring him and his other surviving senior colleagues to justice in a court of law. "Khmer Rouge Heads Want Truth Commission instead of Trial," Agence France-Presse, December 1, 2002.

21. For more detail on Khmer Rouge opinions regarding a genocide tribunal, see Etcheson, *Retribution and Reconciliation*, especially Chapters 2 and 6.

22. Chea Vannath, "Khmer Rouge and National Reconciliation" (Paper delivered at the Stockholm International Forum on Truth, Justice and Reconciliation, April 23–24, 2002); and *The Khmer Rouge and National Reconciliation—Opinions from the Cambodians* (Phnom Penh: Center for Social Development, April 2001).

23. One of the most methodologically competent of these surveys is reported in IFRASSORC, "Doit-on poursuivre les chefs des Khmers Rouges?"

24. However, it is also true that prior to the Khmer Rouge regime, local disputes were often adjudicated at the commune level by the subdistrict chief, who applied the French legal code.

25. For details on how the Eichmann trial helped to spark the first serious na-

tional discussion about the Holocaust among survivors in Israel, as well as among those who had not experienced it themselves, see Helen Epstein, *Children of the Holocaust: Conversations with Sons and Daughters of Survivors* (New York: Penguin Books, 1979).

26. "Vietnam newspaper: Time Cannot Erase Genocidal Khmer Rouge Crimes," Associated Press, January 6, 1999.

27. Tom Fawthrop, "Thai Senator Urges Apology," *Phnom Penh Post*, March 16–29, 2001.

28. "Thaksin Heralds 'New Era of Cooperation' with Cambodia," Associated Press, June 18, 2001.

29. Bilateral Thai–Cambodian relations remained strained for some months following the incident on January 29, 2003, when a mob allegedly enraged by comments attributed to a Thai movie star burned the recently completed new Thai Embassy in Phnom Penh and also torched numerous Thai-owned businesses. See "Thai PM Threatens to Send Commandos to Quell Phnom Penh Mob," Agence France Press, January 29, 2003.

30. UN, *Report of the Group of Experts for Cambodia.*

31. *Joint Communique of 35th ASEAN Ministerial Meeting*, Bandar Seri Begawan, Brunei July 29–30, 2002, para. 45.

32. Scholars estimate that some 50 million people died during various "excesses" in Mao's China. For example, see the chapter on China by Jean-Louis Margolin in Stephane Courtois et al., *The Black Book of Communism: Crimes, Terror, Repression* (Cambridge: Harvard University Press, 1999).

33. See, for example, the comments of Chinese Foreign Minister Tang Jiaxuan in Greg Torode, "Beijing May Veto Genocide Tribunal," *South China Morning Post*, February 6, 1999.

34. "Ex-UN Official: China Tried to Stymie Khmer Rouge Trial," Associated Press, November 12, 2000.

35. See, for example, Ek Madra, "China Forgives Cambodia Khmer Rouge-era Debt," Reuters, November 3, 2002.

36. U.S. Congress, PL 103-236, 108 Stat. 486; 22 USC 2656 (1994), *The Cambodian Genocide Justice Act.* For more information on the origin and implications of the Cambodian Genocide Justice Act, see Chapter 4 of this volume.

37. For background on the CGP, see Chapter 4 in this volume.

38. These U.S. policy initiatives are detailed in Craig Etcheson, "The United States Role in Negotiating Ad Hoc International Criminal Tribunals: The Case of Cambodia" (Paper delivered to the Society of Historians of American Foreign Relations annual conference, Washington, DC, June 6, 2003).

39. For example, see Peter Slevin, "U.S. Would Seek to Try Hussein for War Crimes," *Washington Post*, October 30, 2002.

40. Marlise Simons, "Iraqis Meet with War Crimes Trial Experts," *New York Times*, April 7, 2004.

41. Lorne Craner became assistant secretary of state for democracy, human rights, and labor, and Paul Grove became a foreign policy aide to Republican Senate whip Mitch McConnell.

42. Michelle Knueppel, "Khmer Rouge Tribunal Sought: L.B. Lawmakers Urge Bush to Fund Court That Would Try Regime Chiefs," *Long Beach Press Telegram*, April 3, 2004.

43. At one point, McConnell inserted a provision into the annual Foreign Operations Act conditioning U.S. foreign aid to Cambodia on the Royal Government's cooperation with the international community on bringing about a Khmer Rouge tribunal.

44. See, for example, a January 15, 2003, letter from McConnell and Democratic Senator Patrick Leahy to UN Secretary-General Kofi Annan, arguing that "the 'mixed tribunal' will be doomed to failure." Copy on file with author. See also the "Cambodia Democracy and Accountability Act of 2003," cosponsored by McConnell and Leahy, which proposed to impose restrictions on U.S. support for the Khmer Rouge tribunal. U.S. Senate, *The Cambodian Democracy and Accountability Act of 2003*, 108th Cong., 1st sess., 2003, S.1365.

45. The vote on the General Assembly resolution, A/57/556/Add.2, is recorded in UN, GA/10124, December 18, 2002.

46. Naoko Aoki, "Hun Sen to Resume Talks with U.N. over Khmer Rouge Trial," Kyodo, January 11, 2000.

47. See Luke Hunt, "Tribunal Judges to Come from Eight Countries," Agence France-Presse, August 22, 2001. However, the author's private conversations with Japanese diplomatic officials in March 2004 suggested that the amount of funding Japan is willing to contribute to the Khmer Rouge tribunal had fallen dramatically, to something more on the order of $10 million.

48. UN, A/57/556/Add.2, October 18, 2002.

49. See, for example, "Cambodia Seeks Suggestions on Law to Try Khmer Rouge," Kyodo, November 5, 1999.

50. "Indian PM Said to Consider Providing Judge for Khmer Rouge Trials," BBC Monitoring Service, April 9, 2002.

51. See, for example, Anette Marcher, "National KR tribunal takes shape," *Phnom Penh Post*, November 26–December 9, 1999.

52. The Cambodian first draft of a Khmer Rouge tribunal law is "Loi relative à la répression des crimes de génocide et des crimes contre l'humanité" (Royal Government of Cambodia, Council of Ministers, August 1999, typescript); copy on file with author. The UN's criticism of this draft is detailed in "Comments on the Draft Law concerning the Punishment of the Crime of Genocide and Crimes against Humanity" (Memorandum from UN assistant secretary for legal affairs Ralph Zacklin to the Royal Government, August 27, 1999); copy on file with author.

53. UN, *Report of the Group of Experts for Cambodia*.

54. These negotiations are analyzed in detail in Craig Etcheson, *The Extraordinary Chambers: The Politics of the Khmer Rouge Tribunal* (Manuscript in preparation).

55. The Khmer Rouge tribunal law was promulgated with King Sihanouk's signature on August 10, 2001, and is formally titled the "Law on the Establishment of Extraordinary Chambers in the Courts of Cambodia for the Prosecution of Crimes Committed during the Period of Democratic Kampuchea." An official English translation of the law is available online at http://www.cambodia.gov.kh/krt/english/index.htm. The UN's announcement in 2002 that it would terminate the negotiations included terse criticism of the law; see UN, Press Release, "Daily Press Briefing by the Office of the Spokesman for the Secretary-General," February 8, 2002.

56. For example, on the tenth anniversary of the beginning of the Rwandan genocide, Annan said, "If there is one legacy I would most wish to leave to my successors, it is an Organization both better equipped to prevent genocide, and able to act decisively to stop it when prevention fails." See "10 Years after Rwanda Genocide, Annan Unveils Plan to Stop Future Massacres," UN News Center, April 7, 2004.

57. For example, see Human Rights Watch, *Cambodia: Tribunal Must Meet International Standards*, February 12, 2002; and Amnesty International, *Cambodia: Cambodians Deserve International Standards of Justice*, November 19, 2002.

58. An individual who was present at the meeting confidentially relayed this account to the author.

59. For example, see "Cambodian Premier Meets Newly-Appointed Chinese Ambassador," *People's Daily*, August 30, 2000.

60. A comment about Norodom Sihanouk by his biographer seems to apply equally to Hun Sen: "A dispassionate view bolsters the conclusion that Sihanouk was only rarely able to control courses of action rather than trim his sails to winds he could not control. What is remarkable is the extent to which he has made the most of limited opportunities and in so doing remained in power for so long." Osborne, *Sihanouk*, 10.

61. For example, at ceremonies marking the twenty-fourth anniversary of "Liberation Day" on January 7, 2003, CPP president Chea Sim reiterated the government's call for a genocide tribunal. See "End of Pol Pot Marked, Festivities Marred by Fighting in the Streets," *Bangkok Post*, January 8, 2003.

CHAPTER 10: CHALLENGING THE CULTURE OF IMPUNITY

1. Royal Government of Cambodia, Council of Ministers, "Aide Memoire on the Conversation between Hun Sen, Prime Minister of the Royal Government of Cambodia, and H. E. Kofi Annan, Secretary General of the United Nations," New York, September 17, 1999 [unofficial translation].

2. I am grateful to David P. Chandler for this observation; he notes that this idea is deeply ingrained in Hindu notions of governance, where the word for "govern" is also the word for "consume."

3. For example, see the table on p. 6 of Global Witness, *Going Places: Cambodia's Future on the Move* (London: Global Witness, March 1998) listing the regional military commanders involved in rapacious exploitation of timber resources. Of these influential regional leaders, Prince Norodom Ranariddh says, "It is very difficult to act against the warlords" (ibid., 3). Global Witness argues that "major problems of corruption and impunity persist" in Cambodia. See *The Credibility Gap—and the Need to Bridge It* (London: Global Witness, May 2001), 45.

4. Steve Heder, "Cultures of Genocide, Impunity and Victors' Justice in Cambodia, 1945–1999: Colonial, Communist and Other International Sources" (unpublished typescript, 2000), 5f. For a more detailed view of the same issues, see also David P. Chandler, *The Tragedy of Cambodian History: Politics, War and Revolution since 1945* (New Haven, CT: Yale University Press, 1991).

5. See UN, General Assembly, *The Situation of Human Rights in Cambodia*, A/53/400, September 17, 1998, especially the sections titled "Protection against Political Violence" and "The Problem of Impunity," where the special representative of the secretary-general notes, "The widespread phenomenon of impunity continues." At §68.

6. See, for example, Amnesty International, *Grenade Attack on Peaceful Demonstration*, ASA 23/005/1997 (London, March 31, 1997).

7. For a discussion of the killings, see *The July 26, 1998 Cambodian National Assembly Elections* (Washington, DC: National Democratic Institute for International Affairs, 1999), 48f.

8. Bou Saroeun and Phelim Kyne, "Pelika's Murderers Remain Free Two Years Later," *Phnom Penh Post*, July 6–19, 2001.

9. As Suy Nuo, Cambodia's secretary of state for justice, put it, "Cambodia lacks qualified personnel to act as judges. Some judges in Cambodia have never been lawyers . . . they are not qualified for the job they do. . . . The most serious problem is salaries. Lack of money means that they can't provide 100% justice." Bou Saroeun and Phelim Kyne, "Trials and Tribulations at the Ministry of Justice," *Phnom Penh Post*, August 6–19, 1999.

10. UN, Cambodian Office of the High Commissioner for Human Rights, *Note on Legal and Judicial Reform for the Mid-Term Consultative Group of Donors Meeting*, January 25, 2003.

11. On the origins of Cambodia's current judicial system and the political nature of judicial appointments, see Evan Gottesman, *Cambodia after the Khmer Rouge: Inside the Politics of Nation Building* (New Haven, CT: Yale University Press, 2003), 244f.

12. For example, Amnesty International has argued that a Khmer Rouge tribu-

nal should "be used to assist the continuing program of capacity building and technical assistance in the Cambodian judicial sector." See Amnesty International, *Cambodia: Amnesty International's Preliminary Views and Concerns about the Draft Agreement for the Establishment of a Khmer Rouge Special Tribunal*, ASA 23/003/2003 (London, March 21, 2003).

13. Useful accounts of the war in Yugoslavia include Lenard J. Cohen, *Broken Bonds: The Disintegration of Yugoslavia* (Boulder, CO: Westview Press, 1993); Michael Sells, *The Bridge Betrayed: Religion and Genocide in Bosnia* (Berkeley: University of California Press, 1996); and Chuck Sudetic, *Blood and Vengeance: One Family's Story of the War in Bosnia* (New York: W. W. Norton, 1998).

14. The tribunal was established under the UN Security Council's Chapter VII powers; see UN, Security Council, *Security Council Resolution 827*, S/Res/827, May 25, 1993. See also Aryeh Neier's account of the establishment of the ICTY in his *War Crimes: Brutality, Genocide, Terror and the Struggle for Justice* (New York: Times Books, 1998).

15. For a current summary of the judgments and proceedings of the ICTY, see the court's Web site at http://www.un.org/icty.

16. See Office of the Prosecutor, The Hague, *Statement of the Prosecutor, Carla del Ponte*, F.H./P.I.S./598e, June 29, 2001.

17. For example, see Louise Branson, "With Milosevic on Trial, Reconciliation Becomes a Casualty in the Balkans," *Washington Post*, February 24, 2002.

18. Informative accounts of the Rwandan genocide include Gerard Prunier, *The Rwanda Crisis: History of a Genocide* (New York: Columbia University Press, 1995); Philip Gourevitch, *We Wish to Inform You That Tomorrow We Will Be Killed with Our Families: Stories from Rwanda* (New York: Farrar Straus and Giroux, 1998); and Alison des Forges, *Leave None to Tell the Story: Genocide in Rwanda* (New York: Human Rights Watch, 1999).

19. For a damning account of how the international community turned its back on Rwanda, see the Pulitzer Prize–winning book by Samantha Power, *A Problem from Hell: America and the Age of Genocide* (New York: Basic Books, 2002), especially Chapter 10, "Mostly in a Listening Mode."

20. UN, Security Council, *Security Council Resolution 955*, S/Res/955, November 8, 1994.

21. International Criminal Tribunal for Rwanda, "Jean-Paul Akayesu, summary of the Judgment," ICTR-96-4-T, September 2, 1998. Scholars argue that the Akayesu judgment opened new vistas in genocide prosecution. See Colin Tatz, Peter Arnold, and Sandra Tatz, eds., *Genocide Perspectives II: Essays on Holocaust and Genocide* (Blackheath, NSW: Brandl & Schlesinger, 2003), 10.

22. For example, see Sheenah Kaliisa, "Genocide Survivors' Association Reaffirms Its Suspension of Co-operation with the ICTR," Internews, February 28, 2002.

23. "Tage des Gerichts," *Der Spiegel*, December 2, 2002.

24. In January 2003, the Rwandan government decided to release more than 30,000 genocide suspects who had already served more time in detention than they would if convicted of the charges against them. See "Rwanda to Release over 30,000 Genocide Suspects," Foundation Hirondelle, January 22, 2003.

25. "Gacaca Takes Off Slowly," Foundation Hirondelle, October 14, 2002.

26. IRIN-CEA Update 834 for the Great Lakes, January 6, 2000.

27. "Justice Made in Prison," Foundation Hirondelle, January 20, 2003.

28. See Republic of Rwanda, *Organic Law on Creating "Gacaca Jurisdictions" and Organizing the Prosecution of Offenses That Constitute the Crime of Genocide or Crimes against Humanity Committed between October First, 1990 and December 31, 1994,* October 12, 2000, Kigali, Rwanda.

29. For example, see African Rights, *Gacaca Justice: A Shared Responsibility* (Kigali: African Rights, 2003).

30. Useful accounts of the Derg regime are Africa Watch, *Evil Days: Thirty Years of War and Famine in Ethiopia* (New York: Human Rights Watch, September 1991); and also Africa Watch, *Reckoning under the Law* (New York: Human Rights Watch, December 1994).

31. *Information on Civil Administrators That Served under the Mengistu Regime* (Washington, DC: INS Resource Information Center, January 10, 2000).

32. Much of this summary is based on the author's interviews at the Office of the Special Prosecutor in May 1998 at Addis Ababa, Ethiopia.

33. See, for example, Human Rights Watch, *South Africa Urged to Prosecute Ethiopian Dictator* (New York, December 6, 1999).

34. For an overview of the conflict, see Human Rights Watch, *Sowing Terror: Atrocities against Civilians in Sierra Leone* (New York, July 29, 1998).

35. See statement by James P. Rubin, *Sierra Leone: Rebel Atrocities against Civilians*, U.S. Department of State, May 12, 1998.

36. See, for example, Sierra Leone, Office of the Attorney General and Ministry of Justice Special Court Task Force, *Briefing Paper on Documentation and Conflict Mapping for the Special Court*, January 7, 2002.

37. UN, Security Council, *Security Council Resolution 1315*, S/Res/1315, August 14, 2000.

38. UN, Security Council, *Report of the Secretary-General on the Establishment of a Special Court for Sierra Leone*, S/2000/915, October 4, 2000.

39. UN, Secretariat, Office of Legal Affairs, *Agreement between the United Nations and the Government of Sierra Leone on the Establishment of a Special Court for Sierra Leone,* January 16, 2002; and UN, Secretariat, Office of Legal Affairs, *Statute of the Special Court for Sierra Leone*, January 16, 2002.

40. Special Court for Sierra Leone, Office of the Prosecutor, *Statement by David M. Crane, Prosecutor, Special Court for Sierra Leone*, March 10, 2003.

41. Somini Sengupta, "Sierra Leone Warlord Dies in Custody of War Crimes Court," *New York Times*, July 30, 2003.

42. UN, General Assembly, *Rome Statute of the International Criminal Court*, A/CONF.183/9, July 17, 1998.

43. See, for example, Human Rights Watch, *The ICC Statute: Summary of the Key Provisions* (New York, September 1998).

44. "War Crimes Judges Sworn In," BBC Online News, March 11, 2003; and "War Crimes Tribunal Picks Head Prosecutor," Associated Press, April 21, 2003.

45. "ICC to Investigate Uganda Massacre," Agence France Press, February 23, 2004.

46. Current information on cases at the ICTR can be found at http://www .ictr.org/.

47. For the latest information on ICTY indictments, see http://www.un.org/icty/ cases/indictindex_e.htm.

48. See Chapter 2 for a discussion of the K-5 project and potential criminal culpability associated with that event.

49. For example, fifty-two women from Sa-ang and Kandal Stung Districts of Kandal province consented to in-depth interviews regarding their experiences under the Khmer Rouge, and these interviews contain allegations that there was a high incidence of rape by low-level cadre during the Khmer Rouge regime. Kalyanee Mam, *Crimes Committed against Women in Democratic Kampuchea* (Phnom Penh: Documentation Center of Cambodia, 2000).

50. See, for example, the Akayesu judgment of the ICTR discussed earlier.

51. Royal Government, *Aide Memoire*.

52. Press Release, "A Khmer Rouge Tribunal Brings Hope for Cambodia," British Embassy, Phnom Penh, March 18, 2003.

53. Author's interview with Ok Serei Sopheak, Phnom Penh, December 10, 2001.

54. Author's interview with Chhin Sovann, Prek Tatoch village, Boeung Khyang commune, Kandal Stung District, Kandal Province, July 24, 2002.

55. Author's interview with Um Oeurn, Snay Village, Taches commune, Kompong Tralach district, Kompong Chhnang Province, March 16, 2002.

56. Author's interview with Uon Sokhan, Prek Tatoch village, Boeung Khyang commune, Kandal Stung District, Kandal Province, July 25, 2002.

SELECTED BIBLIOGRAPHY

BOOKS AND MONOGRAPHS

Ablin, David A., and Marlowe Hood, eds. *The Cambodian Agony.* Armonk, NY: M. E. Sharpe, 1990.

Acharya, Amitav, et al., eds. *Cambodia—The 1989 Paris Peace Conference: Background Analysis and Documents.* Toronto: Center for International and Strategic Studies, 1991.

African Rights. *Gacaca Justice: A Shared Responsibility.* Kigali: African Rights, 2003.

Africa Watch. *Evil Days: Thirty Years of War and Famine in Ethiopia.* New York: Human Rights Watch, September 1991.

———. *Reckoning under the Law.* New York: Human Rights Watch, December 1994.

Amnesty International. *Accountability for Gross Human Rights Violations: Open Letter to King Sihanouk and the National Assembly.* September 11, 1996. ASA 23/010/1996.

———. *Grenade Attack on Peaceful Demonstration.* March 31, 1997. ASA 23/005/1997.

———. *Amnesty International Report 1997.* June 18, 1997. AI Index POL 10/001/1997.

———. *Law and Order—without the Law.* March 1, 2000. ASA 23/001/2000.

———. *Cambodia: Flawed trials in No One's Best Interests.* February 11, 2002.

———. *Cambodia: Cambodians Deserve International Standards of Justice.* November 19, 2002. ASA 23/010/2002.

———. *Cambodia: Amnesty International's Preliminary Views and Concerns about the*

Draft Agreement for the Establishment of a Khmer Rouge Special Tribunal. March 21, 2003. ASA 23/003/2003.

Asia Watch. *Violations of the Laws of War by the Khmer Rouge.* April 1990.

—————. *Political Control, Human Rights, and the UN Mission in Cambodia.* September 1992.

Asia Watch and Physicians for Human Rights. *Land Mines in Cambodia: The Coward's War.* September 1991.

Becker, Elizabeth. *When the War Was Over: The Voices of Cambodia's Revolution and Its People.* New York: Simon and Schuster, 1986.

Bekaert, Jacques. *Cambodian Diary: Tales of a Divided Nation, 1983–1986.* Bangkok: White Lotus Press, 1997.

—————. *Cambodian Diary: A Long Road to Peace, 1987–1993.* Bangkok: White Lotus Press, 1998.

Brown, Frederick Z. *Cambodia in Crisis: The 1993 Elections and the United Nations.* New York: Asia Society, May 1993.

Brown, MacAlister, and Joseph J. Zasloff. *Cambodia Confounds the Peacemakers, 1979–1998.* Ithaca, NY: Cornell University Press, 1998.

Caldwell, Malcolm, and Lek Tan. *Cambodia in the Southeast Asian War.* New York: Monthly Review Books, 1973.

Cambodian Genocide Program. *The Cambodian Genocide Program: First Progress Report.* New Haven, CT: Yale Center for International and Area Studies, September 15, 1995.

—————. *The Cambodian Genocide Program, 1994–1997.* New Haven, CT: Yale Center for International and Area Studies, February 1998.

—————. *The Cambodian Genocide Program, 1997–1999.* New Haven, CT: Yale Center for International and Area Studies, April 1999.

Cambodian Human Rights Action Committee. *Press Release.* February 21, 2002.

Carney, Tim. *Communist Party Power in Kampuchea: Documents and Discussion.* Cornell University Southeast Asia Program, Data Paper # 106. Ithaca, NY: Cornell University, 1977.

Center for Social Development. *The Khmer Rouge and National Reconciliation—Opinions from the Cambodians.* Phnom Penh: Center for Social Development, April 2001.

Chanda, Nayan. *Brother Enemy: The War after the War.* New York: Macmillan Publishing Co., 1988.

Chandler, David P. *The Tragedy of Cambodian History: Politics, War and Revolution since 1945.* New Haven, CT: Yale University Press, 1991.

—————. *Brother Number One: A Political Biography of Pol Pot.* 2nd ed. Boulder, CO: Westview Press, 1999.

—————. *Voices from S-21: Terror and History in Pol Pot's Secret Prison.* Berkeley: University of California Press, 1999.

————. *A History of Cambodia.* 3rd ed. Boulder, CO: Westview Press, 2000.

Chandler, David P., and Ben Kiernan, eds. *Revolution and Its Aftermath in Kampuchea: Eight Essays.* New Haven, CT: Yale University Southeast Asia Studies, Monograph Series No. 25, 1983.

Chandler, David P., Ben Kiernan, and Chanthou Boua, eds. *Pol Pot Plans the Future: Confidential Leadership Documents from Democratic Kampuchea, 1970–1977.* New Haven, CT: Yale University Southeast Asia Studies, 1988.

Chhim, Kristina. *Die Revolutionäre Volkspartei Kampuchea 1979 bis 1989. Eine Analyse der politischen Herrschaft einer nach der vietnamesischen Intervention reorganisierten Kommunistischen Partei.* Frankfurt am Main: Peter Lang Verlag, 2000.

Chirot, Daniel, and Martin Seligman, eds. *Ethnopolitical Warfare: Causes, Consequences and Possible Solutions.* Washington, DC: American Psychological Association, 2001.

Clymer, Kenton. *The United States and Cambodia, 1870–1969: From Curiosity to Confrontation.* London: Routledge, 2004.

————. *The United States and Cambodia, 1969–2000: A Troubled Relationship.* London: Routledge, 2004.

Cohen, Lenard J. *Broken Bonds: The Disintegration of Yugoslavia.* Boulder, CO: Westview Press, 1993.

Colm, Sara. *The Khmer Rouge and Tribal Minorities in Northeastern Cambodia.* Bangkok: White Lotus Press, forthcoming.

Courtois, Stephane, et al. *The Black Book of Communism: Crimes, Terror, Repression.* Cambridge: Harvard University Press, 1999.

DeNike, Howard J., John Quigley, and Kenneth J. Robinson, eds. *Genocide in Cambodia: Documents from the Trial of Pol Pot and Ieng Sary.* Philadelphia: University of Pennsylvania Press, 2000.

des Forges, Alison. *Leave None to Tell the Story: Genocide in Rwanda.* New York: Human Rights Watch, 1999.

Documentation Center of Cambodia. *1995 Documentation Center Mapping Reports.* Phnom Penh: Documentation Center of Cambodia, 1995.

————. *1996 Documentation Center Mapping Reports.* Phnom Penh: Documentation Center of Cambodia, 1996.

————. *Mapping the Killing Fields of Cambodia, 1997.* Phnom Penh: Documentation Center of Cambodia, 1997.

————. *Mapping the Killing Fields of Cambodia, 1998.* Phnom Penh: Documentation Center of Cambodia, 1999.

————. *Annual Report.* Phnom Penh: Documentation Center of Cambodia, 2000.

————. *Mapping the Killing Fields of Cambodia, 1999.* Phnom Penh: Documentation Center of Cambodia, 2000.

————. *Annual Report: DC-Cam's Achievements and Progress, 2001.* Phnom Penh: Documentation Center of Cambodia, 2002.

Ea, Meng-Try, and Sorya Sim. *Victims and Perpetrators? Testimony of Young Khmer Rouge Comrades.* Phnom Penh: Documentation Center of Cambodia, 2001.

Ebihara, May M., Carol A. Mortland, and Judy Ledgerwood, eds. *Cambodian Culture since 1975: Homeland and Exile.* Ithaca, NY: Cornell University Press, 1994.

Elliott, David, ed. *The Third Indochina Conflict.* Boulder, CO: Westview Press, 1981.

Epstein, Helen. *Children of the Holocaust: Conversations with Sons and Daughters of Survivors.* New York: Penguin Books, 1979.

Etcheson, Craig. *The Rise and Demise of Democratic Kampuchea.* London and Boulder, CO: Pinter Publishers and Westview Press, 1984.

———. *Retribution and Reconciliation: Healing What Ails Cambodia.* Washington, DC: Project Report to the U.S. Institute of Peace, 2002.

Fawthrop, Tom, and Helen Jarvis. *Getting Away with Genocide? Elusive Justice and the Khmer Rouge Tribunal.* London: Pluto Press, 2005.

Ghosananda, Maha. *Step by Step.* Edited by Jane Sharada Mahoney and Philip Edmonds. Berkeley: Parallax Press, 1992.

Global Witness. *Forests, Famine and War: The Key to Cambodia's Future.* London: Global Witness, 1995.

———. *Going Places: Cambodia's Future on the Move.* London: Global Witness, March 1998.

———. *The Credibility Gap—and the Need to Bridge It.* London: Global Witness, May 2001.

Gottesman, Evan. *Cambodia after the Khmer Rouge: Inside the Politics of Nation Building.* New Haven, CT: Yale University Press, 2003.

Gourevitch, Philip. *We Wish to Inform You That Tomorrow We Will Be Killed with Our Families: Stories from Rwanda.* New York: Farrar Straus and Giroux, 1998.

Haas, Michael. *Cambodia, Pol Pot and the United States: A Faustian Pact.* New York: Praeger, 1991.

———. *Genocide by Proxy: Cambodian Pawn on a Superpower Chessboard.* New York: Praeger, 1991.

Heder, Stephen, with Brian D. Tittemore. *Seven Candidates for Prosecution: Accountability for the Crimes of the Khmer Rouge.* Washington, DC: American University War Crimes Research Office, June 2001.

Heder, Stephen, and Judy Ledgerwood, eds. *Propaganda, Politics, and Violence in Cambodia: Democratic Transition under United Nations Peace-keeping.* Armonk, NY: M. E. Sharpe, 1996.

Hinton, Alexander, ed. *Genocide: An Anthropological Reader.* Oxford: Blackwell Publishers, 2002.

Human Rights Watch. *Sowing Terror: Atrocities against Civilians in Sierra Leone.* July 29, 1998.

———. *The ICC Statute: Summary of the Key Provisions.* September 1998.

————. *South Africa Urged to Prosecute Ethiopian Dictator.* December 6, 1999.

————. *Core Issues in Khmer Rouge Tribunal Law Unresolved.* January 21, 2000.

————. *Human Rights Agenda for Cambodia's Donors.* May 23, 2000.

————. *Cambodia: Tribunal Must Meet International Standards.* February 12, 2002.

Huy, Vannak. *The Khmer Rouge Division 703: From Victory to Self-Destruction.* Phnom Penh: Documentation Center of Cambodia, 2003.

Jackson, Karl, ed. *Cambodia 1975–1978: Rendezvous with Death.* Princeton, NJ: Princeton University Press, 1989.

Jennar, Raoul M. *The Cambodian Constitutions, 1953–1993.* Bangkok: White Lotus Co., 1995.

————. *Cambodian Chronicles: Bungling a Peace Plan, 1989–1991.* Bangkok: White Lotus Co., 1998.

Kamm, Henry. *Cambodia: Report from a Stricken Land.* New York: Arcade Publishing, 1998.

Kiernan, Ben. *The Pol Pot Regime: Race, Power, and Genocide in Cambodia under the Khmer Rouge, 1975–79.* New Haven, CT: Yale University Press, 1996.

————. ed. *Genocide and Democracy in Cambodia: The Khmer Rouge, the United Nations and the International Community.* New Haven, CT: Yale University Southeast Asia Studies, 1993.

Kiernan, Ben, and Chanthou Boua, eds. *Peasants and Politics in Kampuchea, 1942–1981.* New York: M. E. Sharpe, 1982.

Ledgerwood, Judy, ed. *Cambodia Emerges from the Past: Eight Essays.* DeKalb: Northern Illinois University Southeast Asia Publications, 2002.

Luciolli, Esmeralda. *Le Mur de Bambou—Le Cambodge après Pol Pot.* Paris: Régine Deforges Edition, 1988.

Maguire, Peter. *Law and War: An American Story.* New York: Columbia University Press, 2000.

Mam, Kalyanee. *Crimes Committed against Women in Democratic Kampuchea.* Phnom Penh: Documentation Center of Cambodia, 2000.

Mehta, Harish C. *Cambodia Silenced: The Press under Six Regimes.* Bangkok: White Lotus Press, 1997.

Mehta, Harish C., and Julie B. Mehta. *Hun Sen: Strongman of Cambodia.* Singapore: Graham Brash, 1999.

Morris, Stephen J. *Why Vietnam Invaded Cambodia: Political Culture and the Causes of War.* Stanford, CA: Stanford University Press, 1999.

Mysliwiec, Eva. *Punishing the Poor: The International Isolation of Kampuchea.* Oxford: Oxfam, 1988.

National Democratic Institute. *The July 26, 1998 Cambodian National Assembly Elections.* Washington, DC: National Democratic Institute for International Affairs, 1999.

Neier, Aryeh. *War Crimes: Brutality, Genocide, Terror and the Struggle for Justice.* New York: Times Books, 1998.

Newman, Frank, and David Weissbrodt. *International Human Rights: Law, Policy and Process.* 2nd ed. Cincinnati, OH: Anderson Publishing Co., 1996.

Norodom Sihanouk. *War and Hope: The Case for Cambodia.* New York: Random House, 1980.

———. *Prisonnier des Khmers Rouges.* Paris: Hachette, 1986.

Osborne, Milton. *Sihanouk: Prince of Light, Prince of Darkness.* Chiang Mai, Thailand: Silkworm Books, 1994.

Oxfam America. *Cambodia Still Waiting for Peace: A Report on Thai–Khmer Rouge Collaboration since the Signing of the Cambodia Peace Accords.* Boston: Oxfam America, February 1995.

Peou, Sorpong. *Conflict Neutralization in the Cambodia War: From Battlefield to Ballot Box.* New York: Oxford University Press, 1997.

Peschoux, Christophe. *Les "Nouveaux" Khmers Rouges (1979–1990).* Paris: L'Harmattan, 1992.

Phat, Kosal, and Ben Kiernan, with Sorya Sim, trans. *Ieng Sary's Regime: A Diary of the Khmer Rouge Foreign Ministry, 1976–79.* New Haven, CT: Yale Center for International and Area Studies, September 1998.

Power, Samantha. *A Problem from Hell: America and the Age of Genocide.* New York: Basic Books, 2002.

Prunier, Gerard. *The Rwanda Crisis: History of a Genocide.* New York: Columbia University Press, 1995.

Raszelenberg, Patrick, and Peter Schier. *The Cambodia Conflict: Search for a Settlement, 1979–1991.* Hamburg: Institute of Asian Affairs, 1995.

Ratner, Steven R., and Jason S. Abrams. *Accountability for Human Rights Atrocities in International Law: Beyond the Nuremberg Legacy.* Oxford: Oxford University Press, 1997.

Reynell, Josephine. *Political Pawns: Refugees on the Thai–Kampuchean Border.* Oxford: Refugee Studies Program, 1989.

Roberts, David W. *Political Transition in Cambodia, 1991–99: Power, Elitism and Democracy.* Richmond, Surrey: Curzon Press, 2001.

Rodman, Peter W. *More Precious Than Peace: The Cold War and the Struggle for the Third World.* New York: Scribner's, 1994.

Sak Sutsakhan. *The Khmer Republic at War.* Washington, DC: U.S. Army Center for Military History, 1980.

Schabas, William. *Genocide in International Law.* Cambridge: Cambridge University Press, 2000.

Sells, Michael. *The Bridge Betrayed: Religion and Genocide in Bosnia.* Berkeley: University of California Press, 1996.

Shain, Yossi, ed. *Governments in Exile in Contemporary World Politics.* New York: Routledge, 1991.

Shawcross, William. *Sideshow: Nixon, Kissinger and the Destruction of Cambodia.* New York: Simon and Schuster, 1979.

———. *The Quality of Mercy: Cambodia, Holocaust, and Modern Conscience.* New York: Simon and Schuster, 1984.

———. *Cambodia's New Deal.* New York: Carnegie Endowment for International Peace, 1994.

Short, Philip. *Pol Pot: The History of a Nightmare.* London: John Murray, 2004.

Sliwinski, Marek. *Le Génocide Khmer Rouge: un analyse démographique.* Paris: Editions L'Harmattan, 1995.

Slocomb, Margaret. *The People's Republic of Kampuchea, 1979–1989: The Revolution after Pol Pot.* Chiang Mai: Silkworm Books, 2003.

Stanton, Gregory. *The Eight Stages of Genocide: How Governments Can Tell When Genocide Is Coming and What They Can Do to Stop It.* Washington, DC: Woodrow Wilson Center Press, forthcoming.

Sudetic, Chuck. *Blood and Vengeance: One Family's Story of the War in Bosnia.* New York: W. W. Norton, 1998.

Tatz, Colin, Peter Arnold, and Sandra Tatz, eds. *Genocide Perspectives II: Essays on Holocaust and Genocide.* Blackheath, NSW: Brandl and Schlesinger, 2003.

U.S. Committee for Refugees. *Something like Home Again: The Repatriation of Cambodian Refugees.* Washington, DC: U.S. Committee for Refugees, May 1994.

Vickery, Michael. *Cambodia: 1975–1982.* Boston: South End Press, 1984.

———. *Kampuchea: Politics, Economics and Society.* London: Pinter Publishers, 1986.

Ysa, Osman. *Oukoubah: Justice for the Cham Muslims under the Democratic Kampuchea Regime.* Phnom Penh: Documentation Center of Cambodia, 2002.

ARTICLES

Adams, Brad. "The UN Must Stand Firm on Principles for KR Trial." *Phnom Penh Post*, March 17–30, 2000.

Ashley, David. "The Nature and Causes of Human Rights Violations in Battambang Province." In Steve Heder and Judy Ledgerwood, eds., *Propaganda, Politics and Violence in Cambodia: Democratic Transition under United Nations Peace-keeping.* Armonk, NY: M. E. Sharpe, 1996, 159–182.

Banister, Judith, and Paige Johnson. "After the Nightmare: The Population of Cambodia." In Ben Kiernan, ed., *Genocide and Democracy in Cambodia: The Khmer Rouge, the United Nations and the International Community*, New Haven, CT: Yale University Southeast Asia Studies, 1993, 65–139.

Chanda, Nayan. "Cambodia: In Search of an Elusive Peace." *Conference Report on the American–Vietnamese Dialogue.* Aspen Institute, vol. 8, no. 2, February 8–11, 1993.

Chandler, David P. "The Red Khmer and the UN Agreement on Cambodia." *Conference Report on the Challenge of Indochina.* Aspen Institute, vol. 7, no. 3, May 8–10, 1992.

————. "Will There Be a Trial for the Khmer Rouge?" *Ethics and International Affairs* 14 (2000): 67–82.

Chhim, Kristina. "The Reconstitution of the Cambodian People's Party 1979–1989." Paper presented to the 5th Socio-Cultural Research Conference on Cambodia, Phnom Penh, November 6–8, 2002.

Cook, Susan. "Documenting Genocide: Cambodia's Lessons for Rwanda." *Africa Today* 44:2 (April–June 1997): 223–228.

————. "Documenting Genocide: Lessons from Cambodia for Rwanda." In Judy Ledgerwood, ed., *Cambodia Emerges from the Past: Eight Essays*. DeKalb: Northern Illinois University Southeast Asia Publications, 2002, 224–237.

Crocker, David A. "Forgiveness, Accountability and Reconciliation." *Perspectives on Ethics and International Affairs* 2 (2000): 7, 13–14.

Curtis, Grant. "Transition to What? Cambodia, UNTAC and the Peace Process." Workshop on the Social Consequences of the Peace, UN Research Institute for Social Development, Geneva, April 29–30, 1993.

Etcheson, Craig. "Civil War and the Coalition Government of Democratic Kampuchea." *Third World Quarterly* 9:1 (January 1987): 187–202.

————. "The Khmer Way of Exile: Lessons from Three Indochinese Wars." In Yossi Shain, ed., *Governments in Exile in Contemporary World Politics*. New York: Routledge, 1991, 92–116.

————. "The 'Peace' in Cambodia." *Current History* 91:569 (December 1992): 413–417.

————. "The Calm before the Storm." Washington, DC: Report to the Campaign to Oppose the Return of the Khmer Rouge, April 1993.

————. "Genocide Continues as UN Watches." *Vietnam Today* (Spring 1993): 3, 4.

————. "From Theory to Facts in the Cambodian Genocide." *International Network on Holocaust and Genocide* 12:1–2 (1997): 4–7.

————. "The Day I Saw a Monster." *Suitcase: A Journal of Transcultural Traffic* 3:1/2 (1998): 104–116.

Gordon, Bernard. "The Third Indochina Conflict." *Foreign Affairs* 65:1 (Fall 1986): 66–85.

Hannum, Hurst. "International Law and the Cambodian Genocide: The Sounds of Silence." *Human Rights Quarterly* 11 (1989): 82–138.

Heder, Stephen. "The Resumption of Armed Struggle by the Party of Democratic Kampuchea: Evidence from National Army of Democratic Kampuchea 'Self-Demobilizers.' " In Steve Heder and Judy Ledgerwood, eds., *Propaganda, Politics and Violence in Cambodia: Democratic Transition under United Nations Peace-keeping*. London: M. E. Sharpe, 1996, 50–72.

————. "Racism, Marxism, Labeling, and Genocide in Ben Kiernan's *The Pol Pot Regime*." *South East Asia Research* 5:2 (1997): 101–153.

————. "Hen Sen and Genocide Trials in Cambodia: International Impacts, Impunity and Justice." In Judy Ledgerwood, ed., *Cambodia Emerges from the Past: Eight Essays.* DeKalb: Northern Illinois University Southeast Asia Publications, 2002, 176–223.

Heder, Steve, and Judy Ledgerwood. "Politics of Violence: An Introduction." In Steve Heder and Judy Ledgerwood, eds., *Propaganda, Politics and Violence in Cambodia: Democratic Transition under United Nations Peace-keeping.* London: M. E. Sharpe, 1996, 3–49.

Heuveline, Patrick. " 'Between One and Three Million': Towards the Demographic Reconstruction of a Decade of Cambodian History (1970–79)." *Population Studies* 52:1 (1998): 49–65.

———. "L'insoutenable incertitude du nombre: estimations des décès de la périod Khmer rouge." *Population* 3 (May–June 1998): 1103–1118.

———. "Approaches to Measuring Genocide: Excess Morality during the Khmer Rouge Period." In Daniel Chirot and Martin Seligman, eds., *Ethnopolitical Warfare: Causes, Consequences and Possible Solutions.* Washington, DC: American Psychological Association, 2001, 93–108.

———. "The Demographic Analysis of Mortality in Cambodia." In Holly E. Reed and Charles B. Keely, eds., *Forced Migration and Mortality.* Washington, DC: National Academy Press, 2001, 102–129.

Hinton, Alexander. "A Head for an Eye: Revenge in the Cambodian Genocide." In Alexander Hinton, ed., *Genocide: An Anthropological Reader.* Oxford: Blackwell Publishers, 2002, 254–285.

Institut Français de la Statistique, de Sondage d'Opinion et de Recherche sur le Cambodge. "Doit-on poursuivre les chefs des Khmers Rouges?" *IFRASSORC Revue trimestrielle,* Avril 1999, No. 5.

Jarvis, Helen. "Cambodian Genocide Program." *Newsletter* of the Centre for Comparative Genocide Studies, Macquarie University, 2:2 (December 1995–January 1996).

———. "Cataloguing the Killing Fields: The Cambodian Genocide Program." *National Library of Australia News—International Relations Quarterly Supplement* (January 1998): 10–12.

Jarvis, Helen, and Nereida Cross. "Documenting the Cambodian Genocide on Multimedia." New Haven, CT: Yale Center for International and Area Studies, October 1998.

———. "New Information Technology Applied to Genocide Research: The Cambodian Genocide Program." In C. Chen, ed., *New Information Technology '98: 10th International Conference on New Information Technology.* West Newton, MA: MicroUse Information, 1998, 19–26.

———. "CGDB: Cambodian Genocide Data Bases Input Manual." Sydney and Phnom Penh: SISTM, University of New South Wales and the Documentation Center of Cambodia, 1999.

———. "The Cambodian Genocide Program: Australian, Cambodian and U.S.

Cooperation in Research and Documentation." Mekong Perspectives: 1st Annual Conference, (forthcoming).

Jarvis, Helen, and Robert Loomans. "The Cambodian Genocide Program (CGP)." *Proceedings of the Second New South Wales Symposium on Information Technology and Information Systems.* Sydney: School of Information Systems, University of New South Wales, 1997.

Jennar, Raoul. "Before It Becomes Too Late." *Cambodia Chronicles VII*, European Far Eastern Research Center, February 15, 1993.

———. "18 Years Later." *Cambodia Chronicles VIII*, European Far Eastern Research Center, April 18, 1993.

———. "Who Is Really Mr. Hun Sen?" Cambodia Research Center, November 9, 1998.

Jordens, Jay. "Persecution of Cambodia's Ethnic Vietnamese Communities during and since the UNTAC Period." In Steve Heder and Judy Ledgerwood, eds., *Propaganda, Politics and Violence in Cambodia: Democratic Transition under United Nations Peace-keeping.* London: M. E. Sharpe, 1996, 134–158.

Kevin, Tony. "Cambodia vs. the UN." *Far Eastern Economic Review*, November 11, 1999.

Kiernan, Ben. "The Samlaut Rebellion." In Ben Kiernan and Chanthou Boua, eds., *Peasants and Politics in Kampuchea 1942–1981.* New York: M. E. Sharpe, 1982, 166–205.

———. "Cambodia: The Eastern Zone Massacres." Columbia University, Center for the Study of Human Rights, Documentation Series No. 1, 1986.

———. "The Inclusion of the Khmer Rouge in the Cambodian Peace Process: Causes and Consequences." In Ben Kiernan, ed., *Genocide and Democracy in Cambodia: The Khmer Rouge, the United Nations and the International Community.* New Haven, CT: Yale University Southeast Asia Studies Monograph Series, 1993, 191–272.

———. "Bringing the Khmer Rouge to Justice." *Human Rights Review* 1:3 (April–June 2000): 92–108.

McGrew, Laura. "Cambodians Talk about the Khmer Rouge Trial." *Phnom Penh Post*, February 4–17, 2000.

———. "The Thorny Debate on Justice for Pol Pot's Madness." *Phnom Penh Post*, February 18–March 2, 2000.

———. "Truth, Justice, Reconciliation, Peace: The KR 20 Years After." *Phnom Penh Post*, February 18–March 2, 2000.

McGrew, Laura, and Heang Path. "Discussion Guide: Truth, Justice, Reconciliation and Peace in Cambodia: 20 Years after the Khmer Rouge." Phnom Penh, February 2000. Photocopy.

Norodom Sihanouk. "Forging Cambodian Nationhood." *Far Eastern Economic Review*, January 13, 1994.

Pollanen, Michael S. "Forensic Survey of Three Memorial Sites Containing Human

Skeletal Remains in the Kingdom of Cambodia." Mission Report to the Coalition for International Justice, Washington, DC, July 2002.

Quinn, Kenneth. "Explaining the Terror." In Karl Jackson, ed., *Cambodia 1975–1978: Rendezvous with Death*. Princeton, NJ: Princeton University Press, 1989, 215–240.

———. "The Pattern and Scope of Violence." In Karl Jackson, ed., *Cambodia 1975–1978: Rendezvous with Death*. Princeton, NJ: Princeton University Press, 1989, 179–208.

Ramji, Jaya, and Christine Barton. "Accounting for the Crimes of the Khmer Rouge, 1975–1979: Interviews with Cambodians." Phnom Penh: Documentation Center of Cambodia, 1997.

Slocomb, Margaret. "The K5 Gamble: National Defense and Nation Building under the People's Republic of Kampuchea." *Journal of Southeast Asian Studies* 32:2 (June 2002): 195–210.

Stanton, Gregory. "Blue Scarves and Yellow Stars: Classification and Symbolization in the Cambodian Genocide." Montreal: Montreal Institute for Genocide Studies, Concordia University, 1989.

———. "The Khmer Rouge Genocide and International Law." In Ben Kiernan, ed., *Genocide and Democracy in Cambodia*. New Haven, CT: Yale University Southeast Asia Studies, 1993, 141–162.

Suong, Sikoeun. "Forgive and Forget." *On The Record* 13:8 (August 7, 2000).

Tatz, Colin. "Why Denialists Deny." In Colin Tatz, Peter Arnold, and Sandra Tatz, eds., *Genocide Perspectives II: Essays on Holocaust and Genocide*. Blackheath, NSW: Brandl and Schlesinger, 2003, 267–284.

Thion, Serge. "The Pattern of Cambodian Politics." In David A. Ablin and Marlowe Hood, eds., *The Cambodian Agony*. Armonk, NY: M. E. Sharpe, 1990, 149–164.

Turley, William, and Jeffrey Race. "The Third Indochina War." *Foreign Policy* 38 (Spring 1980): 92–116.

Van Schaack, Beth, and Noah Novogrodsky, eds. "Truth and Justice in Cambodia: A Teaching Manual for the Cambodian Genocide Justice Project." Phnom Penh: Documentation Center of Cambodia, 1997.

OFFICIAL DOCUMENTS

Association of Southeast Asian Nations. *Joint Communique of 35th ASEAN Ministerial Meeting*, Bandar Seri Begawan, Brunei, July 29–30, 2002.

Cambodian People's Party. *Memorandum of the Cambodian People's Party Regarding a Draft Resolution 309*, October 28, 1998.

———. *Speech of Samdech Chea Sim, Chairman of the Cambodian People's Party at the 49th Anniversary of the Foundation of the Cambodian People's Party, 28.06.1951–28.06.2000*. [Unofficial translation].

Democratic Kampuchea, S-21. *The Responses of the Contemptible Chhean, Party Secretary of Sector 22, Eastern Region,* June 21, 1978.

Democratic Kampuchea, Ministry of Foreign Affairs, Department of Press and Information. *Black Paper: Facts and Evidences of the Aggression and Annexation of Vietnam against Kampuchea,* September 1978.

Democratic National Union Movement. *Statement of the Democratic National Union Movement on the So-Called "UN Plan."* Pailin, Cambodia, September 2, 1999 [signed by Ieng Sary].

International Criminal Tribunal for Rwanda. *Jean-Paul Akayesu, Summary of the Judgment,* ICTR-96-4-T, September 2, 1998.

Kampuchea Dossier. 3 vols. Hanoi: Le Courier du Vietnam, 1978.

Kingdom of Cambodia, Cabinet of the First Prime Minister. *Speech by Samdech Krom Preah Norodom Ranariddh Made in Conjunction with the International Conference on Striving for Justice: International Criminal Law in the Cambodian Context.* Sofitel Cambodiana Hotel, Phnom Penh, August 21, 1995.

————. *Communique of the Cabinet of H.R.H. Prince Norodom Ranariddh, First Prime Minister of the Royal Government of Cambodia.* New York, October 28, 1997.

Kingdom of Cambodia, Cabinet of the Prime Minister. *Declaration of Samdech Hun Sen, Prime Minister of the Royal Government of Cambodia and Commander-in-Chief of the Cambodian National Armed Forces.* January 1, 1999.

————. *Aide Memoire on the Conversation between Hun Sen, Prime Minister of the Royal Government of Cambodia, and H.E. Kofi Annan, Secretary General of the United Nations.* September 17, 1999, New York. [Unofficial translation].

Kingdom of Cambodia, Council of Ministers. *Projet: Loi relative à la répression des crimes de génocide et des crimes contre l'humanité.* Phnom Penh, Cambodia, August 26, 1999.

————. *Aide Memoire: Second Meeting between the Cambodian Task Force on the Khmer Rouge Tribunal and the Visiting UN Delegation.* Phnom Penh, Cambodia, August 28, 1999.

————. *Presentation and Comments on the Draft Law on the Establishment of Extraordinary Chambers in the Courts of Cambodia for Prosecution of Crimes Committed during the Period of Democratic Kampuchea, by His Excellency Sok An, Minister in Charge of the Office of the Council of Ministers, President of the Task Force for Cooperation with Foreign Legal Experts and Preparation of the Proceedings for the Trial of Senior Khmer Rouge Leaders.* 5th Session of the 2nd Legislature, National Assembly, December 29, 2000, and January 2, 2001. [Unofficial translation by the Documentation Center of Cambodia].

————. *Law on the Establishment of Extraordinary Chambers in the Courts of Cambodia for the Prosecution of Crimes Committed during the Period of Democratic Kampuchea,* August 10, 2001.

Kingdom of Cambodia. *Letter from Co-Prime Ministers to United Nations Secretary General Kofi Annan.* June 21, 1997.

Kingdom of Cambodia, National Assembly of Cambodia. *A Minute on the Session of the National Assembly of the Kingdom of Cambodia, a Draft Law on the Establishment of Extraordinary Chambers in the Courts of Cambodia for Prosecution of Crimes Committed during the Period of Democratic Kampuchea.* December 29, 2000, and January 2, 2001. [Unofficial translation by Documentation Center of Cambodia].

People's Republic of Kampuchea. *People's Revolutionary Tribunal Held in Phnom Penh for the Trial of the Genocide Crime of the Pol Pot–Ieng Sary Clique, August 1979—Documents.* Phnom Penh: Foreign Languages Publishing House, 1990.

People's Republic of Kampuchea. Council of Ministers and Ministry of Interior. *Mastery Plan to Destroy the Enemy Continuously.* Doc. No. 148 S.J.N. March 25, 1986. [Original in Khmer].

People's Republic of Kampuchea. Ministry of Interior. *Directive: Instructions on the Implementation and Reviewing for Amnesty and Acquittal in Favor of the Culprit.* Doc. No. 221 M.Ch. February 21, 1984. [Original in Khmer].

People's Republic of Kampuchea, Research Committee on Pol Pot's Genocidal Regime. *Report of the Research Committee on Pol Pot's Genocidal Regime.* July 25, 1983. [Original in Khmer].

People's Revolutionary Party of Kampuchea, Central Committee, Monitoring Committee. *Instruction: Increase the Work of Monitoring and Discipline in the Party in Keeping with the New Situation.* Doc. No. 250 S.P.N.M.Ch. November 8, 1989. [Original in Khmer].

Republic of Rwanda. *Organic Law on Creating "Gacaca Jurisdictions" and Organizing the Prosecution of Offenses That Constitute the Crime of Genocide or Crimes against Humanity Committed between October First, 1990 and December 31, 1994.* October 12, 2000. Kigali, Rwanda.

Sierra Leone, Office of the Attorney General and Ministry of Justice Special Court Task Force. *Briefing Paper on Documentation and Conflict Mapping for the Special Court.* January 7, 2002. Freetown, Sierra Leone.

Special Court for Sierra Leone, Office of the Prosecutor. *Statement by David M. Crane, Prosecutor, Special Court for Sierra Leone.* March 10, 2003.

State of Cambodia, Ministry of Interior. *Resolution: Organizational Assignment, Role, Task and Rights of the Secret Messenger Network.* Doc. No. 079 L.S.R. February 4, 1991. [Original in Khmer].

———. *Directive: Implementing the Sub-decree on Registration for Military Service for National Defense.* Doc. No. 003 S.R.N.N. May 3, 1991. [Original in Khmer].

United Kingdom, British Embassy, Phnom Penh. *Press Release: A Khmer Rouge Tribunal Brings Hope for Cambodia.* March 18, 2003.

United Nations. Economic and Social Council, Commission on Human Rights,

53rd session. *Situation of Human Rights in Cambodia: Report of the Special Representative of the Secretary-General for Human Rights in Cambodia, Mr. Thomas Hammarberg, Submitted in accordance with Commission Resolution 1996/54.* E/CN.4/1997/85. January 31, 1997.

———. *Situation of Human Rights in Cambodia.* E/CN.4/RES/1997/49. April 11, 1997.

———. *Consideration of Reports Submitted by States Parties under Article 40 of the Covenant, Initial Reports of States Parties due in 1993, Addendum: Cambodia [24 November 1997].* CCPR/C/81/Add.12. September 23, 1998.

UN. General Assembly. *Rome Statute of the International Criminal Court.* A/CONF.183/9. July 17, 1998.

———. *Report of the Secretary-General on the Situation of Human Rights in Cambodia.* A/53/400. September 17, 1998.

———. *Report of the Third Committee.* A/57/556/Add.2. October 18, 2002.

———. *France and Japan: Draft Resolution, Khmer Rouge Trials.* A/C.3/57/L.70. November 13, 2002.

———. *Khmer Rouge Trials.* A/RES/57/228. December 18, 2002.

———. *Report of the Secretary-General on Khmer Rouge Trials.* A/57/769. March 31, 2003.

United Nations. General Assembly, Security Council. *Identical Letters Dated 15 March 1999 from the Secretary-General to the President of the General Assembly and the President of the Security Council.* A/53/850 and S/1999/231. March 16, 1999.

———. *Report of the Group of Experts for Cambodia Established Pursuant to General Assembly Resolution 52/135.* A/53/850, S/1999/231, Annex. March 16, 1999.

United Nations. High Commissioner for Human Rights, Cambodian Office of the High Commissioner for Human Rights. *Note on Legal and Judicial Reform for the Mid-Term Consultative Group of Donors Meeting.* January 25, 2003.

United Nations. Secretariat, Department of Press Information. *The Blue Helmets: A Review of United Nations Peace-keeping.* 1990.

———. *Agreements on a Comprehensive Political Settlement of the Cambodian Conflict.* DPI/1180 92077. January 1992.

United Nations. Secretariat, Office of Legal Affairs. *Comments on the Draft Law concerning the Punishment of the Crime of Genocide and Crimes against Humanity.* Annex to a letter from Assistant Secretary-General Ralph Zacklin to H. E. Sok An, minister of state, Royal Government of Cambodia, August 27, 1999.

———. *Draft: Law on the Establishment of a Tribunal for the Prosecution of Khmer Rouge Leaders Responsible for the Most Serious Violations of Human Rights.* Annex to a letter from Assistant Secretary-General Ralph Zacklin to H. E. Sok An, minister of state, Royal Government of Cambodia, August 27, 1999.

———. *Non-paper on Khmer Rouge Trial.* January 5, 2000.

———. *Letter from UN Under Secretary-General Hans Corell to Minister of the Council of Ministers Sok An.* January 9, 2001.

———. *Agreement between the United Nations and the Government of Sierra Leone on the Establishment of a Special Court for Sierra Leone.* January 16, 2002.

———. *Statute of the Special Court for Sierra Leone.* January 16, 2002.

UN. Secretariat, Office of the Spokesman for the Secretary-General. *Read-out of the Secretary-General's Meeting with Hun Sen, the Prime Minister of Cambodia.* September 16, 1999.

———. *Press Statement by Mr. Hans Corell, Pochentong Airport, Phnom Penh, 7 July 2000.* July 7, 2000.

———. "Daily Press Briefing." January 12, 2001.

———. *Secretary-General Clarifies Position on Cambodian Government Responsibility for Trials of Former Khmer Rouge Leaders.* SG/SM/7868. June 27, 2001.

———. *UN Looks Forward to Receiving New Cambodian Law on Khmer Rouge Trials.* SG/SM/7911. August 10, 2001.

———. "Daily Press Briefing." February 8, 2002.

———. *Press Release.* GA/SHC/3728. November 20, 2002.

UN. Security Council. *Fourth Progress Report of the Secretary-General on the United Nations Transitional Authority in Cambodia.* S/25719. May 3, 1993.

———. *Security Council Resolution 827.* S/Res/827. May 25, 1993.

———. *Report of the Secretary-General on the Conduct and Results of the Elections in Cambodia.* S/25913. June 10, 1993.

———. *Security Council Resolution 955.* S/Res/955. November 8, 1994.

———. *Security Council Resolution 1315.* S/Res/1315. August 14, 2000.

———. *Report of the Secretary-General on the Establishment of a Special Court for Sierra Leone.* S/2000/915. October 4, 2000.

U.S. Agency for International Development. *USAID Assistance Strategy for Cambodia, FY 1994–97.* May 1994. [Draft.]

U.S. Congress. House. *The Khmer Rouge Prosecution Act.* 102nd Cong., 2nd sess., 1992. H.Res. 5708.

———. *The Cambodian Genocide Justice Act.* 103rd Cong., 2nd sess., 1994. H.Res. 2333.

———. *The Khmer Rouge Prosecution and Exclusion Act.* 103rd Cong., 2nd sess., 1994. H.Res. 2333.

———. *Foreign Operations, Export Financing, and Related Programs Appropriations Act, 1995.* 103rd Cong., 2nd sess., 1994. H.Res. 4426.

———. *Expressing Sense of House of Representatives regarding Culpability of Hun Sen for War Crimes, Crimes against Humanity, and Genocide in Cambodia.* 105th Cong., 2nd sess., 1998. H.Res. 533.

U.S. Congress. House, Committee on Appropriations. *Foreign Operations, Export Financing, and Related Programs Appropriations for 1994. Hearings before a Subcommittee of the Committee on Appropriations.* "Avoiding a New War in

Cambodia." Testimony of Craig Etcheson, March 1, 1993. 103rd Cong., 1st sess., 1993.

U.S. Congress. House, Committee on Foreign Affairs. *Statement of Peter Tomsen, Deputy Assistant Secretary of State, Bureau of East Asian and Pacific Affairs.* 103rd Cong., 2nd sess., 1994.

U.S. Congress. Senate. *The Khmer Rouge Prosecution and Exclusion Act.* 102nd Cong., 2nd sess., 1992. S.2622.

―――. *The Khmer Rouge Prosecution and Exclusion Act.* 103rd Cong., 1st sess., 1993. S.1281.

―――. *The Cambodian Democracy and Accountability Act of 2003.* 108th Cong., 1st sess., 2003. S.1365.

U.S. Department of Justice. Immigration and Naturalization Service. *Information on Civil Administrators That Served under the Mengistu Regime.* January 10, 2000.

U.S. Department of State. *Positions and Answers on the Genocide Convention, the Khmer Rouge, and U.S. Rights and Responsibilities as a Signatory to the Convention.* Public submission to the House Committee on Foreign Affairs, September 1989.

―――. *Eagleburger Intervention.* June 21, 1992.

―――. *Statement by James P. Rubin, Sierra Leone: Rebel Atrocities against Civilians.* May 12, 1998.

―――. *Non-Paper on Khmer Rouge Trial.* U.S. Mission to the United Nations, January 5, 2000.

INDEX

ABOUT THE AUTHOR

CRAIG ETCHESON is a principal founder of the Documentation Center of Cambodia. He works with governments, international organizations, and NGOs in the search for ways to help heal nations that are recovering from genocide and other extreme violence. He has been a faculty member at Johns Hopkins University, Yale University, and the University of Southern California. He is the author of several book-length treatises on extreme conflict, including *The Rise and Demise of Democratic Kampuchea* (1984).